A CENTURY OF
TRAINS

CHELTENHAM
FLYER

5043

A CENTURY OF
TRAINS

BASIL COOPER

Brian Trodd Publishing House

First published in 1988 by
Brian Trodd Publishing House Limited
27 Swinton Street, London WC1X 9NW

This edition published 1989

ISBN 1 85361 132 8

Printed in Yugoslavia

CONTENTS

I. TRAINS ACROSS EUROPE

Previous page: Passengers in international trains crossed frontiers, heard unfamiliar languages, and puzzled over strange currencies, but the staff of the Wagons-Lits company remained reassuringly the same in their smart turn-out and the aplomb with which they confronted all problems. The uniforms illustrated belong to the period immediately before World War I.

A CHILD WHO HAD HEARD the bands playing and the crowds cheering at the opening of the Stockton & Darlington Railway on 27 September 1825 would have been only of middle age when the first international sleeping car trains rolled across Europe. The pace of progress in the later years of the 19th century contrasts with the fact that although the Stockton & Darlington was the first public railway to haul trains by steam, it used its locomotives at first for freight. For several more years passengers jogged along the line in a horse-drawn coach. One of them reported that 'at any bends in the road or other place where the view is obstructed, the coachman blows a horn to give warning of his approach to any wagons or vehicles that may be coming or going on the way'.

The steam passenger railway began to take shape with the opening of the Liverpool & Manchester Railway on 15 September 1830. A period of intensive railway building followed in Europe and the United States. In Europe there was a multiplicity of lines within the various national boundaries, and their relations with each other and with neighbouring countries were not always cordial. Railways proliferated in the United States as well, and even though there was not the complication of national frontiers, the idea of co-operation between companies in the running of long-distance through trains was slow to develop.

A young Belgian engineer, Georges Nagelmackers, visited the United States in the 1860s. He studied the railways and noted both the merits and the defects of the Pullman cars that were then coming into service on several lines. He was particularly impressed by the agreements which George Pullman had negotiated with various railways so that his cars could be passed on from one line to another, saving travellers the inconvenience of changing trains which had been a bugbear of American rail travel. At one period the passenger from New York to Chicago had to change five times.

Nagelmackers returned to Europe convinced of two things. He could improve on the comfort of Pullman's vehicles, and he could persuade the European railways to make through working arrangements similar to those established in the United States. Although the lines in Europe had been suspicious of allowing their rolling stock to stray beyond their own territories, they might take a different view about vehicles for which a separate international organisation took responsibility, particularly when they were of a standard which would add prestige to the trains in which they ran. And so the idea for the Wagons-Lits company was born.

The beginnings were difficult. When the Franco-Prussian War broke out in 1870, negotiations were in hand for through sleeping cars between Paris and Berlin, and Nagelmackers had already ordered five cars from a builder in Vienna. They were four-wheeled vehicles with three compartments convertible for day or night use. By day each compartment was furnished with four armchairs and a table. At night the table was folded away, the chairs were pushed together to form two beds, and two upper berths were let down. This arrangement was more agreeable to European tastes than the communal dormitory layout of Pullman's first sleeping cars in the United States.

With the French railways closed to him by war, Nagelmackers looked for another route. At that

time military men and government officials travelling from Great Britain and northern Europe to the East often made the first stage of the journey by train through France to a southern port, so saving time and avoiding the sometimes harrowing passage through the Bay of Biscay. Nagelmackers persuaded a group of railways to work his cars from Ostend to Brindisi by a route which by-passed France, and steamship companies agreed to change to the Italian port. The rail journey was longer, but it proved popular until the war ended and the route through France and Italy to Trieste was again open, and improved by the opening in 1871 of the Mont Cenis Tunnel which avoided the previous change to a mountain railway to cross the pass.

By this time Nagelmackers had ten sleeping cars on his hands and found himself in financial difficulties. Help came from the United States, where Colonel William D'Alton Mann had designed a 'boudoir car' and had tried to compete with Pull-

Dinner is served in the restaurant car of a train de luxe in 1912. The waiters might well be footmen in a stately home.

Train de luxe compartments were convertible for day and night use. Mornings brought competition for use of the washing arrangements but minor irritations were soon forgotten in the elegant surroundings of the restaurant car.

man, but without much success. Mann decided on a European venture and entered into partnership with Nagelmackers in a company they called the Mann Boudoir Sleeping Car Company. Their first success was a Paris-Vienna service begun in 1873. Mann's stay on the European scene was short. He soon returned to America, selling his interest to Nagelmackers. Now in complete control, Nagelmackers revived the company name he had earlier registered provisionally. The Compagnie Internationale des Wagons-Lits came into being.

The suffix 'et des Grands Express Européens' followed in 1885, when it was publicly displayed for the first time on the coaches of the inaugural 'Express de l'Orient' which left the Gare de l'Est in Paris on 4 October in that year with a distinguished party bound for Constantinople (Istanbul). It was not yet a through train, for the Danube had to be crossed by ferry at Giurgiu to pass from Rumania into Bulgaria, where a less impressive train awaited to take the party on to Varna on the Black Sea and the last leg of the journey to Constantinople by steamer. Through-running to Constantinople was not possible until 1889 when re-routeing of the train by the all-rail route saved 14 hours compared with the original schedule. By that time the name of the

train had been changed to 'Orient Express'. It was the first of a family of trains between eastern and western Europe with similar names containing the magic word 'Orient'.

By the end of the 19th century travellers could ride in Wagons-Lits coaches from St Petersburg and Moscow to Madrid and Lisbon. Nagelmackers had planned a single through train in which 'special devices will enable the carriage bogies to be changed in a few minutes so that our rolling stock can pass from French or German tracks to the wider gauge lines of Russia and Spain'. This ambition was not realised in full and the service from the Baltic to the Mediterranean was provided by separate trains – the 'Sud Express' in 1887 and the 'Nord Express' in 1896. On both services a change of train was necessary at the Spanish or Russian frontiers, but the Wagons-Lits company provided the rolling stock on the broad gauge as well as the narrow gauge lines. The 'Nord Express', in particular, was a remarkable feat of organisation, 14 different railway administrations being involved in its running in the early days.

During the second half of the 19th century the European railway network was strengthened by important new links which improved both internal and international routes. The builders were often faced with mountain ranges where coach roads wound their way precariously to wild and exposed passes which were often blocked with snow in winter. One such area was in the eastern ranges of the Alps south-west of Vienna where the mountains barred the way to a railway route from the capital to the port of Trieste. At that time Trieste was in the Austro-Hungarian Empire, whose territory ex-

tended from the Baltic countries to the Adriatic. The Semmering Pass crossed the mountains at an altitude of 3,215 ft (980 m) between Gloggnitz on the Viennese side and Murzzuschlag on the south. It had been a trade route since the 12th century, and by the 1800s as many as 200 horses had to be held in reserve at a posting station to help waggoners' teams as they struggled over the summit.

The Wagons-Lits company put its first bogie restaurant car in service in 1883. In this illustration it carries an 'Orient Express' board and the company's short title. The words 'et des Grands Express Europeens' were added in 1885 when the combined rail/Danube ferry/Black Sea steamer service between Paris and Istanbul was inaugurated.

Patronage of the new bogie restaurant car seems to be slow in this view. Note the interior design, particularly the artistically-decorated vaulted ceiling.

Decorative motifs were as much in evidence in the toilet compartments of Wagons-Lits stock as in other areas. The compartment illustrated shows the style prevailing at the turn of the century.

increase in traffic waiting to cross the pass. There was some criticism of the steam railway proposal on the grounds of difficulty and expense and at one time there was talk of laying rails on which wagons would be drawn by horses. The debate delayed the beginning of work but von Ghega held firmly to his proposal, for which he had the backing of the Minister for Public Works. At length approval was given and construction began on 8 August 1848.

Locomotives had still to be ordered, and when the northern approach to the summit was well advanced the authorities invited locomotive builders to demonstrate their products in a competition with a money prize for the best performance. Four firms designed locomotives for the occasion. The trials took place on 16 September 1851, and the 0-8-0 locomotive *Bavaria* built by Maffei of Munich, gained the award. Belgium's entry, the *Seraing* built by Cockerill, was the least impressive, but it outlived the other three prototypes in service on the Semmering line. The *Bavaria* was rebuilt by Wilhelm Engerth with a gear coupling between the rear locomotive axle and the leading axle of the tender, and coupling rods between the axles of the tender itself. This principle was followed in 26 Engerth locomotives ordered for the Semmering line in 1854 which became the standard type on the route for many years.

The line was 25 miles (41 km) long. By massive engineering works von Ghega kept the maximum gradient to 1 in 40 but 14·25 miles (23 km) were at this inclination. On the northern approach to the summit the line had to climb through 1,781 ft (543 m) while on the southern approach the difference in level was 981 ft (299 m). The length of the 16 tunnels totalled 3·7 miles (6 km), the longest being the Semmering Tunnel with 0·9 mile (1·43 km) at an altitude of 2,940 ft (896 m). Of the 17 viaducts, four were built with two tiers of arches. The most impressive was the Kalte Rinne viaduct, 613 ft (187 m) in length, with 5 arches in the lower tier and 10 above carrying the line at a height of 151 ft (46 m) above the ground. The Semmering is still considered the most spectacular ride in Austria.

The line was opened to goods traffic on 15 May 1854, but had carried its first passenger train on 12 April when the Emperor Franz Joseph travelled over it accompanied by von Ghega to point out its wonders. A full passenger and freight service began on 17 July. In the meantime work was being pressed ahead southwards from Graz until in 1857 the railway reached Trieste and the system of the Austro-Hungarian Empire extended through Europe from its northern to its southern boundary. The first Austrian express train ran on the Semmering line. At first it was a twice-weekly service between Vienna and Ljubljana begun on 1 August 1857, carrying first and second class passengers at supplementary fares. It was later extended to Trieste, the journey with 24 intermediate stops being made at an overall

Gloggnitz is 48·5 miles (78 km) from Vienna. It was connected with the capital on 5 May 1842 by a railway which had been promoted by a private company. When the company failed, with others, in a financial crisis, the line was taken over by the State Railways. At this period the State Railways were planning a rail connection between Vienna and Trieste. The Vienna-Gloggnitz line was a first step. Before it was decided how it could be connected with a railway on the other side of the pass, the engineer Karl Ritter von Ghega was sent to America to study the latest developments there in railway building and locomotives. He returned convinced that the Semmering could be crossed by an ordinary adhesion railway with locomotive traction.

On his return von Ghega's first task was to complete the line from Murzzuschlag to Graz, which was opened on 21 October 1844. One result was a big

average speed of 23 mph (37 km/h). In 1867 the service began to operate daily.

In 1867 the Austrian and Italian railways were linked across the Brenner Pass by a line from Innsbruck which climbed steeply to the frontier station of Brennero some 23 miles (37 km) to the south. There was no summit tunnel, a fact commented upon by J. P. Pearson in his three-volume book, *Railways and Scenery*, recording his worldwide journeys between the 1880s and the First World War. Pearson travelled across the pass in 1895. Of the journey from Innsbruck he wrote:

Continuing now with a general southwardly direction and making two wide curves, we passed the (frozen-over) Brenner-See and reached the Brenner summit (1,370 metres) with mountains visible behind us. This water-parting tops the Arlberg by 60 m, the Mont Cenis by 77, the Gotthard by 217 and the Simplon by no fewer than 666 – yet all these last are in tunnel and the Brenner – highest of all – is *en plein air*.

The history of the Mont Cenis Tunnel as an international route is unusual in that the political situation changed fundamentally between the beginning of the work and its completion. The tunnel was planned to connect the Savoy and Piedmont, both of which were territories belonging to the Kingdom of Piedmont-Sardinia. At the start of the project in 1857, the kingdom's port of Genoa had no direct rail connection with the rest of Europe and its trade was being hit by Marseilles, which had been served by the main line of the Paris, Lyons & Mediterranean Railway since 1855. Moreover, the railways in the Savoy and Piedmont were separated by the Alps. The link-up required a tunnel through the mountains at the Col du Fréjus. This was 8·5 miles (13·6 km) long, and with the rudimentary equipment available at that period it took 14 years to build. By the time it was finished in 1871 the Savoy had been a part of France for 11 years, and Piedmont was on the point of being incorporated into the new Italy.

The railway in the Savoy was now part of the PLM, which with its firm base in Marseilles was not enthusiastic about encouraging traffic to Genoa through the new tunnel, generally called the Mont Cenis Tunnel. For its part Italy had seen in 1870 that the principal flow of trade between northern and southern Europe would move eastwards.

Ten years before the Mont Cenis Tunnel was put in hand, work had begun on extending an existing railway running southwards from Turin to reach Genoa. The project faced similar difficulties to those which had confronted von Ghega on the Semmering route; for 13·7 miles (22 km) from Genoa the line had to cross the Giovi Pass in the Ligurian Appenines, which is at an altitude of 1,545 ft (472 m). At one time two cable-worked sections were proposed but the railway took courage from the example of von Ghega and opted for steam haulage. The 0-4-4-0 locomotives used when the line was opened became known as the 'Giovi Mastofons'.

Taking a route in-tunnel below the pass, the line climbed at nearly 1 in 29 from Genoa to the southern portal, continuing through the tunnel for 2 miles (3·26 km) to a summit of 1,181 ft (360 m) at the northern end. The tunnel was opened on 6 December 1853, and in due course became part of the first main line to Genoa through the Mont Cenis Tunnel.

A second Giovi line on a different alignment was opened on 15 April 1889 to relieve the original route as international traffic through the Mont Cenis Tunnel increased. With 22 tunnels, as compared with 15 on the earlier line, and some massive viaducts, the steepest gradient was restricted to 1 in 62. In the Ronco Tunnel, 5 miles (8·3 km) long and the longest on the new line, the gradient was 1 in 86.

The unification of Germany after the Franco-Prussian War and the frontier changes involved made it clear that the industrial heart of Europe would be in the area of the Ruhr, the Saar, Lorraine and Luxembourg. Plans for a rail connection between Germany and northern Italy via Switzerland

The 'Orient Express' pauses at the Turkish border on its way to the Golden Horn.

had been considered as early as 1838. At first it was proposed to cross into Italy by the Splugen or Lukmanier Passes in the Grisons but the cost of the line was too heavy for Switzerland to carry alone. With the opening of the Brenner route between Austria and Italy a route further west was preferred and it was decided to take the line over the Gotthard Pass. After an international conference at Berne the Gotthard Convention was signed by Switzerland and Italy on 15 October 1869. The German states attended the conference and promised participation, and this promise was ratified on 28 October 1871 by the newly-established German Empire. Austria saw the plan as a challenge to the route between Italy and north-western Europe via the Brenner Pass, which involved a detour through Munich. Its reply was to build a new line from Innsbruck through the Vorarlberg to the Swiss frontier at Buchs, connecting the Brenner line with Zurich and Basle. This connection, opened in 1884, crossed the Arlberg Pass in a tunnel 6·4 miles (10·25 km) long at an altitude of 4,300 ft (1,311 m).

The Gotthard line was the first international railway undertaking in Europe, the original Saint-Gotthard Railway Company being financed jointly by Switzerland, Italy and Germany. The line began

LLSCHAFT

CO

VOITURE - LITS

SCHLAFWAGE

Above: A modern electric train of the Austrian Federal Railways crosses the Krauselklause Viaduct on the historic Semmering line, the first main line in Europe to cross a mountain range. The viaduct is 321 ft (98 m) in length and 118 ft (36 m) high. There is a second row of three arches below those visible in the picture.
Above right: Three-level engineering on the Gotthard line near Giornico.

at Immensee, near Lucerne, where it connected with other Swiss railways. It climbed to a summit of 3,776 ft (1,151 m) inside the Gotthard Tunnel itself, which was entered at Göschenen. The tunnel was 9·25 miles (14·90 km) long. At Airolo, near the southern portal, the descent along the Ticino Valley had already begun, bringing the line to its lowest point at Giubiasco on Lake Maggiore, at an altitude of 754 ft (229·8 m). Continuing along the lakeside, the original main line crossed the frontier into Italy and connected with the Italian railway system at Luino. A branch from Giubiasco ran to Lugano and Chiasso. In later years the branch became the main line and the connection with the Italian railways was at the frontier station of Chiasso. The distance from Immensee to Chiasso was 127·75 miles (205·63 km).

Spectacular engineering work on the northern and southern slopes enabled the steepest gradient to be kept down for the most part to 1 in 38·5 although there were a few stretches at 1 in 35·7. Of the 70 tunnels, 7 were spirals. These could be confusing to the traveller, as Pearson found when he came this way in 1890:

I was quite unaware that on the ascent to the great tunnel, there were any spiral tunnels and the consequence was that I got completely confused as to the lie of the railway on the way up. Especially so was this the case near Wassen, where three levels of the same line (which returns

on itself) were visible at one and the same time. I could not understand at first what the other lines were, it being most unlikely that there were other railways in this Alpine valley, but just before Göschenen it became clear that the curves and twists of the railway line in the valley below were part of the line we had travelled over and, realising this, I was more than ever filled with admiration for this splendid bit of engineering work – the Gotthard Railway. The viaducts, mostly of metal, were magnificent, and crossed affluents of the Reuss at the most dizzy heights.

South of the tunnel the line followed the Dazio Grande Gorge, where the grandeur of the scenery inspired the Swiss writer and Nobel Prizewinner Carl Spitteler to write:

The Dazio Gorge is stupendous Chaos, where Nature has created such confusion that the observer scarcely knows whether he is looking upwards or downwards. The Dazio Grande is the climax of the Gotthard range and the most magnificent part of the Vale of Tessin.

A shuttle service through the tunnel between Göschenen and Airolo began on 1 January 1882, and the line was opened throughout on 1 June of the same year.

In their book *Express Trains English and Foreign* published in 1889, E. Foxwell and T. C. Farrer wrote 'Too much praise can hardly be bestowed on

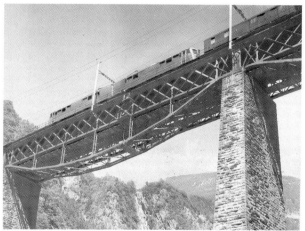

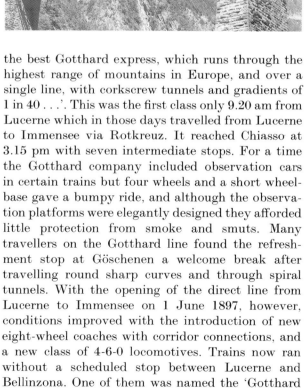

the best Gotthard express, which runs through the highest range of mountains in Europe, and over a single line, with corkscrew tunnels and gradients of 1 in 40 . . .'. This was the first class only 9.20 am from Lucerne which in those days travelled from Lucerne to Immensee via Rotkreuz. It reached Chiasso at 3.15 pm with seven intermediate stops. For a time the Gotthard company included observation cars in certain trains but four wheels and a short wheel-base gave a bumpy ride, and although the observation platforms were elegantly designed they afforded little protection from smoke and smuts. Many travellers on the Gotthard line found the refreshment stop at Göschenen a welcome break after travelling round sharp curves and through spiral tunnels. With the opening of the direct line from Lucerne to Immensee on 1 June 1897, however, conditions improved with the introduction of new eight-wheel coaches with corridor connections, and a new class of 4-6-0 locomotives. Trains now ran without a scheduled stop between Lucerne and Bellinzona. One of them was named the 'Gotthard Express' and classed as a *train de luxe*.

While western Europe was marvelling at the Gotthard route a still more ambitious project was taking shape to the east. Plans for connecting European Russia by rail with its territories in Asia had been under consideration since the 1850s, some of them based on a very superficial understanding

of the rigours of the Siberian climate. The most practical proposal for a Trans-Siberian Railway was made by an American businessman, Peter McDonaugh Collins, who had travelled across Siberia to Chita in 1856–57 and from there sailed down the Shilka, Amur and Ussuri Rivers to the port of Nikolayevsk on the Strait of Tartary, which opens at its southern end into the Sea of Japan. Collins found that the rivers were navigable by steamers as far as Chita and recommended construction of a railway from there to Irkutsk. His idea was discussed from every angle for some 30 years before a final plan was agreed and it was announced in June 1887 that work would shortly begin on building a railway from the Pacific coast at Vladivostok to cross Siberia and join the existing Russian rail system at Ekaterinburg.

There was still more delay before the project was formally launched in a ceremony at Vladivostok on 31 May 1891 when the Tsarevich Nicholas deposited the first shovelful of earth in a wheelbarrow. By the end of the century the line from Vladivostok had reached Khabarovsk. In the west the extension from Ekaterinburg had been completed to Lake Baikal. From Myovsk on the opposite shore of the lake good progress had been made to Sretnsk, from where river transport provided the connection to Khabarovsk. The final development of the original Trans-Siberian project occurred early in the 20th century.

Above: The Karstelenbach viaduct on the Gotthard line showing on the right the Amsteg hydro-electric power station and the aqueduct carrying the conduits supplying water to the turbines.
Above left: Two Swiss Federal Railways locomotives attack the climb to the Gotthard Tunnel.
Left: An inverted 'bowstring' strengthens the main girders on this bridge across an Alpine valley.

2. NEW LINES IN BRITAIN

HALF WAY THROUGH the 19th century the broad outlines of the British railway system seemed to have been fixed. But what might have been the last major development – the opening by the Great Northern Railway of its London terminus at Kings Cross in 1852 – was the prelude to the building of new main lines. The Midland Railway, which had centred its activities on its cross-country route from Leeds to Sheffield, Derby, Birmingham and Bristol, saw the new Great Northern line as a means of reaching London itself. In 1858 it opened an extension from Leicester, via Bedford, to the Great Northern at Hitchin and began running trains into Kings Cross. The arrangement could only be temporary, for the Great Northern line could not cope with the growing traffic of two companies. The Midland therefore obtained powers to build its own line from Bedford to London and in 1868 opened its terminus at St Pancras, close to Kings Cross.

In earlier years Midland trains had reached London over the London & North Western Railway from Rugby. An independent main line to the towns and cities of the Midlands was obviously necessary but the Great Northern and the London & North Western feared the competition. Already the Midland had been looking further north, to Carlisle, where the Glasgow & South Western Railway and the North British Railway were interested in finding a partner to work their traffic to London. The Midland already operated a service between Leeds and Tebay, but it was a shaky arrangement, dependent on the good will of the London & North Western for part of the route. Connections at Tebay for Midland passengers to Carlisle and beyond were poor and a frequent source of complaint, with the underlying suspicion that they were intended to discourage the traffic.

Negotiations failed to bring improvement, and the Midland went to Parliament for powers to build a

From 1876 the Midland Railway challenged the Great Northern and the London & North Western with its own Anglo-Scottish services, using its newly constructed and very expensive line between Settle and Carlisle. Four-coupled express locomotives, as on this express at Carlisle, were always a Midland hallmark, as were its clerestory-roofed coaches.

line of its own to Carlisle from Settle Junction on the old route. The powers were granted, whereupon the Midland looked again at the task it had undertaken. The route would lie through high and sparsely populated moors, brooded over by the sombre heights of Ingleborough, Wild Boar Fell and High Seat. Numerous tunnels and viaducts would be needed to climb to the summit point at Ais Gill 1,169 ft (356·3 m) above sea level, and from Settle Junction there would be only 15 miles (24 km) in which to reach this highest point on the line. The summit was in the desolate expanse of Blea Moor, a rough-hewn plateau approached through Blea Moor Tunnel, 1·5 miles (2·4 km) long.

Contemplating these things, the Midland had cold feet and sought an accommodation with the London & North Western by which traffic might be routed via Tebay on better terms than previously. It was too late. Parliament insisted that the work it had sanctioned should be carried out and the Midland

In 1923 the Midland Railway joined the London Midland & Scottish Group, becoming a partner with its previous West Coast rival for Anglo-Scottish traffic. LMS 'Jubilee' class 4-6-0 No 5568 has toiled up long stretches at 1 in 100 to Ais Gill summit, 1,169 ft (356·5 m) above sea level with a train from Carlisle to Hellifield.

No 192 was the first of J. G. Robinson's (Great Central Railway's Chief Mechanical Engineer), handsome Atlantic locomotives and is here heading a Marylebone-Manchester express composed of coaches of his design. The train is near Denham on the Great Western & Great Central Joint line (note the Great Western lower quadrant signal), about 1913.

In the shadow of the Fells at Kirby Stephen a Leeds-Glasgow relief train in British Railways days. Seen here on the descent from Ais Gill to Carlisle, with surplus steam showing at the safety valves. Ex-LMS 'Black Five' 4-6-0 No 45254.

had to carry on with construction. The Settle and Carlisle line was opened to passenger traffic in 1876, the first public passenger train from St Pancras to Scotland being despatched on 1 May in that year. The Midland's Anglo-Scottish service ran from Carlisle to Glasgow via Dumfries over the Glasgow & South Western, and from Carlisle to Edinburgh via the 'Waverley Route' of the North British Railway through Galashiels. The scenery on this line in the Border Country was on a par with the Settle and Carlisle section. The Midland's route to Scotland was longer than those of the west coast and east coast companies, but many travellers chose it for its scenery and the much-praised comfort of the rolling stock.

One more main line to London was built in the 19th century. The Manchester, Sheffield & Lincolnshire Railway was a cross-country system which connected at several points with the main lines running north and south. In 1892 it opened a small extension southwards to Annesley, near Nottingham, where it joined the Great Northern Railway and handed over the considerable coal traffic from the numerous collieries along its route. The company's chairman was Sir Edward Watkin, who held a similar office on several other railways, among them the Metropolitan. Under his control the Metropolitan had extended far out of London into Buckinghamshire. Watkin was dissatisfied with the role of the Manchester, Sheffield & Lincolnshire as a feeder to other systems for traffic to the south and he planned a new main line to connect Annesley with the Metropolitan Railway at Quainton Road, a few miles north of Aylesbury. A Bill for a London extension was presented to Parliament but rejected after strong opposition by the established railways. On a second attempt in 1892, however, it was approved, and on 28 March 1893 it received the Royal Assent. The Manchester, Sheffield & Lincolnshire in due course changed its name to Great Central and work began on the new line through Nottingham, Leicester and Rugby. Metropolitan tracks were to be used from Quainton Road to West Hampstead, and from there just under 2 miles (3·2 km) of line, mostly in tunnel, had to be built to bring Great Central trains to their terminus at Marylebone. Public services between Marylebone and Manchester began on 15 March 1899.

The Great Central extension to London was the last main line built in England. It provided a more

direct connection between Leicester and Nottingham than by the Midland but its services from Marylebone to Manchester and Bradford duplicated those of the older lines. But the railway never lacked confidence. New locomotives and rolling stock built for the London extension, and an already 20th-century attitude to public relations, changed the pedestrian image of the Manchester, Sheffield & Lincolnshire overnight to the young and dashing Great Central.

3. RAILS ACROSS AMERICA

Previous page : The classic style of the American 4-4-0 showing the elaborate embellishments favoured in its early days.

US Military Locomotive 133, built by Faith and Cooke in 1864 and worked by Nashville and Mathews Railroad.

RAILWAYS IN THE UNITED STATES were still in their infancy when the first proposals were made for a line across the continent. The war between the northern and southern States (1861–65) emphasised the need for national unity, and a transcontinental line to link the widely separated populations on the eastern and western seaboards was seen as both a political and an economic necessity. The first steps were taken while the war was at its height. Theodore Judah, a railway engineer, planned a route from the west coast across the Sierra Nevada into the then largely desert country beyond. Support from business interests in San Francisco was only lukewarm but Judah found financial backing in Sacramento, and on 28 June 1862 the Central Pacific Railroad Company of California was formed.

Judah's energy concentrated the minds of railway promoters in the eastern states and put an end to arguments over where the eastern terminus of a transcontinental line should be. It was decided to start from Omaha, on the west bank of the Missouri River, which was connected by a ferry with Council Bluffs on the opposite shore. Through rail communication between Council Bluffs and Chicago was already in sight. President Lincoln gave his full support to the project and on 1 July 1862 signed an Act authorising the Union Pacific Railroad Company to build westwards from Omaha, and the Central Pacific to put into action its plans for a railway across the Sierra Nevada.

The Central Pacific was first off the mark. It faced formidable terrain, climbing from sea level at Sacramento to a summit of 7,017 ft (2,140 m) in a distance of only 105 miles (169 km). The line was carried up the mountains in deep cuttings hewn out of the rock and over lofty trestle bridges. On one section of 12 miles (19 km) there were 15 tunnels. Barriers and snowsheds to protect against avalanches totalled 37 miles (60 km) in length. Summit Tunnel at the top of the climb was only 162 ft (50 m) long but its construction took from November 1866 to August 1867. In the following December a party of 700 guests was taken by train to the temporary mountain terminus, where they rounded off the more formal celebrations with a snowball fight!

Once over the mountain barrier, easier terrain lay ahead for the Central Pacific and by mid-1868 they had built a little over 186 miles (300 km) of line. There were other problems, however, in that all materials from the Atlantic coast had to be brought

by sea to San Francisco, either round Cape Horn or with land transport across the Isthmus of Panama.

At first the Union Pacific also had supply problems to contend with, its materials being brought by steamer up the Missouri River, but the pace quickened when the rail connection from Chicago to Council Bluffs was completed in November 1867.

The Union Pacific had begun to build its line from Omaha in November 1863. The company had relatively easy terrain until it reached Central Wyoming and crossed into Utah. On the other hand, it was penetrating territory peopled by native Americans who saw the railway and the settlers who followed it as a threat to their way of life. Army detachments gave the rail workers protection, supported by those of the workers who had experience of fighting in the Civil War. Skirmishes with Sioux and Cheyennes were frequent as the rails advanced. By mid-1868, however, more than 620 miles (1,000 km) of track had been laid.

Both companies received grants of land and government bonds in proportion to the length of railway built. There was therefore keen competition in this respect together with the fact that the railway building the greater proportion of the route would be rewarded with a higher proportion of the revenue from traffic. No point of junction had been laid down in the Act, the assumption being that both companies would carry on with construction until their lines met. This vagueness led at length to an absurd situation where both railways were preparing the formation for tracklaying on alignments that overlapped. The government then stepped in and called both sides to a meeting in Washington to decide where the connection would be made. Ogden, east of the Great Salt Lake in Utah, was agreed on as the boundary between the two systems, with the actual meeting point of the tracks at Promontory Summit, a few miles further west. The Ogden-Promontory Summit section was to be built by the Union Pacific and then purchased by the Central Pacific.

The rails from east and west were joined in a ceremony at Promontory on 10 May 1869. After the last rails had been laid a sleeper made of polished laurel was placed beneath them. The Central Pacific representative was handed two spikes made of gold from California and placed them in ready-drilled holes in the sleeper. The Union Pacific man received one spike of silver from Nevada, and one which was an alloy of iron, gold and silver from Arizona. When these had been inserted, the moment came for the four spikes to be ceremonially driven home with silver-plated mallets. It is said that both men missed, not having placed their spikes squarely in the prepared holes, but the telegraphist in attendance flashed the single word 'Done!' over the Union Pacific's wires and the United States rejoiced. The ceremonial sleeper was then removed, an ordinary one substituted, and the rails were secured with standard spikes.

The 4-4-0 locomotives *Jupiter* of the Central Pacific and No 119 of the Union Pacific had been standing each on their own side of the junction. At the end of the ceremony a bottle of champagne was broken on the laurel sleeper and *Jupiter* backed away, allowing No 119 to advance on to Central

The American Standard locomotive, typified by No 119 of the Union Pacific. *Jupiter* and No 119 were the two engines used at the ceremony to mark the joining of east and west rails at Promontory on 10 May 1869.

Right: Jupiter, the first Central Pacific train to travel on Union Pacific territory after the joining of the two railroads' tracks in 1869.

Pacific metals. Then No 119 backed into its own territory, allowing *Jupiter* to cross the divide and enter Union Pacific territory.

For a short time passengers changed between Central Pacific and Union Pacific trains at Promontory, but from the beginning of 1870 the change was made at Ogden. The Central Pacific maintained a locomotive depot at Promontory to provide assistance for heavy trains climbing the eastern slopes of the Sierras. In 1903 the Southern Pacific absorbed the Central Pacific and began construction of a line across the Great Salt Lake from Ogden to Lucin which by-passed Promontory. This was completed in 1904 and from then on took most of the traffic. Today Promontory is known as the 'Golden Spike National Historic site', a preservation order having been made by Congress in July 1965. Some 15 miles (24 km) of the old track are still there, and copies of the locomotives *Jupiter* and No 119 can be seen in steam. They were built in 1979 for a re-enactment of the 'Golden Spike' ceremony celebrating the 110th anniversary of the transcontinental line.

George Pullman, creator of the Pullman Car, was always alert for opportunities to publicise his vehicles. He formed a special train to run on the new transcontinental line and in May 1870 offered it to the Boston Board of Trade to hire for an excursion to San Francisco. As the train crossed the summit of the Sierra Nevada a committee of passengers met in the smoking car to pass the following resolution:

Resolved, that we, the passengers of the Boston Board of Trade Pullman excursion train, the first through train from the Atlantic to the Pacific, having now been a week *en route* for San Francisco, and having had, during this period, ample opportunity to test the character and the quality of the accommodations supplied for our journey, hereby express our entire satisfaction with the

arrangements made by Mr George N. Pullman, and our admiration of the skill and energy which have resulted in the construction, equipment and general management of this beautiful and commodious moving hotel.

There was much more to warm Mr Pullman's heart, particularly the committee's promise to support the further use of 'these elegant and homelike carriages upon the principal routes in the New England States'. No doubt the excursionists had been able to hire trains on advantageous terms.

Another celebrated transcontinental journey took place in 1876. The normal time from the Atlantic to the Pacific was then seven days with four changes of train and some notoriously poor connections. Two theatrical promoters saw a chance for publicity here by hiring a special train to take their star performers from New York in half the usual time to appear in a production of *Henry V* in San Francisco. The Jarrett & Palmer's Transcontinental Express was organised with the co-operation of five railway companies. There was limited accommodation for any of the public prepared to pay the fare in the three-coach formation consisting of a day coach, a Pullman hotel car, and a baggage van. The hotel car was a Pullman with a kitchen compartment from which meals were served in the saloon when converted for day use.

A 4-4-0 of the Pennsylvania Railroad took the train non-stop from Jersey City to Pittsburgh, 438·5 miles (705·6 km). At Chicago, reached in 21 hours, it was already being called the 'Lightning Train'. Welcoming bonfires blazed along its route as it sped on to Omaha. Near Sidney, in Nebraska, the driver eased the pace so that an escort of cowboys could gallop alongside, firing their revolvers. He could afford to, being well ahead of time, but soon news came of a flood near Ogden which had undermined the track. Repair work was already in hand

Until George N. Pullman raised standards of passenger comfort, accommodation for night-time travelling was wooden berths above daytime seating.

By the beginning of the twentieth century the railroads provision of facilities for passengers included every modern convenience. Seen here is the luxurious interior of the observation car of the Oriental Limited.

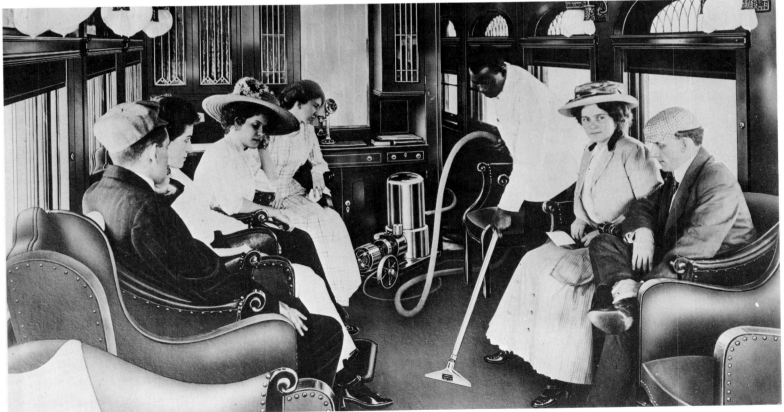

A total of 173 Budd stainless steel cars were needed to equip the daily trains in each direction of the Canadian transcontinental service in its heyday.

and by the time the train reached the site it was able to steam slowly over the restored rails. The Lightning Train pulled into San Francisco 83 hours 39 minutes after leaving New York, headed by a Central Pacific 4-4-0 which had taken charge 879 miles (1,414·6 km) earlier, stopping only to refuel.

The transcontinental flyer of 1876 had an advantage compared with the Boston-San Francisco excursion of 1870 as the Missouri had been bridged between Council Bluffs and Omaha in 1872. Even after the bridge was opened, however, travellers by ordinary services had to change into a train of the Council Bluffs Transfer Company to cross the river. This situation changed in 1887, by which time four main lines from Chicago and the east had converged on Council Bluffs, where the station had been known as 'U.P. Transfer' because of the cross-river connection with the Union Pacific. From that year it was possible to travel in through sleeping cars from Chicago to California. One of the trains put on to handle this traffic began running between Council Bluffs and San Francisco daily from 13 November 1887 under the title 'Overland Flyer'. It earned the approval of Farrer and Foxwell in *Express Trains English and Foreign* who described it as 'quite first rate' because 'It does the 1031 miles from Omaha (1,000 ft above sea level) to Ogden (4,301 ft) over two summits of 8,247 and 7,395 ft respectively (sinking to 6,007 ft between) at 29 miles per hour inclusive, and 31¼ exclusive of stops.'

At the time their book was published a new transcontinental express called the 'Golden Gate Special' had just been introduced. This train had a short life under its original title. It was an all-Pullman service operating between Omaha and San Francisco, and it lasted only from 5 December 1888 to 12 May 1889. After its withdrawal the 'Overland Flyer' was re-equipped to similar standards of comfort. At that time the 'Overland' name was not used west of Ogden, the train being described in the timetables simply as 'Pacific Express' westbound and 'Atlantic Express' eastbound. In 1895 the more familiar 'Overland Limited' title came into use, and in 1899 this name was carried throughout the journey.

The Chicago & North Western also used the 'Overland' name for a Chicago-Council Bluffs train with Pullman sleeping cars which connected with the 'Fast Mail' of the Union Pacific serving points west and conveying a through Pullman sleeper for Denver. The train, which departed at 10.15 pm from Chicago with through cars for Denver, Portland and San Francisco that joined the 'Overland Flyer' at Council Bluffs, was shown in the C&NW timetable as the 'Pacific Limited'. The timetable description of the corresponding eastbound service was 'Overland Flyer – Daily Solid Vestibule train of Baggage Cars, Palace Sleepers, free Chair Cars and Dining Cars Portland to Chicago. Palace Sleeper San Francisco to Chicago'. Travellers making the whole

journey spent two nights in the train. The C&NW also operated a through service between Chicago and Denver called the 'Denver Limited' westbound and the 'Chicago Limited' eastbound.

By the end of the century five transcontinental lines had been built in the United States. Much of their history was made in the board rooms and the stock market as rivals tried to frustrate each other's plans, but there was conflict on the ground as well. To the south of the first transcontinental line, the Southern Pacific had been building eastwards from Los Angeles. By 1883 it had reached El Paso on the Rio Grande, and from there took over a number of local lines to complete a route to New Orleans. In so doing the railway broke the spirit of an agreement with the Texas & Pacific not to build eastwards from El Paso.

The Atchison, Topeka & Santa Fe did not proclaim its transcontinental ambitions at first, confining its proposals to a route from Atchison, on the Missouri River, to New Mexico along the old Santa Fe Trail to the gold and silver mines. In 1876 it had reached Pueblo, where it clashed with the Denver & Rio Grande which was heading south for El Paso. The only practicable route into New Mexico was by the Raton Pass. Surveying parties of both railroads carried arms as they went about their business and seemed likely to do battle. The Atchison's men had the advantage of local support and when the two sides met at the pass the Denver party realised it was outnumbered and withdrew to avoid bloodshed. Continuing over the pass, the Atchison, Topeka & Santa Fe reached its original goal of Santa Fe City and then turned westwards for Los Angeles. The line was opened in 1884.

In the north of the country three railroads based on St Paul had Seattle in their sights. There was much feuding between the Northern Pacific and the Great Northern. The Northern Pacific reached the Puget Sound first, completing its line in 1883, but financial difficulties made it an easy prey for the Great Northern and it was taken over. In 1893 the Great Northern completed its own line to Seattle on an alignment to the north of the Northern Pacific. The third member of the trio in the northern states was the Chicago, Milwaukee & St Paul. Disturbed by the possible effect on its traffic for the west of the Great Northern's growing empire, it was considering a line of its own to the Pacific at the turn of the century. The decision to build to the Puget Sound was taken in 1905 and construction began in the same year. Some 1,400 miles (2,253 km) had to be laid, and there were five mountain ranges in its path, but with work proceeding simultaneously at a number of sites rapid progress was made and the last spike was driven at Garrison, Montana on 14 May 1909.

The Chicago & North Western, which had first linked Chicago with the Pacific coast in collaboration in 1893 with the Union Pacific, also advertised

connections with Seattle by the Northern Pacific route. Passengers on its 10.30 pm 'Pacific Express' from Chicago to St Paul arrived at 12.05 pm and could continue by the 4.15 pm Northern Pacific through train to Seattle, arriving at 12.55 am on the third night of their journey.

In Canada, as in the United States, the political and economic unity of two widely separated territories were the incentive for building a transcontinental railway. A preliminary survey for a route, commissioned in 1857, was in the nature of an exploration, for the parties were literally making their way through the unknown. The work took four years and the conclusions were not encouraging. One positive result was the discovery of a pass in the Rocky Mountains – Kicking Horse Pass – through which a railway might be taken, but the difficulties there as elsewhere were daunting.

No further steps were taken at the time but British Columbia continued to press for a rail link with Canada east of the Rockies. In the 1860s another survey was undertaken for there were murmurs that the province might secede, or even join the United States, if its isolation were not ended. This time a

Construction of the Northern Pacific in western North Dakota in 1880.

route was mapped along which a transcontinental railway might be built and British Columbia was appeased, the Act of 20 July 1871 under which it joined the Dominion of Canada having included a pledge to provide a rail connection to the eastern side of the Rockies within 10 years.

It was soon apparent that the time scale was too short. Political argument and the fall of a government delayed the start of work until 1 June 1875, when the then almost obligatory ceremonial of turning the first sod took place. Two companies had been formed to build the line; they later merged, and in 1881 the combined undertaking was relaunched as the Canadian Pacific Railway Company, incorporated by an Act of the British Parliament.

Enormous difficulties were faced by the builders. Apart from the challenge of climbing to the pass through the Rockies, long stretches of muskeg swamp had to be crossed and a way blasted through rocky outcrops. Some of the most difficult conditions were encountered where the line was taken round the north shore of Lake Superior, a region described by critics of the scheme as 'a rock wilderness'. In winter work had to be carried on in temperatures

which dropped to the minus 40s Fahrenheit, while in the heat of summer swarms of flies and mosquitoes added to the discomforts.

For the management there were financial worries as more and more of their funds were swallowed up. For a long time the government was reluctant to help but in April 1885 there was an unexpected demonstration of how useful the railway could be. A rebellion having broken out in the north-west of the country, the completed sections of the line were put at the government's disposal for hurrying troops to meet the threat. The rebellion collapsed, and government purse strings were loosened in recognition of the railway's help. On 7 November 1885 the last spike was driven home in the Gold Range, British Columbia, by Sir Donald Smith, a Director of the CPR who had committed much of his personal fortune to the project.

On the day after the ceremony the first CPR transcontinental train ran to Port Moody, at that time the western terminus of the line. In the east the railway reached Montreal and Quebec by lines which had been taken over. A regular transcontinental passenger service began in the summer of 1886 between Montreal and Port Moody. The 12-mile (19·3-km) extension to Vancouver was opened in 1887, the inaugural train from Montreal arriving there on 23 May, the eve of Queen Victoria's birthday in her Jubilee year.

An impression of travel through the Kicking Horse Pass on a CPR transcontinental train was recorded by a contributor to *Harper's Magazine.* He wrote:

The legions of spruce, always preserving the same savage independence of poise, perpendicular as masts, now climb six thousand feet above us – climb perhaps even higher still until the hems of the perpetual snows mass over them and hide them from sight. Far above their loftiest outposts, peaks are lifting glaciers to the sun. But we are too close to these immensities to understand all their magnificence. At Stephen we reach the loftiest point of the route; we are nearly five thousand three hundred feet above the sea – but we are still walled up to heaven.

On the original alignment over the pass the average gradient was 1 in 24. Regrading in 1908 reduced this to 1 in 45 but at the expense of adding 4 miles (6·4 km) to the distance. With the building of the Connaught Tunnel, 5 miles (8 km) long, in later years the extra mileage of the previous route was saved.

Central Pacific 60 and Union Pacific 119 meet at Promontory Point on 10 May 1869.

4. POWER, SPEED AND SAFETY

Previous page: A Webb four-cylinder compound 4-4-0 heads a Euston-Birmingham two-hour express of the London & North Western Railway near Harrow.

ARTISTS WHO PRODUCED admirable prints of railway subjects in the early years were often weak on locomotives. Structures, station buildings and contemporary fashions were portrayed convincingly but often the locomotives were represented in a conventional stylised form that did duty for every variety. Some important developments were hidden from the artist's eye, and once the wonder of the 'iron horse' had subsided, interest may have flagged.

A fundamental change in locomotive construction that was not apparent to the observer was the gradual replacement of wrought iron by mild steel which took place between the early 1860s and the end of the century. Over the same period boiler pressures were being increased to around 180 lb per sq in (12·5 bar). Another of these unseen developments concerned the interior of the firebox. In their early days steam locomotives were largely confined to mining districts and they burned coal. In that environment the smoke due to incomplete combustion of the fuel was not important, but it was a different matter when trains began to travel through residential areas. Railways therefore changed to coke, but this was more expensive and also had an abrasive action on the firebox and flue tubes.

Engineers in the United States and Britain experimented with methods of burning coal which would ensure as complete combustion as possible and so minimise smoke, while also improving efficiency. Up to the 1850s some of the combustion air entering the firebox through the dampers or the firehole door had passed straight to the flue tubes. The problem was to make the whole of the air flow pass over the firebed. Two methods were tried. In 1857 G. R. Grigs of the Boston & Providence Railroad put a brick arch over the fire which forced incoming air through the dampers to pass over the firebed before it could curve back over the top of the arch to enter the tubes. A year later the engineer of the Birkenhead, Lancashire & Cheshire Junction Railway fixed a deflector plate in the firebox, above the firehole door, to direct air coming through the door downwards on to the fire. Meanwhile experiments had been made on the Midland Railway under Matthew Kirtley and in 1859, at the suggestion of his assistant Charles Markham, a brick arch and a deflector plate were used together, establishing a practice which lasted for the life of the steam locomotive.

Three-cylinder Webb compound locomotive No 643 *Raven.* An example of Webb's divided drive, the outside cylinders driving the rear axle and the low-pressure cylinder (prominent below the smokebox) driving the axle in front. With a leading pony truck, the wheel arrangement is 2-2-2-0.

Another development of 1859 that persisted in steam locomotive practice was the injector for feeding the boiler with water. Previously boilers had been kept supplied by pumps driven from the motion. If a boiler needed topping up while the engine was not working it had to be driven to and fro on a siding so that the pumps could operate, or at worst it might be necessary to grease the driving wheel treads so that they could spin round without moving the locomotive. The injector was an arrangement of cones that created a high-speed steam jet. Water entrained by the steam was forced into the boiler against the pressure within, and the device could be used whether the locomotive was running or stationary. The injector was invented by Henri Giffard, who had developed a steam-driven airship and was hoping to build a steam-driven aeroplane; its adoption in locomotives was an early example of an idea being borrowed from outside the railway industry – an industry that for the most part was self-sufficient.

With some grades of coal, clinker forming on the firebars was a problem. It could be overcome by mounting the firebars on pivots so that they could be rocked to and fro to break up the deposit by operating a lever. For many years the system was little used in Britain but as the best grades of steam coal were used up it became a useful accessory.

Changes in firebox design were more apparent than some other improvements. The Belpaire firebox, originating in Belgium, was recognisable by its vertical sides and flat top. These surfaces were parallel with those of the inner firebox and made it easier to fit the stays between the inner and outer fireboxes to resist the steam pressure. Limitations on the height of locomotives often made it necessary for the lower part of the firebox to be between the frame plates. In American practice, however, fireboxes might be completely above the frames so that grates could be wider, allowing a large grate area without undue length. By the end of the century wide fireboxes were being fitted on 4-4-0 locomotives above driving wheels of 7 ft (213·36 cm) diameter but for still bigger grates the firebox had to be behind the rear driving axle and supported by a trailing axle or truck.

By mid-century the Stephenson link motion and Walschaerts valve gears were well established. The Stephenson system was the most widely used in Britain and America up to about 1900. From 1879 a valve gear developed by David Joy was fitted to some 4,000 locomotives of the London & North Western and Lancashire & Yorkshire Railways but was not adopted to a significant extent elsewhere. It differs from both the Stephenson and Walschaerts gears in having no eccentrics or return crank, the movement of the valves being derived through a linkage from the connecting rod.

In the Stephenson gear the 'lead' (the point at which steam is admitted to the cylinder before the piston ends its stroke) increased as the cut-off of steam was made earlier. Before superheating was introduced, however, engines were not worked at the early cut-offs which made this effect a drawback. In the Walschaerts gear the lead was constant at all cut-offs and as superheating became general this type of valve gear gained in favour.

As to the valves themselves, the conventional slide valve caused considerable friction, being pressed down by the steam pressure on the surface over which it worked. Experiments were carried out with valves having cylindrical heads – piston valves – but there were difficulties with steam leakage. This problem was tackled more energetically when superheating became general in the next century, because the hot, dry steam increased the friction. Improved piston ring design overcame the problem.

While these detailed improvements in the generation and use of steam were being made, engineers were considering a more fundamental change. In the simple-expansion locomotive, even when early cut-offs made the best possible use of the expansive property of steam, energy was lost in the exhaust. Compound working, in which the steam exhausted from a high-pressure cylinder worked again in a low-pressure cylinder before escaping to atmosphere, was widely used in stationary engines. It was first applied in a practical locomotive by the Swiss engineer, Anatole Mallet, who designed an 0-4-2 tank engine with one high-pressure and one low-pressure cylinder for the Bayonne-Biarritz Railway. Three of these locomotives were built by the French firm of Schneider in 1876. In Germany August von Borries designed a 2-2-0 tank engine which was delivered to the Prussian State Railways in 1880 and by 1884 had produced a 2-4-0 passenger design for the same system. A 4-4-0 express locomotive followed in 1893, a prelude to larger and more powerful Prussian compounds in the next century.

These locomotives all had one high- and one low-pressure cylinder. There was an inherent difficulty in obtaining a high tractive effort at starting because the low-pressure cylinder could not contribute until the high-pressure cylinder had exhausted. Both Mallet and von Borries devised methods of supplying high-pressure steam to the low-pressure

cylinder to improve the starting performance. In Britain F. W. Webb of the London & North Western Railway chose a three-cylinder system with two high-pressure cylinders on the outside driving the rear axle, and an inside low-pressure cylinder driving the front one. With a single-axle pony truck leading, the wheel arrangement was 2-2-2-0 as the driving axles were not coupled. This introduced a different starting problem in the shape of a strong tendency to slip in greasy rail conditions. Webb's compounds are remembered rather unfairly for this characteristic, which in extreme cases could lead to the two driving axles revolving in opposite directions, and for stories of men with crowbars standing by at stations to lever them on their way if necessary. None the less, they behaved staunchly during the Race to Aberdeen of 1895. Webb's first compounds came out in 1882 and his last class, the more successful and swifter 'Teutonics' in 1897.

A Webb 'Dreadnought' class three-cylinder compound takes water from the troughs near Bushey while working a heavy train. The 'Dreadnoughts' were designed in 1884 as a more powerful version of the earlier 'Experiment' class compounds to handle increasing loads on the main line between London and Carlisle.

The compound locomotive was developed to a high state of efficiency in France in later years. A first step was taken in the 19th century when Alfred de Glehn, a Director of the Chemin de fer du Nord, proposed an experiment in compounding to the company's chief mechanical engineer, Gaston du Bousquet. It took shape in the 2-2-2-0 compound No 701, placed in service in January 1886. This was a four-cylinder locomotive with two high-pressure inside cylinders driving the leading axle and two low-pressure outside cylinders driving the second axle. Here, too, the divided drive made the locomotive prone to slip at starting and in its successors the axles were coupled. A four-wheel bogie replaced the original single carrying axle under the smokebox in 1892 and in this form the locomotive has been preserved at the Mulhouse Railway Museum.

During 1888 and 1889 No 701 was tested in comparison with a contemporary simple-expansion

2-4-0 and showed a 14 per cent economy in fuel consumption. In the de Glehn-du Bousquet system the cut-offs in the high-pressure and low-pressure systems were individually adjustable by the driver. When the Paris, Lyons & Mediterranean Railway took up compounding in 1889 in some 2-4-2 locomotives it used the Henry-Baudry system in which the high-pressure and low-pressure valve gears were linked and controlled together. The PLM profited from the experience of the Nord with No 701 and coupled the driving axles.

In the last resort the effectiveness of improvements in the generation and use of steam depended on the ability of the locomotive to exert a useful tractive effort on its load. The weight on the driving axles was an important factor in providing the good adhesion between wheel and rail necessary for this purpose, but this weight was limited by what the rails and bridges could safely carry. It was logical, therefore, to distribute the weight between two or more driving axles. As railways competed more keenly for passenger traffic, speed also became of increasing importance. Right up to the turn of the century some engineers preferred the locomotive with a single driving axle for fast passenger work. The argument was that the wear of driving wheels was unequal, but if they were coupled all would be forced to revolve at the same speed although their diameters might differ slightly. This would increase the loads on the coupling rods. By the 1890s, however, the locomotive with a two-axle leading bogie and two coupled axles had become the most widespread type for fast passenger work. It was so general in the United States that the 4-4-0 was often known as the 'American' type.

There was also some hesitancy at first in changing from a single carrying axle at the leading end of the locomotive, with sideplay for negotiating curves, to the pivoted four-wheel bogie. It was feared that the bogie would be liable to derailment. Experience soon showed that stability depended on proper positioning of the pivot and providing it with sideplay controlled by springs. Attention to these points soon overcame the objections.

Engines with single and coupled driving axles, with single carrying axles at the front end and with bogies, took part in the two periods of railway 'racing' in Britain in the 1880s and 1890s when the companies forming the east coast and the west coast routes to Scotland vied with each other in reducing journey times from London first to Edinburgh and then to Aberdeen. The Edinburgh contest took place in 1888. Up to that time the west coast day train from Euston reached the Scottish capital in 10 hours, and the corresponding service from Kings Cross in 9 hours. The distance from Euston was 399·7 miles (643·2 km) and from Kings Cross 393·2 miles (632·8 km). At the end of the racing period both routes had shown that the journey could be made in about 7·5 hours. Actual fastest times were 7 hr 27 min from Kings Cross and 7 hr 38 min from Euston.

As to maximum speeds, a 2-4-0 of the North Eastern Railway was timed to cover successive quarter miles at 75·7, 76·2, 76·5 and 76·5 mph (121·8, 122·6, 123·1, 123·1 km/h) in running down the bank from Chester-le-Street towards Newcastle. In general, contemporary records show point-to-point averages rather than maximum speeds but from these it is probable that Patrick Stirling's celebrated 4-2-2 8-foot (2.4-m) 'Singles' and 2-2-2s did not much exceed 70 mph (112 km/h); however, 72 mph (116 km/h) has been calculated for the Caledonian Railway's 4-2-2 No 123 on the descent from Harburn to Edinburgh. On that occasion No 123 was recouping 45 minutes lost south of Carlisle on the west coast route by a failure of the London & North Western engine on the climb to Shap Summit.

At the end of August 1888 the east coast companies had achieved the fastest time from London to Edinburgh, 7 hr 27 min. The best time by the west coast route was 7 hr 38 min on 13 August. Ample proof had been given of the ability of both 'Singles' and coupled engines to run fast and hard.

The Race to Aberdeen of 1895 was a still more hectic occasion, with the competitors changing their schedules overnight and without warning, which must have been confusing for the ordinary traveller. The trains concerned were the night expresses from Euston and Kings Cross with distances to cover of 540 and 524 miles (869 and 843 km) respectively.

On 21 August the east coast route train reached Aberdeen from London in 8 hr 40 min, after which Kings Cross and its allies reverted to the normal timetable. The west coast route made a final effort on the following night with an electrifying 8 hr 32 min. By this time compound locomotives were in the picture on the LNWR and the train was hauled from Euston to Crewe by the 4-2-2-0 *Adriatic* of the Teutonic class, which averaged 64 mph (103 km/h) start-to-stop. The most dramatic performances, however, were by the 2-4-0 'Precedent' class engine from Crewe to Carlisle, and the Caledonian 4-4-0 No 17 from Perth to Aberdeen. Again maximum speeds can only be estimated but there is reason to think that on the descent from Shap to Carlisle the Precedent *Hardwicke* was running at above 80 mph (129 km/h). On the Caledonian line 4-4-0 No 17 covered 89·7 miles (144·4 km) from Perth to the Aberdeen ticket platform in 80·5 minutes, averaging virtually 70 mph (112 km/h).

The suitability of the coupled locomotive for high speeds had been convincingly demonstrated but the 'Single' had not lost all support in Britain. Slipping had been a drawback as the weight of trains increased, but when an improved method of sanding the rails had been developed, using steam pressure instead of gravity, the Midland Railway built several series of 4-2-2s between 1887 and 1901 to the designs of S. W. Johnson, and on the North Eastern Railway T. W. Worsdell used the same wheel arrangement in a two-cylinder compound class

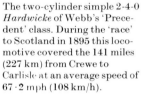

The two-cylinder simple 2-4-0 *Hardwicke* of Webb's 'Precedent' class. During the 'race' to Scotland in 1895 this locomotive covered the 141 miles (227 km) from Crewe to Carlisle at an average speed of 67·2 mph (108 km/h).

built between 1886 and 1892. A maximum speed of 90 mph (145 km/h), a record for the nineteenth century in Britain, was claimed for both classes.

In the United States the 4-4-0 was reaching its zenith. Speed rivalry flared between the New York Central and the Pennsylvania on their New York–Chicago routes in 1893 when the World's Columbian Exposition was held in Chicago. Both railroads scheduled trains between the two cities in 20 hours. George H. Daniels of the NYC had a luxury train of special stock built by the Wagner Palace Car Company to form the 'Exposition Flyer' and a high-

speed 4-4-0 with 7 ft 2 in (2·184 m) diameter wheels was turned out from the shops to the designs of an existing class but with increased diameter. On 9 June 1893 this high-speed 4-4-0 (No 999) was claimed by the guard of the train to have touched 102·8 mph (165 km/h) while making up lost time before Buffalo. Two days later there was another whirlwind descent of the 1 in 350 gradient and this time a maximum of 112·5 mph (181 km/h) was claimed. Daniels was not the man to look too closely at figures he would like to believe. He proudly announced a record. The public received it with enthusiasm and the doubters held their peace. It is now thought that the maximum was probably closer to 81 mph (130·3 km/h).

The 'Exposition Flyer' ran for less than a year, being withdrawn when the exhibition closed, but it had provided experience which enabled the company to introduce a regular 20-hour train between New York and Chicago in 1902, the 'Twentieth Century Limited'.

A rival 20-hour service between New York and Chicago was operated during the exhibition by the Pennsylvania Railroad. The train was called the 'Pennsylvania Special' and as far as posterity is concerned its behaviour has been eclipsed by the exploits on the New York Central. Subsequently the Pennsylvania went back to its old 28-hour timing between the two cities, but in 1902 the 20-hour schedule was revived to keep level with the 'Twentieth Century Limited' on the rival route. The train ran for a year-and-a-half until increasing freight traffic in the Pittsburgh area made timekeeping problematic. Measures to ease the problem were already in hand, and in 1905 an 18-hour schedule was announced and the 'Pennsylvania Special' name revived. The Pennsylvania had been building 4-4-2 (Atlantic) locomotives since 1899, and an engine of that type headed the inaugural train out of New York on 11 June 1905. A hot box near Mansfield, Ohio disabled it and a freight engine had to be

After *Hardwicke*'s record run from Crewe to Carlisle, the Caledonian Railway 4-4-0 No 17 completed the journey to Aberdeen with a final dash over the 89·7 miles (144·4 km) from Perth at an average speed of almost 70 mph (112 km/h).

requisitioned to take the train on to Crestline, where another Atlantic, No 7002, was waiting to take over. With 26 lost minutes to make up the new driver went all out and No 7002 is credited with having covered the 131·4 miles (211·4 km) from Crestline to Fort Wayne in 115 minutes which works out at an average speed of 68·56 mph (110·31 km/h). Observers who noted the times at which the train passed AY Tower and Elida claimed that over those 3 miles (4·83 km) it had been travelling at 127·1 mph (204·5 km/h). Passing times taken at the lineside with ordinary watches are shaky evidence of speed and this 'record' by No 7002 met with more disbelief than the more modest claim made for No 999 of the New York Central.

Traffic on the 'Pennsylvania Special' did not come up to expectations in spite of the dramatic debut. In 1912 the train reverted to a 20-hour schedule and was renamed the 'Broad Way Limited'. This was an allusion to the six tracks of the Pennsylvania main line between New York and Philadelphia. In the same topographical vein the New York Central called its New York-Chicago main line the 'Water Level Route' because it ran close to the lakes instead of climbing through the mountains like the Pennsylvania's main line west of Philadelphia. The 'Broad Way' illusion was probably lost on most of the

Pennsylvania's customers. Soon the railroad changed the name to 'Broadway Limited' so that the train has ever since been associated with New York's Great White Way.

By the end of the century the six-coupled (three coupled axles) locomotive was coming on the scene. In many countries this was to be the most numerous express type although in America the 4-4-2 (Atlantic) was preferred because the trailing axle enabled a wide firebox to be used, so that a large grate area could be provided in a grate of average length. The next step from the Atlantic was direct to the Pacific (4-6-2), again with carrying wheels at the rear to support a wide firebox.

Some duties made four or even five coupled axles desirable, but many engineers were wary of the rigidity of long coupled wheelbases where there was severe curvature. Often sharp curves and steep gradients occurred together and various types of articulated locomotives were built for these conditions. Karl Gölsdorf, on the Austrian State Railways, favoured the alternative of a long coupled wheelbase with increased sideplay for certain axles. His first

venture in this direction was the Class 170 compound 2-8-0 of 1893, a replacement for older passenger locomotives on the Arlberg line. His ideas were vindicated by the ease with which the new class negotiated sharp curves at speed, and at the same time the adhesion with four coupled axles enabled loads to be doubled. In these engines two of the coupled axles were allowed sideplay. In practice the stability on curvature was not matched by the behaviour on straight track or less severe curves, and after a time the sideplay of the rear axle was eliminated.

When new locomotives for heavy freight on the 1 in 27 gradients of the line from Klostergrab to Moldau were required, Gölsdorf applied his principles in an 0-10-0. Here he allowed a sideplay of a little over 1 inch (2·54 cm) in each direction in the first, third and fifth axles. The drive was taken to the fourth axle, which was fixed, and to avoid a long and

heavy connecting rod Gölsdorf extended the piston rod and placed the slidebars in line with the second coupled axle. As in his 2-8-0, the sideplay in the last coupled axle was found to be unnecessary and was eliminated. The Gölsdorf 0-10-0, Class 180, influenced the design of ten-coupled locomotives throughout Europe. Classes 170 and 180 were both two-cylinder compounds with the high-pressure cylinder outside the frames on one side, and the low-pressure on the other. In his later compounds Gölsdorf changed to four cylinders.

Several locomotive builders in America developed compound systems towards the end of the 19th century. The Vauclain system, named after the chief engineer of the Baldwin Locomotive Works,

Atlantic (4-4-2) locomotives were staple express power on the Pennsylvania Railroad in the early years of competition with the New York Central for New York-Chicago traffic. A 'Pennsy' class E3a Atlantic crosses the Schuylkill River bridge, Philadelphia, on a train of wooden Pullman cars in 1907.
Inset: The driver of a Pennsylvania Atlantic poses for the camera. Several series of locomotives with this wheel arrangement were built for the railroad between 1899 and 1914 and three of the last batch survived until 1955.

The high-speed 4-4-0 No 999 specially built for the New York Central's 'Exposition Flyer' of 1893. Some rebuilding has taken place, and with smaller driving wheels the small splasher originally over the leading pair has been removed. No 999's career as a 'racehorse' was short-lived. A correspondent to *The Railway Magazine* in 1902 reported that the engine 'has come down to hauling a train composed of eleven milk cars and a caboose on the "West Shore" between Albany and Oneida'.

was distinctive in having the high-pressure and low-pressure cylinders on each side of the locomotive arranged one above the other, the piston rods of each pair driving a common crosshead. Vauclain Atlantics of the Philadelphia & Reading Railroad distinguished themselves in the fierce competition with the Pennsylvania Railroad when the Reading company scheduled its trains to run the 55·5 miles (89·3 km) from Camden to Atlantic City in 50 minutes at a start-to-stop average speed of 66·6 mph (107·2 km/h). On 17 occasions in 1898 one of these engines ran at a start-to-stop speed of 70 mph (112·6 km/h). For many years the world's fastest trains ran on this service.

As the power of locomotives and the speed of trains increased, some flaws in the safety of railway operation became apparent. Early braking systems were rudimentary. Trains were equipped with brakes on the locomotive, often acting only on the tender wheels, and on one or more guard's vans. Code signals were sounded on the engine whistle when the driver wanted the brakes on the vans to be applied. By the 1870s some progress had been made in braking systems that operated throughout a train, and were not dependent on physical effort by

the crews in screwing brake blocks against the wheels, but they were not necessarily automatic in action. The runaway coaches involved in a notorious accident at Armagh, Northern Ireland on 12 June 1889 had the vacuum brake, but the brakes were not applied automatically when the coaches were detached to lighten the load on the engine in climbing a stiff gradient. When the runaways collided with a following train, 80 passengers were killed and some 250 injured. After the Armagh accident the British Parliament passed the Regulation of Railways Act which, among other important requirements, insisted on all railways fitting automatic continuous brakes on passenger trains.

There were two types of automatic continuous brake – the air brake and the vacuum brake. The air brake was the invention of an American engineer, George Westinghouse, but it was not originally an automatic brake. As first introduced in 1869, a break in continuity of the pipe supplying air to the brake cylinders resulted in loss of braking power, and might go undetected until the driver had to apply the brakes.

In 1871 Westinghouse visited Britain, where his attention was drawn to an article in the journal *Engineering* which set out the requirements for a fail-safe braking system, one of which was that if the air supply was interrupted in any way, the brakes would be applied automatically. It followed from this that if vehicles were detached from a train, as

had occurred at Armagh, or broke away accidentally, the brakes would be applied on both halves of the train.

Westinghouse acknowledged that his system was inadequate in this respect and on his return to the United States he set about redesigning it. His revised system still had an air compressor on the locomotive and a pipe running through the train, with flexible hose connections between the coaches, but now a reservoir on every vehicle was connected to the train pipe and kept charged with air to a pressure of some 70 lb per sq in (5 kg per sq cm).

When the driver moved his brake handle to apply the brakes, air was released from the train pipe; the drop in pressure operated an automatic valve on each vehicle which disconnected its

reservoir from the train pipe and allowed air to enter the brake cylinders, where it acted on the pistons so that through a system of rodding and cranks the brake blocks were pressed against the wheels. When the braking force was sufficient, the driver moved his handle to another position in which the escape of air from the train pipe was stopped and the pressure which had built up in the brake cylinders was maintained. In the 'release' position of the handle the reservoirs were reconnected to the train pipe and recharged with air, while the air in the brake cylinders was exhausted.

With the system described, the driver could control the brake pressure applied, but the brakes could only be released fully. This was a disadvantage in descending long gradients, where a partial

The American express steam locomotive begins to assume the massive proportions familiar in later years.

A Class E2 Atlantic leads the 'Pennsylvania Special' Pullman across the Schuylkill River Bridge, Philadelphia.

release would enable speed to be maintained on sections where the gradient was less severe. Later developments enabled the degree of release to be controlled and improved both the speed of release and of application. The original form of Westinghouse brake in which air was supplied direct to the brake cylinders from a reservoir on the locomotive is still used as a locomotive brake, acting in conjunction with automatic systems on the train and is often called the 'straight' air brake. Before the automatic brake took over, 'straight' systems with certain safety features were used for a time for train braking. In Britain the underground District Railway fitted all its stock in the early 1870s with a straight air brake in which the train pipes were duplicated. If one became unserviceable, the driver could switch to the other, and automatic valves isolated the faulty line from the brake cylinders.

The alternative form of automatic continuous brake was the vacuum brake. A train pipe ran through the train as in the air brake system, and one end of each brake cylinder was connected to it. While the train was running an ejector or vacuum pump on the locomotive maintained a partial vacuum in the pipe and in the cylinders. The piston in each cylinder incorporated a ball valve which in low-pressure conditions allowed the pressure on both sides of the piston to equalise. To apply the brakes air was admitted to the train pipe and entered the cylinders at one end. The ball valves were forced on to their seatings, sealing one side of the pistons from the other, and the difference between atmospheric pressure on one side and the partial vacuum on the other provided the force to move the pistons and apply the brakes.

The brake was automatic because any leakage of air into the system applied the brakes in the same way as when the driver made an application with his brake handle. The ejector which maintained the

vacuum was a high-velocity steam jet device. Sometimes the vacuum was maintained while the train was running by a vacuum pump driven from part of the motion, the ejector being used for quick release of the brakes with the train at a standstill. Degrees of vacuum were usually expressed in inches (that is the height of the column of mercury that the pressure would sustain). In Britain, the largest user of the vacuum brake, the usual figures were 21 inches or 25 inches (53·34 cm or 63·5 cm) comparing with about 30 inches (76·2 cm) at normal atmospheric pressure. The vacuum of 25 inches was favoured by the Great Western Railway. When the British railways were formed into four large groups in 1923, vacuum-braked vehicles outnumbered air-braked by three to one. After the nationalisation of the British lines in 1948 a decision had to be taken on a standard braking system. At first the vacuum brake was chosen, but the decision was reversed in favour of the air brake in 1968. The indecision may be seen as an echo of the comment made by Sir Douglas Galton who, as President of the Institution of Mechanical Engineers, promoted a series of comparative trials of the vacuum and air systems in 1878–79 and was unable to decide on their relative merits. He wrote 'A series of experiments which touch upon the interests of rival inventors who have invested large sums of money in their respective enterprises cannot be carried out by a private individual' and he suggested a Government Commission to assess the two types.

As well as laying down rules for braking, the Regulation of Railways Act of 1898 required the railways in Britain to adopt the block system of signalling. This system divides the line into block sections, and only one train is allowed into a section at a time. There had been a variety of practice before the block system became mandatory, and vestiges of the old time interval signalling lingered. Under time interval working a train was allowed to pass a signal when it was judged that sufficient time had elapsed for a preceding train to get far enough ahead for there to be no risk of collision.

About 1850 an instruction to operating staff on the London & North Western Railway told them to 'give instructions to the policeman i.e. signalman in charge of the down main home signal at Wolverton to stop the 9 a.m. express every day, and tell the driver and guard how long the third class has left'. Even when block working assisted by the electric telegraph was introduced on this line the principle of one train per section was considered too restrictive and could be waived if heavy traffic was causing bottlenecks. Signalmen could let a driver enter a section that might still be occupied if they warned the driver to proceed with caution. Drivers interpreted 'caution' in their own ways and collisions sometimes occurred when they caught up unexpectedly with the train in front. If not serious, such episodes seem to have been treated casually, for the

A Golsdorf two-cylinder compound of Class 170 designed in 1893 for the Arlberg line in Austria.

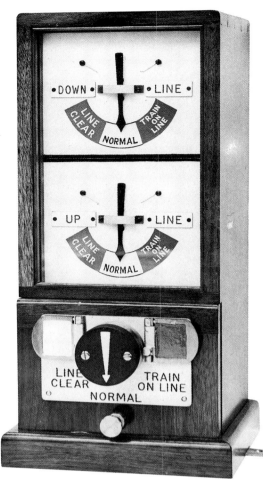

report of an incident near Wolverton in 1862 simply remarked that the train ahead had been 'running too slow', and the one behind it 'too fast'.

Railways and the telegraph grew up together. As early as 1837 Sir Charles Wheatstone and F. W. Cooke had demonstrated their apparatus between Euston and the winding engine house at the top of Camden Bank, the trains at that time being hauled up the incline and lowered into the terminus by cable. Cooke published a pamphlet, 'Telegraphic Railways', in 1842 showing how the telegraph could improve the safety of working single lines, but the principles of the telegraph were soon applied to railways on a more general basis, both for business purposes and the control of traffic.

Specialised instruments were developed for block working. They were provided with a key or plunger for transmitting the code of bell signals by which trains were offered and accepted from signalbox to signalbox, and with indicators to show the successive steps in the procedure, an indication set up by the signalman in one box being reproduced automatically on the corresponding instrument in the other. When the man who had accepted a train by repeating back the bell signal put his instrument at 'line clear', the same indication appeared in the box from which the train had been offered. On receiving the 'train entering section' bell, the signalman would set his indicator at 'train on line' and again the

instrument in the preceding box would change to the same indication.

Safety with the block system depended on rigorous observance of the procedure. The block instruments themselves did not prevent a false move, and there were occasions when a signalman disbelieved the message of his instrument and admitted a train to an occupied section. The basic block telegraph was therefore extended to prevent mistakes by electrically locking levers and instruments. In this form it was known as 'lock and block'. It took various forms, one of the most widely used being the Sykes lock and block system. Here a signalman could not signal a train into a section until the signal lever had been released electrically by the man in the next box. He in his turn could not send the release until the train ahead had passed a specified signal, that signal had been returned to 'danger', and the train had proceeded a safe distance beyond the signal. This last condition was confirmed when the train passed over a treadle in the track, actuating contacts in an electric circuit.

The treadle was an early form of 'train detection'. It preceded the track circuit, which was to become the most significant step forward in railway signalling. Early work on track circuits began in the 1860s but it was not until the turn of the century that the principle became firmly established and accepted.

The West Side signalbox at Liverpool Street station, London, in the days of mechanical signalling with levers and locking frames.
Block telegraph instruments of the type illustrated were an early application of the electric telegraph to railway working and remained in service as long as mechanical signalling survived.

5. THE CHOICE OF GAUGE

A Great Western Railway 7 ft (2·1 m) single locomotive hurries the first British corridor train through Acton on its way to Birkenhead. Locomotive and coaches are standard gauge, and running on mixed gauge track. The photograph was taken in 1892 before the final abandonment of the broad (7 ft/12·1 m) gauge.

Previous page: A broad gauge train passes Twyford in 1892 while work on converting the gauge is in progress.

FOR MOST OF THE 19th century Britain was unique in having a railway built to the gauge of 7 ft 0¼ in (2·14 m). This was the Great Western Railway, whose first chief engineer, Isambard Kingdom Brunel, chose the broad gauge on the grounds that the locomotives would be less cramped and therefore more efficient, while for smooth running he devised a track in which the rails were supported continuously by longitudinal sleepers. This departure from the gauge of 4 ft 8 in (1·422 m), later 4 ft 8½ in (1·435 m), to which Stephenson built his first locomotives caused much inconvenience as points of contact between the Great Western and railways built to the 4 ft 8½ in (1·435 m) gauge increased. Brunel and his supporters stoutly defended the broad gauge before a Gauge Commission in 1846, but the Commission decided that future public railways in Britain should use the 4 ft 8½ in standard gauge. Its report, however, left several loopholes and broad gauge tracks continued to be laid in the Great Western's sphere of influence. In the mid-1860s the Great Western had 1,040 miles (1,674 km) of broad gauge and 387 miles (623 km) of mixed gauge, in which a third rail was laid between the other two so that both broad and standard gauge locomotives and rolling stock could use the line.

The last broad gauge train did not leave Paddington until 20 May 1892. A programme of gauge conversion had been in progress since 1868 and at the end 171 miles (275 km) remained to be converted.

The task was completed in two days. In the broad gauge period the Great Western established a reputation for the speed of its principal trains, although this was not characteristic of the service as a whole. Some of its expresses impressed the public enough for them to be known generally by unofficial names like the 'Zulu', the 'Flying Dutchman' and the 'Cornishman'. When introduced in 1890 the 'Cornishman' was a broad gauge train. In the summer of 1896 its standard gauge successor was booked to run non-stop from Paddington to Plymouth, 245·5 miles (394·6 km), which at that time was the longest regular run without a stop in the world. From 1906 the erstwhile 'Cornishman' was officially named the 'Cornish Riviera Express', one of the world's famous trains and in direct descent from the days of Brunel's broad gauge.

Early American railways were built to a variety of gauges. On the outbreak of civil war in 1861 the gauges in use on a substantial scale included 4 ft 8½ in, 5 ft (1·524 m), 5 ft 6 in (1·676 m) and 6 ft (1·83 m). The war underlined the inconvenience and delays of transhipment and by 1865 a process of standardisation to 4 ft 8½ in was well under way. Acceptance of 4 ft 8½ in as standard divided the rest of the gauges into narrow gauge or broad gauge according to whether they were below or above that dimension. In Europe, Spain and Portugal adopted a gauge of approximately 5 ft 5½ in (1·664 m); Ireland chose 5 ft 3 in (1·60 m), and Russia, after a preliminary

An excursion train on the Rio Grande Southern narrow gauge line crosses a trestle bridge at Ophir, Colorado, on 30 May 1947.

The Westland Express of the Western Australian Government Railways pulls away behind a PR class Pacific from a stop in the country. The gauge is 3 ft 6 in (1·067 m).

A pick-up freight train of the Western Australian Government Railways is braked down the incline through the 'grand canyon' near Zig Zag by a D-53 class 2-8-0.

A narrow-gauge Denver and Rio Grande Western freight train near Alamosa gives out a sculptured plume of smoke.

essay with 6 ft (1·83 m), standardised at 5 ft (1·524 m). In metric measurement the standard gauge of British Railways has become 1·432 m, equivalent to 4 ft 8⅜ in.

During the full tide of railway building in the 19th century there was much interest in narrow gauges for economy in construction, particularly in difficult terrain. Often narrow-gauge systems existed alongside a standard gauge network. In the United States the Denver & Rio Grande Railroad had a line of 3 ft (0·9 m) gauge from Denver to Ogden in the 1880s which climbed to an altitude of 7,440 ft (2,268 m) in crossing the Rockies in Colorado. South of Denver the railway extended to New Mexico, and in conjunction with the Rio Grande Southern had by 1891 formed a circular route 675 miles (1,086 km) in extent known as the Narrow Gauge Circle. This system remained unbroken until part of the circle was closed in 1949. It had a named train, the 'San Juan', between Alamosa and Durango until 1951 when passenger working ceased, and continued freight operations until 1968, steam-worked to the end. When the Western Pacific Railroad from San Francisco reached Ogden in 1909 the Denver & Rio Grande had been taken over, becoming the Denver & Rio Grande Western. Converted to standard

Four Fell-type locomotives work a Masterton-Upper Hutt excursion over Cross Creek Summit on the 1 in 15 Rimutaka Incline, New Zealand Government Railways.

gauge, the Denver-Ogden section became part of an important east to west route.

There were numerous branches on the Narrow Gauge Circle. The branch from Durango to Silverton, 45·5 miles (73·2 km) long, was opened in 1882 to serve a mining community. After closure of the rest of the system it continued to be operated in summer by the D&RGW as a tourist attraction using its old passenger coaches and steam locomotives. After the 1980 season it was taken over by another operator and maintained the tourist service under the title Durango & Silverton Narrow Gauge Railroad. In 1970 the 64 miles (103 km) of the old Circle between Antonito and Chama were bought by the railroad authorities of Colorado and New Mexico and reopened as a steam-worked tourist line – the Cumbres & Toltec Scenic Railroad.

Railway building in Australia began in New South Wales on the standard gauge in the 1850s. The British Government was anxious to see uniformity throughout the sub-continent, but the various states had their own ideas. Queensland and Western Australia chose 3 ft 6 in (1·067 m) and some sections of the South Australian system were built to the same narrow gauge, all with economy of construction in mind. As the railway network grew

South Rangitikei viaduct on the Mangaweka-Ulika on the North Island main trunk line in New Zealand.

Weissen viaduct on the narrow-gauge Rhaetian railway in Switzerland. The transalpine routes have produced some remarkable feats of engineering.

and previously isolated sections met, the inconvenience of breaks of gauge became all too apparent. By the end of the century there was still a gap of 1,085 miles (1,746 km) between the South Australian Government Railways at Port Augusta and the Western Australian Government Railways at Kalgoorlie. At both places the gauge was 3 ft 6 in. In 1901 the Commonwealth of Australia was formed, and the building of a transcontinental railway to bridge the gap was a Commonwealth project. The choice of standard gauge in spite of breaks of gauge at each end can be seen as a strong hint at the desirability of establishing a national standard gauge network. The transcontinental line was completed in 1917, but it was not possible to travel from Sydney to Perth without changing trains until 1970.

When a national programme of railway building in the North and South Islands of New Zealand was launched in 1870, the 3 ft 6 in (1·067 m) gauge was specified. The same gauge was adopted in South Africa, and was carried through into Rhodesia (Zimbabwe), as was necessary if Cecil Rhodes' dream of a Cape to Cairo Railway was to be fulfilled.

By 1897 the 3 ft 6 in gauge was continuous from Cape Town to Bulawayo. Already, however, the Cape-to-Cairo project was unattainable for political reasons. The Foreign Office in London had accepted German objections in 1895 to a railway 'corridor' between the Congo and German East Africa which would have been necessary to reach Uganda. Separated as they were from the system in South Africa and Rhodesia, the railways of both Uganda and Kenya were built to the metre gauge.

India adopted the 5 ft 6 in (1·676 m) gauge for the principal main lines but from the first envisaged numerous narrow gauge feeder lines of metre gauge to reduce the costs of construction. A network of 2 ft 6 in (0·76 m) lines was built by private under-

Signals of unmistakably British inspiration beckon an East Indian Railway 0-8-0 forward with its freight train after a pause at Lhaksar Junction in the United Provinces in 1941.
Inset : A standard Pacific of the Indian Railways heads the 'Punjab Mail' on its run of 519 miles (835·25 km) between Peshawar and Mughal Sarai.

takings under government incentive schemes. Japan began its railway development in the 19th century on the 3 ft 6 in gauge and did not build to standard gauge until the high-speed electric lines of the 1960s.

Many metre gauge lines were built in South America, together with others of both standard and broad gauges. By 1930 the metre gauge represented about one-tenth of the total world railway mileage of some 700,000 miles (126,540 km). The 3 ft 6 in gauge was in third place with 47,000 miles (75,637 km).

Narrow gauge motive power often needed to combine several coupled axles for good adhesion with the ability to take curvature considerably more severe then on standard gauge lines. A locomotive for these conditions was designed and patented by Robert W. Fairlie of the Londonderry & Coleraine Railway in 1864. The Fairlie locomotive was formed of two boilers back to back with a common

firebox and a central cab, each boiler supplying a separate steam bogie. In 1869 Fairlie's 0-4-4-0 *Little Wonder* for the 1 ft 11½ in (0·6 m) gauge Ffestiniog Railway in North Wales attracted worldwide attention and made engineers look more seriously at the narrow gauges. Fairlie himself was as ardent in their support as Brunel had been of his own 7 ft broad gauge. His book *Railways or no Railways* published in 1872 could have harmed a good case by overstatement. While being built mainly for the narrow gauges, Fairlie-type locomotives were adopted by some standard gauge lines and even by the broad gauge Trans-Caucasus Railway in Russia. The Mexican Railway was a large user of Fairlies from the 1890s and the Trans-Caucasus Railway had them in service over the 1 in 22 gradients of the Suram Pass.

Of ten 0-6-6-0 Fairlies built by the Yorkshire Engineering Company, five were equipped for the Russian gauge and shipped out to the Trans-

Electric locomotives and rolling stock on the 25 kV AC electrified line of the State-owned FC Electrico al Pacifico in Costa Rica, connecting the capital, San Jose, with the port of Punta Arenas.

South African Railways Class 15CA 4-8-2 No 2837 stands in Monument Station, Cape Town, after bringing in the 'Rhodesia Limited'.

Gouritz River Bridge, Mossel Bay, in the Cape Province of South Africa.

Caucasus line. Records show that only four were put into service and it is assumed that one was lost on the voyage. The other five were standard gauge locomotives and put into store to await a purchaser. They were bought in 1881 by the metre gauge Nitrate Railways of Chile and converted accordingly. The conversion included the addition of a carrying axle at each end, giving the 2-6-6-2 wheel arrangement. This was one of the rare examples of a Fairlie with leading and trailing carrying axles, the locomotives being used mainly for heavy freight trains at low speeds at which the additional guiding forces were unnecessary.

An alternative to the 'double Fairlie' with two boilers and a central cab was the 'single Fairlie' with a conventional boiler and cab layout, one steam bogie under the boiler, and a rear four-wheel bogie. Single Fairlies with the 0-6-4 wheel arrangement were supplied to the New Zealand Government Railways by the Avonside Engine Company in 1878, a first order for 15 being followed by three more in the next year. Having a driving wheel diameter of only 3 ft (91·44 cm) they were intended mainly for freight traffic and mixed trains not exceeding 25 mph (40 km/h) but were occasionally put on express passenger work with good results. On a test run in 1879 with eight goods wagons, a passenger coach and a brake van one of these locomotives held a top speed of around 53 mph (85 km/h) for over 2·75 miles (3 km), probably a unique performance con-

sidering the small wheel diameter and the 3ft 6 in (1·06 m) gauge.

The name of Anatole Mallet, the compounding pioneer, is generally associated with giant articulated locomotives in the United States, but the first locomotive in which Mallet combined his systems of compounding and articulation was built in 1887 to the 2 ft (61 cm) gauge. This little 0-4-4-0 was to meet a requirement for a locomotive with an axle-load of 2·95 tons (3 tonnes) capable of hauling useful loads on gradients of up to 1 in 12·5 with curves of 65 ft (20 m) radius. Mallet's locomotive weighed 10·83 tons (11 tonnes) distributed over four axles and could haul 9·84 tons (10 tonnes) on the specified gradient and curvature. Most of the Mallets built in the 19th century were for narrow-gauge lines.

Mallet's patents for an articulated locomotive were granted in 1885, and compounding was inherent in them. They described a locomotive with one pair of cylinders acting on fixed axles at the rear, and the other pair driving the axles of a leading swivelling truck with its pivot point at the front of the fixed frames. In his first designs the two high-pressure cylinders drove the fixed axles while the low-pressure pair were on the swivelling truck. This was a practical advantage at a time when flexible pipe joints for high-pressure steam were a problem. The first standard gauge Mallets were built in 1892. By 1900 over 390 Mallets were at work, 173 of them on the narrow gauges.

6. THE EARLY COMMUTERS

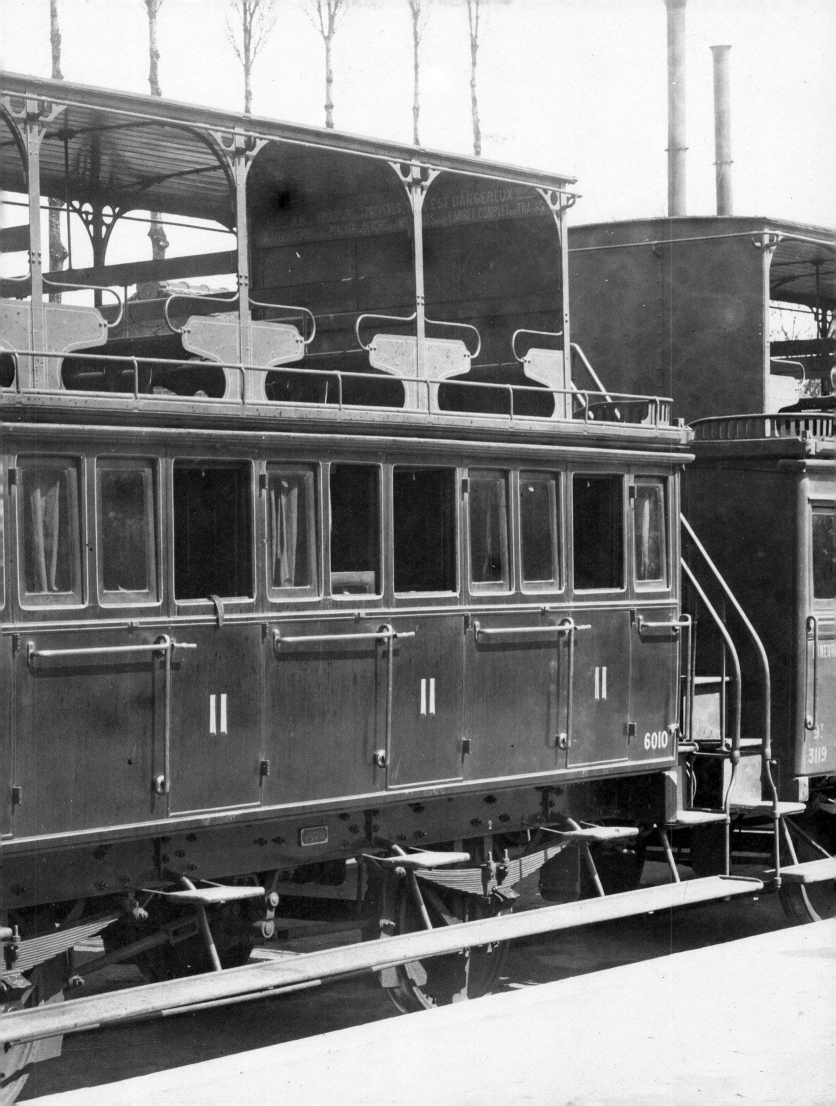

Previous page : The first New York elevated railway was opened in 1867 and steam locomotives were used. Chicago opened its first elevated line in 1892.

Below right : AT and Santa FE No 493, train 468 San Bernardino local, built in Rhode Island 1900 and seen here at Los Angeles in 1935. *Below :* The first train equipped with Westinghouse air brakes, No 728 Pennsylvania Railroads at West Philadelphia, with commuter coaches (photographed in 1886). *Right :* Pages from Illinois Central's publicity pamphlet of 1881, advertising the Railroads' new services.

LIVING IN THE SUBURBS and travelling to work in town used to be considered a typically British lifestyle. Today it has spread worldwide and is conveniently called 'commuting', a word imported from the United States. An Illinois Central Railroad timetable of the 1880s quoted 'commutation rates' for 19 stations in the Chicago suburban area at distances up to 17 miles (27·4 km) from the city terminus on its main line to the south. A footnote extolled the advantages and pleasures of commuting:

The very perfect system of Suburban Trains now run by this Company over their 4 Track Route along the Lake Front invites the suburban dweller to the choice locations now to be had near this line, and but a few minutes' ride from the business portion of the city.

Seated in their comfortable cars, the business man, after a hard day's work in the city, finds the homeward ride along the beautiful Lake Front a pleasure rather than a task, as he waits for no draw-bridges, Railroad crossings, or other annoyances.

This was an idealised picture of suburban travel. Most trains were all-stations, and the journey to the limit of the commuting area took closer to an hour than the 'few minutes' of the blurb. But there were a few trains morning and evening making only one or two stops, and travellers were warned that 'Trains will Stop only at Points where Time is given'.

In the second half of the 19th century British railway companies were making provision for the daily traveller both by season tickets and by cheap workers' fares. The Artisans' and Labourers' Dwellings Act of 1868 recommended that railways running into London should provide transport at the rate of one penny for 7 or 8 miles (11·3 or 12·9 km). Many dwellings had been demolished to make way for the railways as they penetrated to their London termini and the occupants had been obliged to move further out and travel daily to and from their work. Some of the Acts empowering companies to build their lines had themselves stipulated cheap travel for workers before this general recommendation was made.

The City of London was a magnet for railways south of the River Thames. The London & Brighton Railway had its terminus at London Bridge, and from its opening in 1842 provided a fast morning service from the coast to London, returning in the evening. For many years these trains were first class only, although there was the proviso that second class carriages would be attached 'for Servants travelling with their Employers'. This was commuting for the upper crust, but by the middle 1850s the London, Brighton & South Coast Railway was

THE SHORTEST ROUTE
And the ONLY ONE running THROUGH TRAINS between

CHICAGO

—AND—

DUBUQUE, INDEPENDENCE,
WATERLOO, CHARLES CITY,
CEDAR FALLS, ACKLEY,
FORT DODGE and SIOUX CITY,

MAKING DIRECT CONNECTIONS AT

SIOUX CITY

TO AND FROM

Sioux Falls, Beloit and Yankton

The BEST ROUTE from

NORTHERN IOWA AND ILLINOIS
TO ST. LOUIS.

A DIRECT ROUTE

BETWEEN

CHICAGO

—AND—

Pontiac, Chatsworth, Gibson, Farmer City, Mt. Pulaski and Springfield.

THIS IS THE

ONLY LINE
From CHICAGO to the

West & South

That enters and departs over the great

4 TRACK ROUTE

Along the Lake Front, with no Streets, Draw Bridges, or other Railroad Tracks to cross.

NOVEMBER, 1881.

ILLINOIS CENTRAL
RAILROAD

THE QUICK ROUTE

— BETWEEN —

CHICAGO & ST. LOUIS

Without Change of Cars.

PULLMAN PALACE SLEEPING CARS

Between Chicago and St. Louis.

Making direct connections at St. Louis, in Union Depot, to and from Kansas City, Atchison, Leavenworth, St. Joseph and all Points West.

NO OTHER LINE

MAKES QUICKER TIME

— BETWEEN —

CHICAGO & ST. LOUIS

ELEGANT SLEEPING CARS. FINE DAY COACHES,

ENTERS AND DEPARTS OVER THE

Great 4 Track Route

ALONG THE LAKE FRONT.

NOVEMBER, 1881.

THE
ILLINOIS CENTRAL
RAILROAD

GRAND ENTRANCE

INTO THE

CITY OF CHICAGO

OVER THEIR GREAT

4 TRACK ROUTE

ALONG THE

LAKE FRONT

NO STREETS, DRAW BRIDGES
OR RAILROAD TRACKS TO CROSS.

A. H. HANSON,
General Passenger Agent.

J. F. TUCKER,
Traffic Manager.

Rand, McNally & Co., Printers and Engravers, Chicago.

quoting season ticket rates to London from Croydon, Epsom and intermediate stations. These relatively short-distance seasons were second class only, the first class patronage being assumed to dwell in the further regions of Surrey and Sussex.

Sir William Acworth was much impressed by the season ticket traffic on the Brighton line. In *The Railways of England* (1889) he wrote:

> If on a given day all the season ticket holders in Great Britain were confined to their houses for a space of four-and-twenty hours, the fact would make little difference to the appearance of the 'Dutchman' or the 'Flying Scotchman' (*sic*) or the other great expresses. . . . But the best trains of the Brighton Company would be little better than strings of empty coaches. Let anyone travel by, for example, the 8.45 a.m. from Brighton, or the return train at 5 p.m., and notice the pleased surprise with which the ticket collectors accept the tender of an ordinary ticket, and he will appreciate the dimensions to which the Brighton season ticket traffic has already grown.

Acworth noted that in the 13 years previous to publication of the first edition of his book season ticket receipts on the LB&SCR had grown from £129,000 to £189,000. By the time he published a second edition in 1899 they had grown further to £235,000.

The lure of living at the seaside also brought a heavy season ticket traffic to the London, Tilbury &

Southend Railway which served a number of towns on the north shore of the Thames Estuary. Its terminus at Fenchurch Street was the first actually in the City of London. On this route the shorter-distance commuter traffic was dealt with as far as Barking by the District Railway, whose tracks were parallel with the LT&S, and so the latter was able to run some fast trains to the estuary towns. A time of 45 minutes for the 35 miles (56·3 km) from Fenchurch Street to Westcliff-on-Sea required hard work for the locomotives, but they were specially designed for the job.

In its early years the London, Chatham & Dover Railway had only a West End terminus in London,

The Central Pacific Depot at Sacramento, California, 1883.

occupying one half of Victoria station. Its aspirations to reach the City were realised in 1856 when it was granted powers to build a line from Herne Hill, on the route to Victoria, to Blackfriars and on to a junction with the Metropolitan Railway near Farringdon Street. Blackfriars was reached on 1 June 1864, and on 1 January 1866 the connection with the Metropolitan Railway was made at West Street Junction, near Farringdon Street. To reach the underground lines the LCDR trains had to descend a gradient of 1 in 39. In the meantime, on 1 June 1865, a station had been opened at Ludgate Hill. Editorial staff and printers of the great daily newspapers in nearby Fleet Street knew it well for the

services it provided to the south-eastern suburbs in the early hours of the morning after their night's work was finished.

A terminal station for the LCDR trains was opened at Holborn Viaduct on 2 March 1874, reached by a spur only some 792 ft (241·4 m) long from the line to West Street Junction. Most of the local services continued to run to and from the Metropolitan line and beyond but they served the Holborn Viaduct area by two platforms in a deep cutting. This station was first called Snow Hill but the name was changed later to Holborn Viaduct Low Level. Passenger traffic through Snow Hill fell off as Underground and bus services increased but for many years the line continued to be an important link for freight traffic between railways north and south of the Thames. British Railways announced in 1983 that its restoration for through cross-London passenger services was being considered.

A remarkable feature of the LCDR City line was the number of stations in a short distance. Blackfriars station on the south bank of the Thames was closed in 1885 but a new station called St Paul's was opened on the opposite bank on 10 May 1886. This, like Holborn Viaduct, was a terminus adjacent to the through line, and it reminded the public that the London, Chatham & Dover was in the Continental business by listing 54 destinations on the stones of the entrance walls to which the company was prepared to take the traveller. They were a strange mixture, with Beckenham and Bickley sharing the honours with Baden Baden and Brindisi. St Paul's was renamed Blackfriars by the Southern Railway in 1937. It might also be claimed that one feature of the line made it among the best known stretches of railway in the world. The bridge across Ludgate Hill, with Saint Paul's Cathedral in the background, was to be seen in countless picture postcards of London,

Right: LMS engine No 6870 at Watford Junction.

often with the engine of a cross-London freight train passing over it.

Development of suburban traffic on the LB&SCR had followed an opposite sequence. The company's first terminus was at London Bridge and its trains did not reach Victoria until 1860. Victoria and London Bridge were linked by the South London line, traversing inner suburbs where soon the railway was in keen competition with the new electric tramways.

The busiest of the stations in the City was Liverpool Street. The Great Eastern Railway was one of those obliged to make fare concessions for workers under their Acts, and a year after it had opened its first terminus at Bishopsgate, that station had handled 2·14 million passengers. With the numbers still increasing, the railway obtained powers to extend to a larger site at Liverpool Street, where local services began in February 1874.

Broad Street station, next door to Liverpool Street was the terminus of the North London Railway. This line and the Great Eastern were largely responsible for the spread of suburbs northwards, although their traffic was different in character. The North London was the line of the growing army of what we now call 'white collar workers'. It was not obliged to carry third class passengers until 1875. The Great Eastern on the other hand was once described in a London County Council report as 'especially the workman's London Railway – the one above all which appears to welcome him as a desirable customer'.

The North London extended through the northern suburbs and then turned south to terminate on the Thames at Richmond. It was an all-suburban line, as indeed the country extension of the Metropolitan Railway from Baker Street had seemed to be at first. But, as has been seen earlier, the Metropolitan's Chairman, Sir Edward Watkin, had other plans and

pushed the line north-westwards through Hertfordshire and Buckinghamshire until it met the Great Central at Quainton Road, beyond Aylesbury. Once the connection was made, both main line and outer suburban trains shared the same tracks as far as West Hampstead. The arrangement was inconvenient, particularly for Great Central freight traffic, and early in the next century the Great Central and Great Western combined in building a new line that by-passed the Metropolitan for the Great Central and provided a shorter route to Birmingham for the Great Western. At the same time it opened up new country for the London commuters making their homes in Buckinghamshire and among the Chiltern Hills.

Outside London new lines and extensions were built for suburban traffic around the great provincial cities but for the most part they served other purposes as well. One example was the Birmingham West Suburban Railway, built in 1876 and adapted to carry main line traffic in 1885. On the other hand the Nottingham Suburban Railway of 1889 did not have a dual role and proved a costly failure, to the chagrin of the Borough Council which had contributed to its construction. It was on exclusively suburban routes that the railways first felt competition from the trams, horse-drawn at first but soon electrified, and around London, Manchester, Liverpool and Newcastle the railways' reply was to electrify their own suburban lines. Manchester and Liverpool were like London in having detached 'suburbs' on the coast. The Lancashire & Yorkshire Railway claimed its electrification from Liverpool to Southport as the first main-line electrification in the country, although on the grounds of Southport being a town in its own right, rather than on the distance of only 19 miles (30·6 km). Many Manchester businessmen lived in Blackpool and commuted daily over the 35½ miles (57 km). This service was never electri-

A previously unpublished picture of the L & Y steam rail motor.

fied but it had some fast steam trains which started a fashion by providing special 'club' coaches for a group of businessmen who travelled together daily and paid for private accommodation. Similar groups of regular travellers were also formed on the Manchester-Llandudno and Manchester-Windermere services, and between Bradford and Morecambe.

As cities all over the world grew in size the pattern that had been so pronounced in Britain at an early date was seen elsewhere. Early electric traction development was predominantly for suburban traffic conditions. The same conditions had been met previously by specialised steam locomotive designs with powers of rapid acceleration so that trains could follow each other at short intervals. William Stroudley's 0-6-0 tank engines, popularly called 'Terriers', were among the best known and made their mark on the South London line between Victoria and London Bridge although were soon to be seen all over the spreading London, Brighton & South Coast suburban network. James Holden's standard tank engine for the Great Eastern suburban services was also an 0-6-0. When the management was harassed by demands for electrification, Holden and his assistant, F. V. Russell, designed and built an 0-10-0 that could match the electric train's ability to accelerate to 30 mph (48 km/h) in 30 seconds. This 'Decapod' never went into regular service. It saved the management's face but did poor service to the Liverpool Street commuter. The railway continued to operate its ever more intensive suburban services with small steam locomotives, achieving something of a triumph in terms of railway operation under pressure but denying the commuter the speed and cleanliness of the electric suburban railway until after the Second World War.

In 1890 the first electric tube railway in the world was opened in London from a station near the Monument to Stockwell – the City & South London Railway. Tube and underground lines later reached far into the London suburbs, running considerable distances at ground level. The only tube railway in Britain outside London was the Glasgow District Subway, opened as a cable-operated circular route in 1896. Ten years earlier, however, an important steam-worked underground line had opened in the provinces when traffic began on the Mersey Railway in 1886. At first the line simply linked Liverpool and Birkenhead, tunnelling under the River Mersey and offering an alternative to the ferries, sometimes it is said at the risk of asphyxiation by steam and smoke. In 1888 the line was extended to Birkenhead Park, where it surfaced alongside the Wirral Railway, which served a growing suburban area on the Wirral Peninsula. Wirral passengers could now change into the underground trains and reach the centre of Liverpool. From 1891 a Mersey Railway branch to Rock Ferry gave connections for Chester and the south, while in 1892 it penetrated further into Liverpool to a new terminus under the Liverpool Central station of the Cheshire Lines.

The lively performance of suburban tank engines was partly due to the relatively light loads, for the rolling stock provided only the bare essentials. A visitor to London from the Midlands in 1893 was not impressed. His first experience on the Metropolitan evoked the comment, 'Well, I had seen some "old stuff" on the Great Western but nothing to equal the narrow, bare boxes of this Metropolitan train'. At Broad Street 'the horrible screech of the whistles did not appeal at all, any more than did the cushionless open thirds'. District Railway rolling stock was

LMS locomotive No 2135, one of a number of 'Tilbury Tanks' built for the outer suburban and Southend Express trains.

judged 'if anything less attractive than that of the Metropolitan, the carriages being equally comfortless four-wheelers . . .'. At Charing Cross 'the carriage stock did not impress me at all; even the latest types had no cushions for the back in the third class compartments, while the majority had bare boards for seats. Some of the stock, also, was of old design, very low in the roof and with small windows'.

Victoria fared little better, for 'the carriages, largely four-wheelers and very scantily upholstered, did not at all appeal to me'. The London, Chatham & Dover side of the same station was similarly criticised. The carriages struck him as 'comfortless in the third class compartments and very poor in those of the second class. Some, especially those on the

Crystal Palace train, were so low in the roof that a tall man could not have stood upright in them'.

This was the unglamorous side of London rail travel, it took a poet to look beyond the uninviting facade. In his poem 'The King' written in 1894, Rudyard Kipling made a comment on commuting that is often quoted, though usually only the last line:

'Romance!' the season tickets mourn,
'*He* never ran to catch his train
'But passed with coach and guard and horn –
'And left the local – late again!'
Confound Romance! . . . And all unseen
Romance brought up the nine-fifteen.

The ornamentation of first class coaches reached its peak in the second half of the nineteenth century. As commuter trains became established, the interior design of carriages tended towards a more functional approach to accommodate the increasing passengers.

7.GROWTH CONTINUES

Previous page: Ansbuae Federal Railways and German Federal Railway electric locomotives climb through the Gastein Valley to the Tauern Tunnel with a Munich-Klagerfurt Express.

VISITORS TO THE Paris Universal Exhibition in 1900 could sit in a railway restaurant car and watch a panorama of a journey from Europe into Asia unfolding past the windows. This was Georges Nagelmacker's preview of the 'Trans-Siberian Express', which would convey passengers from Moscow to Vladivostok in the solidly reassuring environment of the International Sleeping Car Company's rolling stock. The project ceremonially launched by the Tsarevich Nicholas in 1891 was taking shape. At the eastern end of the route the line had been built northwards for some 500 miles (805 km) to Khabarovsk and would turn west to join other sectors of construction. The detour to the north had been necessary to keep the railway within Russian territory.

As we have seen building from the west had reached Lake Baikal near Irkutsk, and from the eastern shore of the lake the railway extended to Sretnsk. A train ferry across the lake and river transport from Sretnsk to Khabarovsk filled the gaps. Already a 'Trans-Siberian Express' ran between Moscow and Irkutsk once a week. In winter the lake crossing and river passage were made by sledge. Accommodation on the trains was spartan. A passenger in 1900 who joined a train at Sretnsk after the river passage from Khabarovsk reported that his carriage with wooden seats and three tiers of bunks for sleeping was 'the best on the train'. The rest of the accommodation was in vans with no seats.

Conditions were better on the other side of the lake. A few months after the Paris exhibition new State-built rolling stock began running between Moscow and Irkutsk. The usual formation of the train was a luggage van, restaurant car, and one first class and one second class sleeping car. Compartments were carpeted, and a table, reading lamp and a bell to summon the attendant created something of an hotel atmosphere. The Wagons-Lits Company, however, had second thoughts about the commercial possibilities of the 'Trans-Siberian Express' and did not put the vehicles it had exhibited in Paris in service on the line but supplied a train of its standard stock.

Meanwhile, Russia had been granted a concession to build the Chinese Eastern Railway through northern Manchuria, which shortened the journey from Vladivostok to Lake Baikal by some 350 miles (560 km) compared with the route via Khabarovsk. When this by-pass became available in 1903, through coaches between Moscow and Vladivostok, 5,437 miles (8,750 km), could be run in summer when the train ferry was operating across the lake.

But a storm was gathering over the presence of Russian troops in Manchuria. During construction

Troubled days on Russian railways – Red Guards with an armoured train defending the approach to Tsaritsyn (now Volgograd) in 1918.

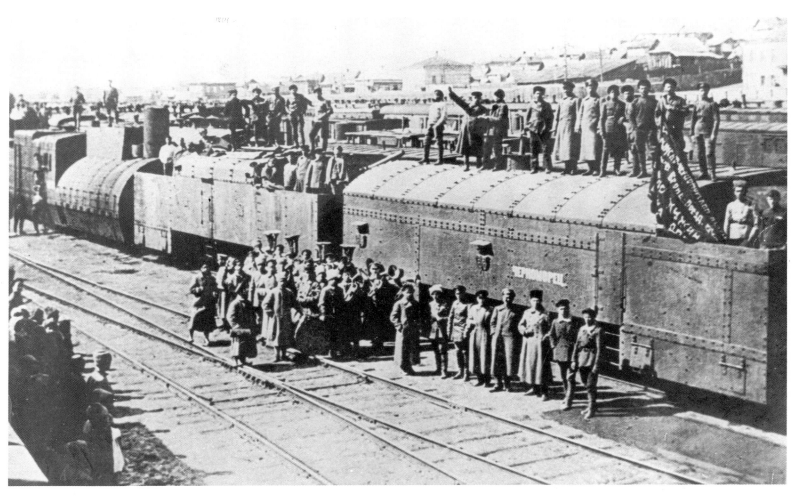

of the Chinese Eastern Railway they had provided protection for the workers, but they had not been withdrawn when the job was done. Japan, always suspicious of the Russian presence in the Far East, claimed that Russia had reneged on an agreement. The troops remained where they were in spite of protests, and in January 1904 Japan and Russia went to war. Immediately the Lake Baikal crossing presented a problem in the transport of reinforcements and supplies to the war zone. The train ferry, although an ice-breaker, could not cope with ice 5 ft (1·5 m) thick. Rails were laid across the ice but unsuspected warm currents reduced the thickness in places. A locomotive plunged in and was lost. The line across the ice had to be relaid with wider sleepers to spread the load, and rolling stock and locomotives were hauled over the lake with painful slowness by teams of men and horses.

The war emergency hastened the construction of a line through the difficult terrain south of the lake to connect with the railway to Sretnsk and eliminate the ferry crossing. The Sretnsk line also gave access to the Chinese Eastern Railway, and from the end of the Russo-Japanese War in 1905 to the outbreak of the First World War the 'Trans-Siberian Express' ran through between Moscow and Vladivostok via the Chinese Eastern Railway. A branch from this line at Harbin served Dalny (Dairen) and Peking. Steamers sailed from Vladivostok to Japan, and from Dairen round the coast of China to Shanghai.

These were the golden years of the railway. It enjoyed considerable popularity among globe-trotting tourists, enough of whom were attracted by the idea of an overland journey from Europe to Peking for Nagelmackers to open an hotel there. Others travelled to Japan via Vladivostok and the shipping lines. All enjoyed the experience of riding in a train from one continent to another as the 'Trans-Siberian Express' crossed the border between Europe and Asia in the Ural Mountains.

In 1909 Wagons-Lits offered some additions to its standard facilities. An announcement of the period stated: 'The Restaurant Cars contain a Library with Illustrated Papers and Games – Dominoes, Chess &c. Of the Conductors, one is a Barber and another an Infirmary Nurse. Arrangements can be made for a Doctor to visit the Train during its stoppage at the principal stations. A Medicine Chest is carried on each train'. In the same year the company put on a special train between Warsaw and Moscow as a connection between the Warsaw portion of the 'Nord Express', from Ostend and Paris, and the Trans-Siberian train. The train from Warsaw arrived in the Brest station at Moscow, and passengers crossed the city to the Koursk station to join the 'Trans-Siberian Express', which left an hour or so later. In the reverse direction passengers spent the night in a Moscow hotel. If the Trans-Siberian train was very late, as happened not infrequently, passengers

Wood-burning locomotives head a mixed train of freight vans and passenger cars in Siberia in 1919.

might find themselves seeking an hotel in the small hours. In due course arrangements were made for the train in these circumstances to be taken on from the Koursk to the Brest station, passengers being able to stay in their sleeping cars on payment of a supplement, taking dinner and breakfast in the restaurant car. A new timetable in 1911 scheduled the 'Trans-Siberian Express' to run to and from the Brest station regularly.

A traveller's diary suggests that restaurant car facilities between Moscow and Lake Baikal were overtaxed, noting that 'after giving an order one sometimes had to wait from an hour to an hour and a half before getting served'. Some travellers complained that Russian officers on the way to and from their regiments monopolised the tables, staying long after they had finished their meals. The restaurant car staff seemed to be in awe of them, never asking them to move. But others found them 'capital fellows, full of life and gaiety'. There was a similar problem in the lounge section of the dining car, which housed the library. All seats were liable to be occupied because 'card playing went on all the time . . . if a Russian sits down to a game of cards nothing but a matter of life or death will induce him to stir from it until it is finished'.

A much-pictured feature of the 'Trans-Siberian Express' is the church car, or 'ambulatory basilica'. This was not primarily for passengers' devotions but had been put on the expresses of state-built stock in the early days to provide church services at settlements and construction sites along the line where as yet there was no church or priest. If anything the coaches built by the state for the Trans-Siberian service were more luxurious than the Wagons-Lits cars. Their library section included a piano, and there was a bathroom, but travellers could never be sure they would find all the facilities on their train and their bath might be a wooden tub in the baggage car. Certainly the service aimed at comfort rather than speed. An early timetable shows Moscow to Peking taking ten days.

While shortening the journey to Vladivostok and providing a connection with the South Manchurian Railway to Dalny, the Chinese Eastern Railway through Manchuria brought the route into an area of political tension between Russia, China and Japan. Russia therefore reverted to the original plan of a line wholly in its own territory and in 1908 began closing the gap between Sretnsk and Khabarovsk by building a railway along the Amur Valley. It was completed in 1916, the distance from Moscow to Vladivostok by this new and longer route being 5,787 miles (9,413 km). By this time the First World War was at its height, and Russia was soon to be plunged into the turmoil of revolution. The Trans-Siberian line emerged much battered but intact. Post-war travellers found the Wagons-Lits stock, which had been confiscated by the Russians, still in service but lacking its former elegance. One of them described the soup in the restaurant car as 'greasy hot water poured over pieces of fish which had been cooked earlier in bulk'. Carpets were torn and windows cracked; none the less, riding in these vehicles was considered a privilege and reserved for officers and important visitors. The ordinary traveller rode in coaches with hard wooden benches and struggled for refreshments in the scrummage at stations, or prepared his or her own *en route*. The problems foreseen on the Chinese Eastern Railway were now a reality, the Russians and Chinese disputing its ownership. It was a long time before stability was restored and the development of railway communication between Russia in Europe and the Asiatic territories was resumed.

While the first trains were running on the Trans-Siberian line, a new international route was being developed on the other side of Europe. In Switzerland the Jura-Simplon Railway connected Vallorbe, on the French frontier, with Lausanne, Montreux, and Brigue at the entry to the Simplon Pass into Italy. The line followed the Rhone Valley – a traditional route from Italy to France. For the railway to reach its full potential a connection with Italy was necessary but the Italian response to suggestions of supporting construction of another tunnel through the Alps was lukewarm at first. There were already routes to the north through the Gotthard and Mont Cenis tunnels. The Jura-Simplon proposal, however, had a new element in being an east-west rather than a north-south route, and there were prospects of the line being joined at Brigue by a new connection from Berne which would tunnel through the Bernese Alps. A further factor was the likelihood of competition with the established routes keeping the rates for carriage low. Accordingly an agreement between Switzerland and Italy for building a railway from Brigue to Domodossola was signed at Berne on 25 November 1895. The work was entrusted to the Jura-Simplon Railway, which began construction of the Simplon Tunnel between Brigue and Iselle in 1898. It was completed, however, by the Swiss Federal Railways, the Jura-Simplon company having been bought out by the Swiss Confederation in 1903.

The first Simplon Tunnel was a single-track bore 12·3 miles (19·8 km) long, and at that time was the longest railway tunnel in the world. Construction

A station scene in Kirgizia, Asiatic Russia, at the turn of the century. This territory, near the border with China, is now the Kirgiz Socialist Soviet Republic.

was interrupted several times by the inrush of water. Some 2·5 miles (4 km) from the southern portal a torrent of cold water poured into the workings in September 1901, and 3 miles (5 km) further on hot springs with temperatures between 46° and 54°C were encountered. One of these flowed at a rate of 18·5 gal (85 litres) per second. Over the years some of these sources have dried up and others have reduced their flow but a considerable volume of water is still discharged at both ends of the tunnel.

The final rock barrier was pierced on 24 February 1905, and the first train ran through the tunnel from Brigue to Iselle on 25 January 1906. Regular traffic began on 1 June in the same year. Electric locomotives hauled the trains through the tunnel, the line between Brigue and Iselle having been electrified on the three-phase alternating current system. At first through trains between Italy and France had to reverse at Pontarlier in France, but in 1915 Pontarlier was by-passed, and the journey shortened, by the opening of a direct line from Frasne to Vallorbe which crossed the Jura Mountains in the Mont d'Or Tunnel, 3·75 miles (6 km) in length. By this time traffic had increased to an extent that made a second Simplon bore necessary. It was begun in 1912 but work was delayed by the First World War and it was not opened to traffic until 1922. The new bore was parallel to the first and 55·75 ft (17 m) from it. It was connected with the original one by crossovers inside the tunnel at the half-way point, with a signalbox controlling them and the block sections in each direction, which were approximately 6·2 miles (10 km) long. In the short distance between the crossovers, trains passed the frontier between Switzerland and Italy.

As soon as work on the first Simplon Tunnel went ahead, plans for a connection from Berne were translated into action. A concession for a railway from Frutigen to Brigue had been granted in 1891, a line from Berne to Frutigen being already in existence. The concession was taken up by the Canton of Berne, and after a detailed study of the route the Bernese Alps Railway Company was formed in 1906. From Frutigen the line was taken up the Kander Valley and then entered a tunnel through the Bernese Alps which brought it out into the valley of the Lonza. This was the Lotschberg Tunnel, and the railway was generally known as the

Two Re 4/4 locomotives of the Berne-Lotschberg-Simplon Railway pass Blausee-Mitholz with freight bound for Italy via the Lotschberg and Simplon Tunnels.

One of the 12-wheeled electric railcars which was pushed up to a speed of 130·5 mph (210·1 km/h) in the Marien-felde-Zossen experiments of 1903.

Berne-Lotschberg-Simplon Railway (BLS). The tunnel was 9 miles (14·6 km) long – a not inconsiderable proportion of the distance of 37·5 miles (60·3 km) from Frutigen to Brigue. The highest point in the tunnel was at an altitude of 4,068 ft (1,240 m), or 292 ft (89 m) higher than the Saint-Gotthard. From the southern portal the line entered the Lonza Valley, also known as the Lotschthal, and so into the Rhone Valley, descending its rocky northern slopes on a ruling gradient of 1 in 37 for some 12 miles (19 km) to Brigue station. The scene on emerging from a tunnel into the valley with the river far below and the surrounding mountains has

Harlowton, Montana was the eastern extremity of the Rocky Mountain Division which the Chicago, Milwaukee St Paul & Pacific RR electrified at 3 kV DC in 1915.

been described as one of the railway sensations of Switzerland. Construction of the Lotschberg Tunnel began in 1906 and was not completed until 1913. During the work part of the excavation was inundated and the tunnel had to be taken on a new course. The new line formed an important link in the Swiss railway network, shortening the distance from Berne to Brigue by 79 miles (127 km) compared with the previous route via Lausanne, and from Berne to Milan by 51 miles (82 km) compared with the Saint-Gotthard route via Lucerne.

The new line was opened to traffic on 15 July 1913 and worked by electric traction on the single-phase alternating current system. Three-phase current continued to be used through the Simplon Tunnel until 1930.

Further to the east, in Austria, Alpine ranges obstructed direct communication from the north with the port of Trieste. Proposals to take a line southwards from Salzburg through the Tauern range had been discussed since the 1870s but work did not begin until 1901. Only 49·7 miles (80 km) of new construction was necessary to link up with an existing line on the other side of the mountains but a tunnel 5·3 miles (8·6 km) long had to be built. Over half the route was at a gradient of 1 in 35·7. The tunnel was not completed until 1910, by which time two new lines had been opened to eliminate a previous long detour eastwards from Klagenfurt for traffic from the South Tyrol to reach Trieste, skirting the eastern end of the Karawanken mountains. The new lines, both opened in 1906, were the Karawanken Bahn from Klagenfurt to Assling (now Jenice), and the Wocheiner Bahn from Assling to Trieste. They also shortened the journey to Trieste from Vienna via the Semmering line, the previous route having been southwards through Graz and Marburg (Maribor) before turning west to reach the port via Laibach (Ljubljana). Although far to the

north of these new works, the Pyhrn Bahn was associated with them in that it opened a new direct route to the south from Linz, shortening the journey from Berlin, the spas of Bohemia, and Prague to Trieste via Linz and Klagenfurt. This link, too, was opened in 1906. The Karawanken, Wocheiner, Tauern and Pyhrn lines were all the work of the engineer Karl Wurmb, whose achievements are commemorated by a statue in Salzburg. The tunnels, bridges and viaducts rank among the finest and at the same time the most difficult works of their kind undertaken in the period of the Austro-Hungarian Empire. On the Tauern line alone there were 17 tunnels, a snow shed, and 41 bridges and viaducts with spans of more than 82 ft (25 m); on the Kara-wanken and Wocheiner lines there were 53 tunnels and a great number of bridges, among them the largest masonry viaduct in Europe, near Gorz, with a main arch 279 ft (85 m) wide.

The Tauern Tunnel was opened to traffic in 1909. The Tauern line itself began at Schwarzach-St Veit, south of Salzburg, and ended at a junction with a line from the Italian frontier at Spittal-Milstattersee. Trains for Trieste then followed this line to Villach where they joined a new westward extension, 16·8 miles (27 km) long, of the Karawanken Bahn. They joined the main Klagenfurt-Jesenice section of the Karawanken Bahn at Rosenbach and then entered the Karawanken Tunnel. With the opening of these new lines there were many improvements in services to Trieste up to the First World War. In May 1914 there were four day trains and two at night from Vienna to Trieste, one of them with sleeping cars.

The Salzburg-Trieste service had two through day trains and two at night. One of the day trains included a Pullman-style observation car. Eight of these vehicles had been built in Austria under agreements with the Canadian Pacific company whose liners were calling at Trieste. The cars were available to first and second class passengers on payment of 5 Kronen, equivalent at that time to $1. The night trains conveyed through sleeping cars from Munich, Stuttgart and elsewhere. One of the day trains was combined at Rosenbach with a through train from Linz.

An early Swiss electric loco-motive: built by Brown Boveri for the Burgdorf-Thun line in 1910.

Among the first electrifica-tions in Italy, completed in 1902 was the Valtellina line into the foothills of the Alps: one of its 10 four-motor rail-cars is seen at Lecco in 1904.

8. EARLY ELECTRIFICATION

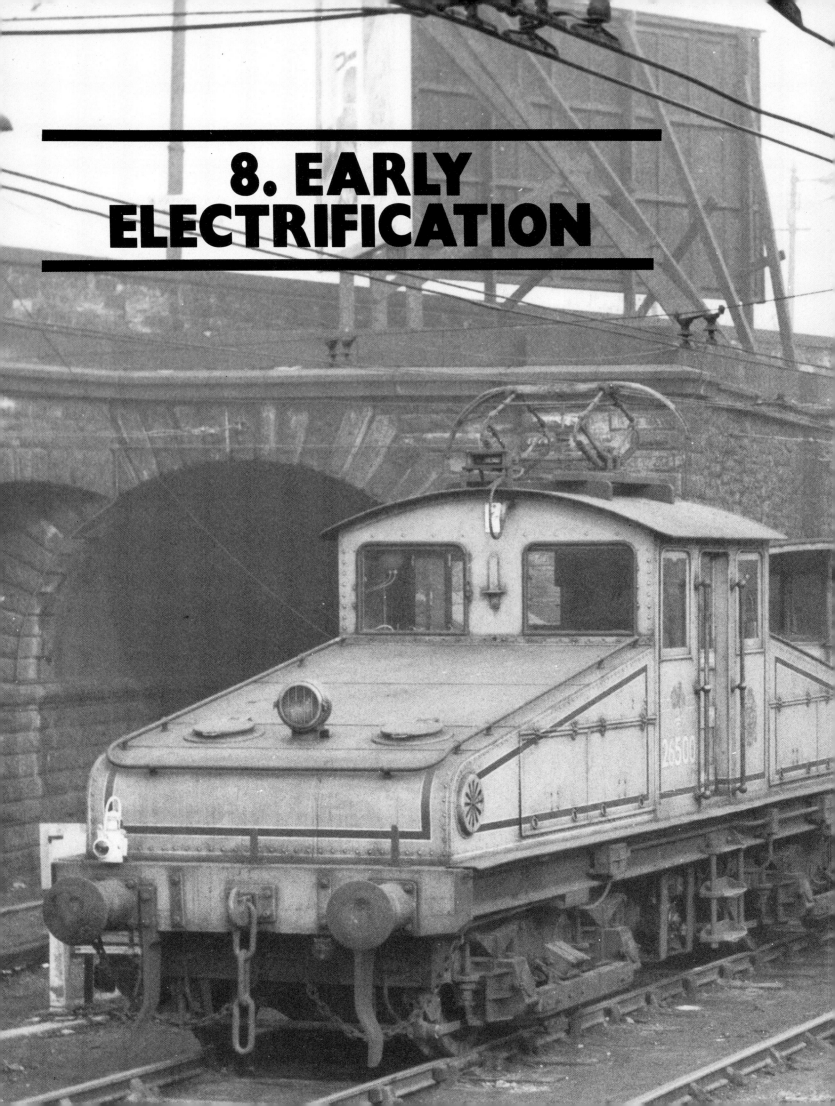

EXPERIMENTS WITH ELECTRIC TRACTION began as early as the 1840s, making use of the recently discovered property of electromagnetism. The power sources were primary cells, which were the first means of making an electric current flow continuously.

In the Science Museum in London there is a poster advertising 'Mr Robert Davidson's exhibition of electro-magnetism as a moving power, to be held under the patronage of the Royal Scottish Society of Arts in the Egyptian Hall, Piccadilly'. It is undated, but believed to have been published about 1843. A principal exhibit was 'A Locomotive Engine carrying passengers on a circular railway'. This was presumably the battery locomotive known to have been demonstrated by Davidson on the Edinburgh & Glasgow Railway in 1842. In this machine electromagnets attracted iron bars attached to drums on the axles, Davidson's machine is said to have attained a speed of 4 mph (6·4 km/h). It seems to have been successful enough to cause alarm in some quarters for it was apparently destroyed either by 'angry workmen' fearing job losses among locomotive firemen, or by 'jealous rivals'. These interchangeable endings have given an undeserved air of myth to an episode that was a serious attempt at electric traction with the resources available at the time.

Early batteries were composed of primary cells, and so could not be recharged when they ran down. They were too heavy, and without the reserves of power necessary for practical electric traction, which could not make progress until the dynamo provided the means of converting the energy of a stationary steam engine into electrical energy.

In 1820 Michael Faraday had shown how an electric voltage was induced in a conductor moving in a magnetic field, and how a conductor carrying a current and situated in such a field was acted on by a force. These were the fundamentals of the electric generator and the electric motor. Practical electric traction based on these principles is generally accepted as dating from the little railway exhibited in Berlin in 1879 by Werner von Siemens. The track was 900 ft (328 m) long and laid in an oval. The four-wheeled locomotive collected current from the rails, the power being supplied from a stationary steam-driven generator. It was propelled by a 3 hp (2·23 kW) electric motor. At that time the carbon brushes through which the current passed to the revolving armature had to be reset each time the direction of running was reversed. Since this was inconvenient in a locomotive, Siemens' motor ran continuously in the same direction and drove the wheels through a mechanical reverse gear.

There was much activity in electrification both in Europe and the United States in the 1880s. The earliest applications were on tramways, beginning with the experimental line at Lichterfelde, a suburb of Berlin, in 1881. This was the first commercially

successful street tramway electrification. It operated over a route of approximately 1·5 miles (2·5 km). In 1883 Magnus Volk opened a short electric railway on the sea front at Brighton. This was the first public electric railway in the British Isles. In the United States Lee Daft built a number of experimental electric locomotives and in 1884 electrified 2 miles (3·2 km) of line in Baltimore. The line was operated with electric traction for two years and is generally accepted as the first successful electrification of a public railway in the USA. A new era began in 1890 when the first underground electric railway in the world was opened in London – the City & South London Railway.

These early systems used direct current at low voltage. As the length of lines increased there were advantages in using higher voltages because of voltage drop in the rails, so that when trains were at the end of the line remote from the power station the motors were operating below their rated voltage, with consequent loss of power.

At this period the distribution of electric power in the form of alternating current at high voltage was being developed. Electric power being the product of

voltage and current, the higher the voltage the lower is the current for a given power. Low currents can be transmitted long distances over conductors of small cross section, which reduces the cost of power networks. Voltages suitable for economic transmission are too high for use in traction motors, but the voltage of alternating current can be raised or lowered in transformers. This brought the possibility of transmitting power at high voltage to feeder points spaced along the railway, and installing transformers at these points to lower the voltage to a value suitable for supply to the trains.

But here another problem arose. Ordinary traction motors operated on alternating current of normal industrial frequencies (50 or 60 Hz) are subject to severe sparking at low speeds and when working hard, which results in burning and rapid wear of the commutators. Commutation is the process by which the direction of current in the revolving motor windings is switched so that a continuous turning force is exerted on them. The force proceeds from the interaction between a magnetic field surrounding each coil of the winding, set up by the current flowing through it, and the field

produced by the poles of the stationary electromagnet system. The commutator is in effect a rotary switch, the brushes being the fixed contacts.

For satisfactory conduction of current to the revolving windings it is essential for the commutator surface to be truly cylindrical. Sparking pits the surface, which aggravates the problem and requires frequent maintenance. There were two ways of overcoming the problem at that time:

1 The alternating current could be converted to direct current at the feeder points.
2 Current could be generated at a lower frequency, or converted to such a frequency before being supplied to the overhead system of the railway.

Railways soon divided into two groups: the direct current (DC) railways using method (1); and the alternating current (AC) railways using method (2). Both systems might be used in the same country, short-distance lines being dc and long-distance main lines AC.

Countries with hydro-electric power, where railways could generate their own low-frequency supplies economically, tended to favour AC. The voltage in the overhead wires from which the trains

Swiss Federal Railways 1-B-B-1 locomotive No 12339 pauses at Erstfeld before beginning the climb to Goschenen and the Gotthard Tunnel.

collected their supply could be as high as 15,000 volts but this was reduced to a few hundred volts by transformers in the locomotives or motor-coaches before reaching the motors.

The DC railways converted high voltage AC into DC in rotary converters installed in substations at the lineside. If the supply was to be collected by the trains from a live rail at ground level the voltage did not normally exceed 750. Where higher voltages, usually 1,500 or 3,000 volts, were used, collection was from overhead wiring. At first the DC railways had a similar problem to that of the AC lines because early rotary converters would not operate satisfactorily on industrial supplies. The difficulty was soon overcome, but not before many railways had built their own power stations or had made arrangements with electricity undertakings to be given a low frequency supply. In England the changeover on the large DC system of the Southern Region of British Railways to taking power from the national network was not completed until the 1960s.

At first the advantages of electric traction were most apparent on suburban lines. Rapid acceleration is necessary on services where trains follow each other at short intervals. This requires high tractive efforts, but the effort that can be applied at an axle is limited by its adhesion on the rail. If this limit is exceeded, the wheels slip. In the electric train a high tractive effort was made available by distributing it among several axles, each powered by a relatively small motor. Another big advantage was that the electric train could be driven from either end. On arriving at a terminus there was no locomotive to detach, run round the train, and couple on at the other end, requiring several signalling operations. On some intensive steam services, locomotives were held in sidings, ready to couple on to a train for its next journey out of the terminus as soon as it had unloaded its passengers, but this involved complex trackwork and it still left the problem of disposing of the locomotive that had brought the train into the terminus, and so led to still more shunting movements.

At first current for all the motors in the train passed through the driver's controller and was led by cables running through the train to the motors on the rear car. The most important technical development in the early period of suburban and underground railway electrification was the multiple-unit control system introduced by Frank J. Sprague in the United States, and soon adopted worldwide. As well as being concerned with early electric railway experiments, Sprague was involved in electric lifts. His work in that area gave him the idea for his control system in electric trains. The principle of multiple-unit control is that all the control switchgear in a train, distributed among the various motor-coaches, is operated by a low-voltage electrical supply from a 'master controller' in the leading cab. The motorcoaches collect current individually, but all motors respond to the signals sent from the master controller.

Multiple-unit trains are formed of units, each consisting of one or more motor-coaches and one or more trailers. The number of units that can be coupled together is largely limited by operating considerations, such as the length of station platforms and sidings. Because the motors in each unit contribute to the total power, the ratio of power to weight is constant for any length of train and the performance is unaffected when coaches are added. This is a very different situation from adding coaches to a steam-hauled train, when the extra vehicles were simply deadweight. The Sprague multiple-unit control system was first applied in regular service on the South Shore Elevated Railway in Chicago in 1898.

The United States also claims the first electrified main line in the world. It was a modest affair, only about 3 miles (4·8 km) long, but it formed part of a connection between two previously separated main line sections of the Baltimore & Ohio Railway in the city of Baltimore, and carried both passenger and freight traffic. A gradient of 1 in 125 northbound would have caused problems with steam traction because over 1·25 miles (2 km) of the line had to be in tunnel under an important thoroughfare, and the city authorities would not allow openings at street level through which smoke and steam might be discharged. A contract was therefore placed with the General Electric Company of America to electrify the line through the tunnel. A 2,000 kW steam generating plant was built near the southern portal to supply the trains at 660V DC. The first three locomotives were four-axle centre-cab machines developing 1,440 hp (1,074 kW). Electric working began on 1 July 1895 and the full freight and passenger service came into operation in May 1896 when the third locomotive was delivered.

Freight trains were normally propelled through the tunnel with the steam locomotive still at the head but not working. On emerging from the northern portal steam and electric power worked together to tackle a steepening gradient, the electric locomotive falling behind at the summit ready to coast downhill to the southern end of the tunnel. Passenger trains were hauled through the tunnel to a station at its northern end. Southbound passenger and freight trains simply coasted down the gradient through the tunnel without electric assistance.

Soon after the turn of the century two more important low-voltage DC electrifications of main lines came into operation in the USA. In New York, the New York Central approached the Grand Central terminal through 2 miles (3·2 km) of tunnel under Park Avenue. After a serious collision in the smoke-filled tunnel on 8 January 1902 the railroad was ordered to stop using steam locomotives south of the Harlem River as from 1 July 1908. A major electrification was planned to meet this requirement,

the four-track main line being electrified for 34 miles (54·7 km) to Croton-on-Hudson, while the double-track Harlem Division was electrified from its point of divergence at 138th Street to North White Plains, 24 miles (38·6 km) from Grand Central. A 660V system with third rail was chosen and two power stations generating AC at 25,000 volts were built. This supply was converted to DC in eight substations. Main line trains were hauled by loco-motives of 2,200 hp (1,640 kW) individually but capable of working in pairs on the Sprague multiple-unit system when necessary. In addition there was a fleet of multiple-unit trains for suburban services. Traffic began on 30 September 1906, handsomely beating the deadline.

Trains of the New York, New Haven & Hartford Railroad shared Grand Central Terminal with the New York Central, joining the NYC electrified tracks at Woodlawn, 12 miles (19·3 km) out. The New Haven line had to meet the same deadline as the NYC in changing to electric traction. This company, however, was engaged on a more extensive electrifi-cation, having decided in 1905 to electrify its main line as far as Stamford, 33 miles (53 km) from Grand Central, in the first instance, continuing to New Haven when the system had been proved. But on its own metals from Woodlawn the railroad's electri-fication was to be at 11,000 volts, 25Hz. Its trains would therefore have to operate both on high-voltage AC and low-voltage DC, but this was not a

serious problem. The most generally used AC traction motor differs from the DC machine only in details of construction and will run on either supply. Trans-formers in the New Haven locomotives reduced the ac to 660 volts when under the high-voltage catenary, while inwards from Woodlawn the same voltage was collected from the third rail.

The Pennsylvania was the next railroad to work its trains into central New York with electric traction. Until this electrification, Pennsylvania trains had terminated in Jersey City and passengers for Manhattan had to cross the Hudson River by ferry. It was a vast project, involving tunnels under the Hudson, a magnificent new station in the heart of New York, and a continuation under the East River to a junction with the Long Island Railroad. The electrification began in New Jersey at a station called Manhattan Transfer where the new line branched from the old and descended to the Hudson River tunnels. The new Penn Station was 9 miles (14·5 km) from Manhattan Transfer, and the total length of the electrification to the rolling stock sidings at Sunnyside Yard and the junction with the Long Island system was 13·4 miles (21·5 km). Power supply was 675V DC to a third rail, the same as on the Long Island so that that company's trains could serve Penn Station. Manhattan Transfer was the point of exchange between steam and electric traction for the Pennsylvania's main-line trains. Motive power continued to be changed here until the

The mountains close in on the main line at the approach to Goschenen on the Gotthard line.

DC electrification was converted to high-voltage AC with overhead contact wire in 1932 and electric trains ran through to Washington.

The Manhattan Transfer-Penn Station, Sunnyside electrification went smoothly into action on 27 November 1910 after two weeks of trial operation of a full service but not carrying passengers. Several prototype locomotives had been tested previously. The design selected was a two-unit machine, the equivalent in wheel arrangement to two 4-4-0 steam locomotives coupled back to back. In each unit a single 2,000 hp (1,490 kW) motor was coupled to the two driving axles through a jackshaft and side rods. It was a remarkably successful and long-lived design. After AC electrification into Penn Station in 1932 the locomotives remained at work on the Long Island's DC lines, the last two surviving until the early 1960s. Penn Station featured in innumerable cinema films but the electric locomotives were rarely seen. A shot of a departing train was usually followed by one of a steam locomotive at speed, so that their existence was unknown to many cinemagoers.

The choice of ac by the New York, New Haven and Hartford as early as 1905 reveals how fast development of that form of traction had gone ahead. Two systems had been studied from the 1890s. By that time the transmission of electric power as three-phase AC at high voltage was becoming established. A three-phase system carries three alternating currents of the same frequency, but going through their cycles out of step with each other. Consumers can be connected to the three phases, as in industry, or to one of the phases, which is the usual practice for domestic electricity supplies. Both methods were investigated by railways in Europe and the USA.

When three-phase current is supplied to suitably connected electromagnets a rotating magnetic field is set up. If a system of interconnected electrical conductors is pivoted in such a field it will start to rotate and approach the speed of the field. This is the essence of an electric motor which is simple both in principle and construction. The principle is the fundamental one that every action produces an equal and opposite reaction. Here the action is the induction of currents in the pivoted conductors as the lines of magnetic force sweep through them. The reaction is for the conductors to revolve in the same direction as the field and try to catch up with it for if conductors and field revolve at the same speed the inductive effect stops. In practice the rotary system always lags by an amount called the 'slip'. The slip produces a torque, or turning effort, and so the arrangement constitutes an electric motor.

A motor of this kind is simple in construction because there need be no physical connection between the revolving rotor and the stationary electromagnets. The commutation process with the problems it brings is dispensed with. It is little wonder that engineers have always been attracted by the idea of using induction motors in locomotives.

There are also drawbacks. A three-phase supply requires three conductors. On a railway this means two overhead contact wires instead of one and using the rails as the third, or 'neutral', conductor. The two contact wires complicate the overhead system where there are points and crossovers.

The speed of an induction motor is closely linked to the supply frequency and the number of poles in the magnet system. The supply frequency being fixed, speed has to be controlled by fairly complex switching to change the effective number of poles and the interconnections between motors. On the credit side there is the fact that if, when running downhill, the motors revolve faster than the magnetic field, they automatically return power to the supply instead of absorbing it.

The Hungarian firm of Ganz in Budapest was active in three-phase development at an early stage and by 1896 had a three-phase locomotive on trial. In Switzerland the branch from Burgdorf to Thun, 28 miles (45 km), was electrified with three-phase current at 750V, 40Hz, in 1899 and was the first standard gauge three-phase railway to provide a regular and reliable service. The branch had gradients as steep as 1 in 40.

Three-phase traction has been associated mainly with modest speeds on steeply graded lines, but it briefly took on a more dramatic aspect. About 1900 a Study Group for High Speed Railways was formed in Germany with the participation of the leading electrical and mechanical engineering companies and the support of the Deutsche Bank. The sum of 1·5 million Marks was allocated to an experiment to investigate various aspects of electric traction and to establish the maximum speed that could be attained. The Group equipped the Marienfelde-Zossen military railway with an experimental 10,000V three-phase installation. Two railcars were prepared for the tests, one equipped by Siemens and the other by AEG. Both were powered by four motors with a rating of 670 hp (500 kW) at 55Hz. The three conductors of the three-phase supply were mounted alongside the track, one above the other, and the railcars carried side-contact current collectors on their roofs. Speed was controlled from the trackside by supplying the conductors with a range of frequencies. On 7 October 1903 the Siemens railcar for the first time reached the target speed of 125 mph (200 km/h). It was then decided to aim higher still, and on 23 and 27 October both railcars attained speeds of 128·4 mph and 131·7 mph (206·7 km/h and 210·3 km/h), repeating the performance on both occasions. A record speed on rails had been attained that was not broken until the Kruckenberg propellor-driven railcar surpassed it by maintaining 143 mph (230·1 km/h) for 6·25 miles (10 km) on 21 June 1931.

Italy chose three-phase at 3,000V, 15Hz, for electrification of the Valtellina line in 1903. The

original electrification was from Lecco to Sondria and Chiavenna but it was later extended to Monza on the main line from Milan to the Gotthard, a total of 90 miles (145 km). The same system was adopted for the Giovi lines between Genoa and Turin. Both electrifications were carried out by Ganz, and locomotives were supplied by Ganz and Brown Boveri. Eventually 1,082 miles (1,742 km) of the Italian State Railways were electrified on the three-phase system. Most of the lines were steeply graded and advantage was taken of the regeneration of power when running downhill. The return of power also had a retarding effect, holding the speed steady when descending long inclines with important savings in the wear and tear of brakes. On the Giovi lines, where the maximum gradient was nearly 1 in 28, the downhill speed of a train weighing 324·79 tons (330 tonnes), with a locomotive at front and rear, was approximately 33 mph (53 km/h) and each locomotive returned between 600 and 800 kW to the supply system. Speed uphill in similar circumstances was about 30·3 mph (48·8 km/h).

The Italian electrifications were watched with interest in the United States, particularly by the Great Northern Railroad. This was the most northerly of the transcontinental lines, and while it had found a relatively easy route across the Rockies there was a more severe barrier in the Cascade Mountains, some 600 miles (965 km) further west

before descending to the coastal strip. At first the railroad struggled over the range with gradients as steep as 1 in 25 while a tunnel was being built to reduce the maximum gradient to 1 in 45 and shorten the distance by 9 miles (14·5 km). Opened in 1900, the tunnel relieved the situation to some extent but ever-increasing loads and larger steam locomotives created almost intolerable conditions inside the tunnel for the train crews. The Great Northern therefore decided to electrify through the tunnel with three-phase ac so as to be in a position to reap the benefits of regeneration when the electrification was extended later.

The Cascade Tunnel electrification, 4 miles (6·4 km) long, extended through the tunnel and over its approaches to yards at each end. A hydro-electric plant was built on the Wenatchee River, some 30 miles (48 km) from the line, generating 6,600V at 25Hz. The voltage was stepped up to 33,000V for transmission to the railway substation, where it was reduced to 6,600V again for feeding into the overhead system. The locomotives were carried on two two-axle motor bogies, the four motors producing 1,500 hp (1,118 kW). Transformers on board reduced the line voltage to 500V for the motors. Three-phase operation lasted from 1909 to 1927, when the line was converted to single-phase ac and the electrification was extended to cover the 72·9 miles (117·3 km) between Skykomish and Wenat-

A train from Italy emerges from the Simplon Tunnel at Brigue. This is the portal of the second tunnel, opened in 1921. The earlier bore of 1906 is alongside.

chee. A new Cascade Tunnel on a different alignment was opened in 1929.

The Italian three-phase experience also influenced events in Europe. While the Simplon Tunnel was being built it became apparent that early plans for ventilation had been inadequate and that steam traction would not be practicable. Plans for electrification were put in hand in 1905. The Italian State Railways were partners in the Simplon undertaking and they agreed to loan three of their Ganz-built Valtellina locomotives for a trial of three-phase electrification and to release two more similar locomotives, that were being built for them by Brown Boveri, for the same purpose. Brown Boveri undertook to electrify the line through the tunnel from Brigue to Iselle at its own expense on the understanding that if the equipment was not retained it would remain the company's property. It carried out the work between December 1905, when the decision to use three-phase ac at 3,300V, $16\frac{2}{3}$Hz was taken, and the opening of the tunnel on 1 June 1906. The three-phase system was extended to Sion in 1919, bringing the distance electrified up to 47·2 miles (76 km) and remained in use until displaced on 15 May 1930 by the single-phase system at 15,000V, $16\frac{2}{3}$Hz which had become general in Switzerland.

In single-phase traction the motors are similar in principle to DC traction machines but are subject to the commutation problems mentioned earlier. These are mitigated by the low frequency of $16\frac{2}{3}$Hz but further refinements were necessary to make the ac traction motor a generally acceptable alternative to its DC counterpart. The most important steps in this direction were embodied in patents granted in 1904 to the Oerlikon company in Switzerland. In 1902 Oerlikon was granted the use of 14·3 miles (23 km) of Swiss Federal Railways' line between Seebach and Wettingen for its single-phase experiments. At first the line was electrified at 15,000V.

50Hz and Oerlikon's first experimental locomotive contained a rotary-converter which changed the AC supply into 700V DC for the traction motors. On 16 January 1905 this locomotive began its trials between Seebach and Affoltern on the Wettingen line. It is of historic importance in foreshadowing the converter principle which some 50 years later became the all but universal method of operating locomotives on a single-phase supply at the industrial frequency of 50Hz, although by that time rectifiers were replacing rotary machines for AC/DC conversion.

The true ancestor of the modern ac locomotive operating on a special low-frequency supply was the second Seebach-Wettingen prototype, which began its trials on 11 November 1905. This was powered by AC motors, and the supply frequency was reduced to the now standard $16\frac{2}{3}$Hz. At that time the railway authorities were not prepared to set up their own low-frequency power system and the Seebach-Wettingen experiments were discontinued. The distance electrified was also too short for a true assessment to be made of the economics of electrification. In the summer of 1909 the equipment was dismantled and the locomotives went into store. Ten years later they emerged when the Federal Railways had embarked on their single-phase electrification programme, at first on light freight duties and then as shunters.

The Seebach-Wettingen experiments were the source of the main stream of single-phase traction, but in Germany the Winter-Eichberg type of single-phase traction motor had been developed and found applications in the early years. In 1903 the Prussian-Hessian State Railways decided to experiment with AC traction and electrified the line from Niederschöneweide to Spindlersfeld, near Berlin, a distance of 2·5 miles (4·1 km). The electrification was single-phase at 6,000V, 25Hz, and two motor-coaches were equipped with Winter-Eichberg motors of 100 hp (74·6 kW). No further electrification was undertaken for some time while the results of the experiment were being studied. The Niederschöneweide line was the first single-phase electric railway in the world. It was also the first to use catenary suspension of the contact wire.

There were two early single-phase AC electrifications in England. Both used 6,600V at 25Hz. The first in service was on the Midland Railway branch lines connecting Lancaster, Morecambe, and Heysham, about 13 miles (21 km) in all. Traffic began in 1908, services being worked mainly by three-coach trains consisting of a motorcoach and two trailers (one of them being a driving trailer with master controller for remote control of the motor-coach). These lines were used for the first British experiments with industrial frequency ac traction in 1952.

The second AC electrification was on the London, Brighton & South Coast Railway. Electric services between the company's termini at Victoria and

The southern exit from the Lotschberg Tunnel, near Goppenstein on the descent to the Rhone Valley at Brigue. A view taken soon after the opening of the tunnel in 1913.

The Alte Trisannabrücke on
the Arlberg line of the Austrian
Federal Railways.

London Bridge began in 1909 in a bid to secure for the railway traffic which was being lost to electric tramways in South London. Extensions from Victoria and London Bridge to Crystal Palace followed in 1911 and 1912. Both services were worked by three-car trains, those on the South London line consisting of two motor-coaches and an intermediate trailer, while the Crystal Palace trains were formed of one motor-coach and two trailers. At this period there were rivals to the series AC motor developed by Oerlikon and the LBSC trains were powered by Winter-Eichberg repulsion motors. Extensions of the AC system to Sutton and Cheam, and down the main Brighton line to Coulsdon were deferred by the First World War. They took place in the post-war years, but after the LBSC had been absorbed into the Southern Railway in 1923 all these lines were converted to low-voltage DC with third rail supply.

The last ten years of the 19th century can be considered as the period of 'urban' electrification in Great Britain, for the City & South London opening in 1890 was followed by the Liverpool Overhead electric line in 1893, the Waterloo & City underground line in London in 1898, and the underground Central London Railway in 1900. Trains on the Liverpool Overhead and the Waterloo & City were powered by motor-coaches from the start.

On the Central London small electric locomotives were used at first but this line changed to motor-coach operation in 1902. At that time motor-coach working did not necessarily imply a multiple-unit system on the Sprague pattern. On the Liverpool Overhead and Waterloo & City lines the motors on the front and rear motor-coaches of a formation shared a common control equipment and were interconnected by power cables. This practice would no longer be countenanced on an underground line like the Waterloo & City.

The British main-line railways began to electrify certain suburban routes early in the 1900s, and systems were developed around London, Manchester, Liverpool and Newcastle-upon-Tyne. Most of them worked in the 600–700V DC range with third rail supply, but in 1913 the Manchester-Bury line of the Lancashire & Yorkshire Railway adopted 1,200V DC with a special type of shoegear and protected third rail. A short experiment with 3,500V DC and overhead contact wire was conducted by the Dick, Kerr company on the 3·75 miles (6 km) of the branch from Bury to Holcombe Brook in 1913. The equipment was later dismantled and in 1918 the 1,200V system which had been adopted between Manchester and Bury was extended to Holcombe Brook.

Liverpool saw the first conversion of a British steam railway to electric working, the changeover taking place on the Mersey Railway in 1903. As we have seen the Lancashire & Yorkshire Railway's Liverpool-Southport electrification of 1904 is sometimes claimed as the first electrification of a British main line although the distance was only 19 miles (30·6 km). However, some of the business trains made only one stop and covered the distance in 25 minutes. The contemporary North Tyneside electrification of the North Eastern Railway was similar in providing fast electric trains between residential suburbs on or near the coast and the business centre of a city, in this case Newcastle-upon-Tyne. A section of track forming part of the east coast main line to Scotland was included in this scheme, giving rise on occasion to more 'first main-line electrification in Great Britain' claims.

In 1913 the North Eastern Railway began electrifying a cross-country freight line between Shildon and a marshalling yard at Newport for conveying coal to the yard from collieries in the Bishop Auckland area. The system chosen was 1,500V DC with overhead contact wire. Traffic began in 1915, and after the war, in 1919, provisional approval was given by the NER Board to electrification of the company's main line between York and Newcastle on the same system. Vincent (later Sir Vincent) Raven, the company's Chief Mechanical Engineer, had a main-line electric locomotive built for this project but by the time it left the works in 1922 the North Eastern was on the point of being absorbed into the London & North Eastern Railway and the electrification of the main line never went ahead. The 1,800 hp locomotive, the electric equivalent in wheel arrangement to a 4-6-4, carried the unpropitious number 13. It made some trial trips on the Newport-Shildon line and then went into store. When the LNER decided to electrify the main line between Sheffield and Manchester under a government-assisted scheme in the late 1930s there seemed to be a prospect of No 13 returning to active life. But by the time the Sheffield-Manchester electrification was reactivated after suspension during the Second World War the design of No 13 had become outdated and the locomotive was broken up in 1950.

On the eve of the First World War the London & South Western Railway had begun a programme of suburban electrification at 600V DC, the first section opening in 1915 between Waterloo and Wimbledon via East Putney. This was the nucleus of the Southern Electric system which expanded rapidly after the war under the General Manager of the Southern Railway, Sir Herbert Walker. Its extensions to Brighton, Eastbourne, Hastings and Portsmouth gave Britain an electric main-line system in southern England in the 1930s but it was entirely a passenger operation, with multiple-unit trains. The first British main line with all traffic worked by electric traction did not come into operation until the Manchester-Sheffield line had been converted throughout in 1954.

The DC railways were restricted in the voltage they could use by what the traction motors would accept without flashovers between 'live' components at different potentials. In practice the limit was about 1,500 volts, but higher voltages could be used in the contact wire if at least two motors were always connected in series so that the voltage could be shared between them. This arrangement was used on the Butte, Anaconda & Pacific Railroad in the USA, electrified in 1913 at 2,400V. The railroad was built to carry copper ore from Butte, Montana, to the smelter at Anaconda, 26 miles (41·8 km) away. It connected at Butte with the Chicago, Milwaukee, St Paul & Pacific where the one daily BA&P passenger train in each direction shared the Milwaukee's station. This arrangement, and the fact that the two companies had a director in common, justified the '& Pacific' part of the BA&P's title. On electrification the traffic was taken over from 2-8-0 and 4-8-0 steam locomotives by 1,280 hp (954 kW) electrics.

Butte to Anaconda was a prelude to the great 3,000V DC electrification of the Chicago, Milwaukee, St Paul & Pacific Railroad on 645 miles (1,038 km) of its transcontinental main line. There were two electrified sections, the first from Harlowton to Avery, 438 miles (705 km), taking the line through the Belt Mountains in Montana; and the second from Othello in the State of Washington to Tacoma, a distance of 207 miles (333 km), crossing the Saddle Mountains. They were separated by 216

miles (347·6 km) of more easily graded route which were never electrified. Harlowton-Avery was completed in 1916, and Othello-Tacoma in 1920. A final phase was the electrification of 10 miles (16 km) from Black River Junction to Seattle in 1927.

Steep gradients, severe curvature and many tunnels were only part of the operating problem faced with steam locomotives. In winter the temperature in the mountains might drop to 40 degrees of frost and there were numerous motive power failures, sometimes through sheer inability to maintain adequate steam pressure in such conditions. As to gradients, eastbound trains faced a steady 1 in 100 for 49 miles (79 km) through the Montana Canyon in the Belt Mountains, while from Beverly, in the State of Washington, there were 18·9 miles (30·4 km) of nearly 1 in 45 to the summit in the Saddle Mountains.

The Milwaukee's electrification was a success from the start. The first winter of operation was the harshest recorded but an official comment was: 'There were times when every steam locomotive in the Rocky Mountain District was frozen, but the electric locomotive went right along. The electrification had in every way exceeded our expectations.

This is so not only as respects tonnage handled and mileage made, but also the regularity of operation'.

A US tradition of massive, many-wheeled electric locomotives was born with this electrification. The first Milwaukee electrics were twin-unit machines with a four-wheel bogie at each end and eight driving axles in four groups of two (2-B-B+B-B-2), measuring 112 ft (34·1 m) overall. The eight traction motors, operating in pairs at 1,500V each, totalled 3,640 hp (2,714 kW) at the one-hour rating. Publicity for all aspects of the electrification was uninhibited, and not surprisingly the first locomotive left the General Electric works with banners on its sides proclaiming it to be 'the largest electric locomotive in the world'. Of more interest to technical observers was the provision for regenerative braking. On a test run two locomotives held a train of 2,755·76 tons (2,800 tonnes) to 17–18 mph (27–29 km/h) during a descent of 21 miles (32 km) with gradients as steep as 1 in 50 on the western slope of the Continental Divide.

In later years the 3,000V DC system was adopted in South America, South Africa, the Soviet Union and elsewhere in Europe. In Italy it steadily replaced the early three-phase electrifications.

Former North Eastern Railway 2-Co-2 electric locomotive, No 26600, on tow in 1951 after withdrawal. The locomotive was built to the designs of Sir Vincent Raven when it was proposed to electrify the North Eastern main line from York to Newcastle with 1500V DC. When the NER was absorbed into the London & North Eastern Railway in 1923 the plans were dropped and the locomotive never saw commercial service although it made trial runs on the Newport-Shildon electrified freight line.

9. ENGINES TO MATCH THE TRAFFIC

Previous page: Great Central Atlantic No 1086 heads the 3.35 pm from Manchester and Sheffield to Marylebone near Northwood on the Metropolitan & Great Central Joint line in 1906. The coaches are still in the French grey and brown livery of the early days of the Great Central's London Extension.

FROM THE BEGINNING of the 20th century until the eclipse of steam by other motive power, steam locomotive designers were continually meeting demands for more power and higher efficiency to work both heavier and faster trains. Superheating and compounding were two fundamental developments that came to the fore in the early years and retained their importance throughout. Compounding was a controversial subject, and was strongly supported in some quarters and viewed with less enthusiasm in others, but there was no division of opinion on the importance of superheating.

When steam enters the cylinders of a steam locomotive it is cooled by contact with the cylinder walls and condensation takes place, resulting in some of the energy being lost. If steam is admitted at a higher temperature it will not be cooled enough for condensation to begin. Early experiments in raising steam temperature by superheating were restricted by the lubricants and packing materials available, which deteriorated in high-temperature conditions, but by the end of the 19th century these difficulties were being overcome. The superheating system developed by Wilhelm Schmidt in Kassel was given its first practical application in two 4-4-0 locomotives of the Prussian State Railways in 1897.

In these early superheaters the high steam temperatures still caused problems, but by 1899 an improved design fitted to the S3 class 4-4-0s yielded encouraging results. One of these locomotives showed a fuel saving of 12 per cent on trial runs between Berlin and Breslau. This was satisfactory enough for superheaters to be fitted in 104 more 4-4-0s ordered by the Prussian State Railways between 1902 and 1909, and with the Prussian P8 class 4-6-0 of 1906 the decisive step was taken of making the superheater standard equipment.

Originally the superheater elements were in the smokebox inside a special tube through which the hot gases flowed from the fire. Further work by the Belgian engineers Flamme and Bertrand led to the more usual arrangement of extending the elements back into the boiler inside the flue tubes, some of which were of larger diameter for this purpose. This type of superheater was first used by the Belgian National Railways in 1901.

The unusual 2-8-4 wheel arrangement was chosen for express locomotives in Austria in 1928. In their day they were the most powerful locomotives in Europe, hauling loads of up to 600 tons (610 tonnes) on the Vienna-Salzburg line.

Superheating was sometimes seen at this period as an alternative to compounding, which was attracting equal attention. In 1908 the Class S3/6 4-6-2s of the Bavarian State Railways gave a convincing demonstration of what could be done by combining the two techniques. These were the celebrated Maffei Pacifics, of which 159 were built over a period of 22 years. After the various State railway systems in Germany were merged into the Deutsche Reichsbahn in 1920 the Maffeis were to be seen all over its main lines. They have been acclaimed in German literature as the most handsome of the country's locomotive fleet, and made a strong impression on all who saw them. C. Hamilton Ellis had memories of them from student days in Munich between the world wars and devoted a chapter to 'The Maffeis' in his book *The Engines that Passed* (Allen & Unwin, 1968). He wrote:

Indeed, this was one of the truly great designs of the early 20th century. Fuel economy was exemplary; no other big German types could

touch the engines in this respect and they would stroll quietly away from Munich with enormous trains that stretched far out of its great, old station. The only fuss I ever knew when watching them was the occasional rush of wet steam from the cylinder drain cocks, and blowing off was rare. Kronawitter quotes a run on which one of the 1927 series (Reichsbahn No 18.518) took a 670-tonne train up the 1 in 128 bank between Treuchtlingen and Donauworth at a sustained speed of 43·5 mph (70 km/h) and kept up a steady 72 mph (116 km/h) on the level stretches to the south.

Hamilton Ellis recalls that on the last run of one of the Maffei Bavarian Pacifics in public service, on 29 May 1965, 'she was garlanded with flowers like a May Queen'. There had been an earlier mark of public esteem when Munich celebrated its eighth century in 1958. A specimen of the class preserved in the Deutsches Museum was taken out and towed through the streets on a trailer in triumphant procession.

Compounding had gone far since the de Glehn system first made its impact in the 4-2-2-0 No 701 of the Nord. The prototype was followed by a series of 4-4-0s which gave excellent service on their home ground and on the metals of other companies which had purchased them. In 1900 the first of the Nord Atlantics appeared, forerunners of a famous class that maintained their tradition of speediness up to the outbreak of the Second World War. The de Glehn system of compounding was versatile. Either pair of cylinders could be isolated; the hp cylinders could exhaust direct to atmosphere; or the lp cylinders could be supplied with live steam at reduced pressure as a reinforcement.

The Paris, Lyons & Mediterranean Railway had followed its early compound 2-4-2s with the 4-4-0 *Machines à bec*, so-called from the fairings on the smokebox and between chimney and dome which were supposed to reduce wind resistance when battling with the Mistral wind in the Rhone Valley. In contrast with the de Glehn locomotives, those of the PLM worked permanently in the compound mode. The reverser varied the hp cut-off but the cut-off in the lp cylinders was fixed permanently at 63 per cent. A very long hp cut-off was used at starting and live steam was admitted to the lp cylinders to reinforce the steam exhausted from the hp cylinders.

In Austria Gölsdorf was now building four-cylinder compounds. His first design was the Class 108 4-4-2 of 1901, which showed the influence of a visit to Great Britain in 1899 and his appreciation of how British locomotive engineers were combining power with elegance in their designs. Gölsdorf's work on multi-coupled designs continued, reaching its climax in his Class 100 2-12-0 of 1911. By that time the increasing weight of trains on the Tauern line was taxing the existing 2-10-0 designs to their limit. The axle-load being limited to 13·78 tons (14 tonnes) Gölsdorf could only increase adhesion by introducing a sixth coupled axle. Again he had to allow considerable sideplay, and for the sixth coupled axle this was 1·6 in (40 mm) in each direction. This was too much to be accommodated by normal coupling rod bearings and so a universally-jointed arrangement was used. Where Gölsdorf could keep within a stipulated axle-load without going to such lengths, he was expert in saving weight in locomotives of more conventional wheel arrangements. His Class 110 2-6-2 of 1905, with four cylinders, 6 ft (182·9 cm) coupled wheels, a grate area of 43·1 sq ft (4 sq m) and 2,856 sq ft (265·2 sq m) heating surface, weighed no more than 66·93 tons (68 tonnes) in working order, an achievement claimed as a world record. It was followed in 1910 by a superheated version, Class 10, which was at work for nearly 50 years on the best Westbahn trains. The choice of a single leading axle instead of a two-axle bogie, with its heavy frames, was an important contribution to weight saving in these locomotives.

No more 2-12-0 locomotives were built for Austria. Improvements to the infrastructure of the main lines allowed heavier axle-loads, and after the First World War electrification was being planned. No 100 was broken up in 1928. The design lived on, however, 44 similar 2-12-0s being built for the Wurtemberg State Railways. In due course they became Class 59.0 of the Deutsche Reichsbahn and gave outstanding service during the Second World War. Some remained at work on the Semmering line until the 1950s.

Gölsdorf continued to go against the general trend towards two leading carrying axles in his Class 210 unsuperheated 2-6-4 of 1908, and the superheated version, Class 310 of 1911. The trailing bogie allowed a wide, deep firebox of simple construction to be installed; the wheel arrangement also reduced the length of the locomotive, which more than compensated for the weight of the Krauss-Helmholz bogie which carried the leading axle and the first coupled axle. Austrian pioneering in the 2-6-4 wheel arrangement for large express locomotives earned the type the name 'Adriatic', for in those days Austria had an Adriatic coastline.

Compounding never won general acceptance on the British railways, where the restricted loading gauge made it difficult to accommodate large-diameter low-pressure cylinders. On the North Eastern Railway T. W. Worsdell built two-cylinder compounds of various wheel arrangements between 1886 and 1892, and contemporary comment has recorded them as being more reliable than Webb's compounds on the LNWR. Worsdell was succeeded as Chief Mechanical Engineer by his brother, Wilson, who also built a two-cylinder compound but in 1898 this was rebuilt under the direction of the North Eastern's chief draughtsman, W. M. Smith as a three-cylinder compound with the low-

pressure cylinders outside. Smith also designed two four-cylinder compound Atlantics, built in 1906, putting the high-pressure cylinders outside and taking the drive from all cylinders to the leading coupled axle. A proposal to build ten more when Vincent Raven had succeeded Wilson Worsdell as CME was dropped because of legal difficulties over royalties for using Smith's designs.

On the Great Central Railway J. G. Robinson was now building Atlantic locomotives for the company's new main line to London and in 1905–06 he used the Smith system in four three-cylinder compounds with this wheel arrangement. The high-pressure cylinder between the frames drove the front coupled axle, while the two outside low-pressure cylinders drove the second axle. These engines had the characteristic Smith starting valve for admitting high-pressure steam at reduced pressure to the low-pressure cylinders when extra 'boost' was needed.

On the Great Western Railway G. J. Churchward experimented with French-built compound Atlantics but decided that the 4-6-0 wheel arrangement was better suited to GWR requirements, and that application of the principles he was developing for four-cylinder simple locomotives would produce the performance he required. The most numerous

Austria first turned to the 4-8-0 wheel arrangement for express traffic in 1915. Later versions of the design built after the First World War were the backbone of main line passenger services from Vienna to Italy and Yugoslavia by the Semmering line until replaced by diesels.

British compounds were on the Midland Railway where in 1903 S. W. Johnson built five three-cylinder compound 4-4-0s with the Smith starting valve arrangement. In the first two locomotives the cut-offs in the high-pressure and low-pressure cylinders were controlled separately, but in the remainder of the batch the two sets of valve gear were linked.

When R. M. Deeley succeeded Johnson in 1904 he built more compounds but did not use the Smith starting valve (also called the 'reinforcing' valve because it could be used to boost the power in other circumstances), and arranged for automatic change-over from simple to compound working as the regulator was opened. Driving was simplified, but it has been suggested that this was at the expense of achieving optimum performance. In 1913 one of the Midland compounds was superheated and in due course this was extended throughout the class. If the earlier simplification had reduced the best that could be got out of these engines the effect was evidently not serious in practical terms, for a standard Midland compound proved the most economical engine in trials conducted by the London, Midland & Scottish Railway between 1923 and 1925 of various types of locomotives from its constituent companies. The Midland had been absorbed into the LMSR under the Railways Act of 1921. As a result of the trials the LMSR made the Midland type of three-cylinder compound 4-4-0 a standard express passenger type for the whole of its system.

Superheating was adopted hesitantly at first on the railways of Great Britain. A big impetus was given in 1910 when a superheated 4-4-2 express tank engine of the London, Brighton & South Coast Railway began working over the London & North Western Railway between Willesden and Rugby with through trains between the south coast and the north. The LNWR Chief Mechanical Engineer, C. J. Bowen-Cooke, was so impressed by its economy and performance that he decided to build a super-heated version of his already very successful 'Precursor' class 4-4-0. The resultant 'George the Fifth' class became one of the classic British 4-4-0 express locomotives and the superheater was soon firmly established.

On the Great Western Railway G. J. Churchward adhered to the simple-expansion engine with large-diameter piston valves, a long valve travel, and careful proportioning of piston stroke to cylinder bore. He once said: 'The long stroke in relation to the bore is the only way we know of making the simple engine equal in efficiency to the compound engine'. By careful application of his principles, Churchward produced two-cylinder and four-cylinder 4-6-0 locomotives of outstanding performance. The value of large-diameter piston valves was generally recog-nised because they provided adequate port areas for free flow of steam but it was difficult to make them steam-tight. Churchward had his own design which, although relatively complex, could be manufactured economically in large numbers. The long valve travel gave him flexibility in timing events in the

Great Western 4-4-0 No 3717 *City of Truro* is recorded to have touched 102·3 mph (165 km/h) near Wellington, Somerset, on 9 May 1904 while working an Ocean Mails special from Plymouth to Bristol, where another locomotive took over to complete a record run to London. *City of Truro* is preserved in the Great Western Museum at Swindon.

cylinder so that the changes in the moment of steam admission which occurred as a link motion valve gear was notched up were turned to good account. His two-cylinder 'Saint' class locomotives with link motion were notably smooth runners at speed and on occasions could pull harder than his later four-cylinder 'Stars' with Walschaerts valve gear, with which the moment of admission was the same at all cut-offs. The characteristics of Great Western steam locomotive design under Churchward and his successor, C. B. Collett, were summed up by a well-known commentator on locomotive practice: '. . . Great Western design was sound in the basic essentials, which are to provide plenty of space for air, water and steam to go where they ought to go and to prohibit them from going where they ought not to go and moreover, to employ such materials and constructions that 50,000 miles of running caused only small departures from this ideal'.

In the United States the typical 'American' 4-4-0 was being phased out in the closing years of the 19th century, and the Atlantic wheel arrangement was coming into vogue for express locomotives. The 4-6-0 was relatively little favoured because trailing wheels allowed designers to use wide and deep fireboxes suitable for burning the quality of coal available. There was therefore a rapid change to the Pacific (4-6-2) wheel arrangement at the turn of the century. At the same time US engineers were turning away from the compound system to the most straightforward and rugged form of simple-expansion steam engine – two outside cylinders with outside Walschaerts valve gear. The Pennsylvania Railroad was a pioneer in the development of the US express passenger Pacific. On the highly competitive New York-Chicago service the PRR had a more difficult route than its New York Central rival. The Pennsylvania route was 58 miles (93·3 km)

shorter but it had formidable gradients and curvature where it crossed the Alleghenny Mountains. Double-heading by 4-4-0 locomotives had been necessary on the principal expresses. In 1907 a non-superheated Pacific (4-6-2) was built for the railroad by the American Locomotive Company (ALCO) in anticipation of the heavier loads soon to come when the railroad would be obliged to form its trains to and from New York of all-steel stock to minimise fire risk in the tunnels under the Hudson River. The new Penn station in Manhattan was opened in 1910 and in that year the Pennsylvania began a programme of building Pacifics in its own shops at Altoona. In 1913 the railroad adopted superheating as standard practice for all new main-line locomotives and began converting existing types. An 's' suffix to the class designation indicated 'superheated', and so when several series of Pacifics were followed by the prototype of a new design in 1914 this locomotive was classified K4s. War interrupted production of the new engines in quantity but from 1917 they began rolling off the production lines to form a fleet that remained the railroad's standard express motive power for nearly 30 years.

The K4s Pacific can be considered as an enlarged and lengthened version of the Pennsylvania's highly successful E6 class Atlantics, which had been superheated in 1913, but it could exert 42 per cent more tractive effort. In the course of time mechanical stokers and power reverse gear were added, and various external fitments broke up the clean lines that had characterised the prototype, but the basic design was unchanged to the end, when the heaviest and fastest trains of the 1930s needed two, and sometimes three, K4s Pacifics at the head on the steepest section of the New York-Chicago route.

As express locomotives grew in stature, the goal of travel at 100 mph (160·9 km/h) beckoned in the countries that measured speeds in miles per hour. Early in the new century there was a crop of high-speed claims in the United States, some of them since proved to have been beyond the bounds of possibility. Often they were based on passing times noted by lineside observers at different points, whose watches were unlikely to have been carefully synchronised. Although analysis has discredited 'records' of this kind, they continued to be quoted for many years. As late as 1935 the Vice-President of the Baldwin Locomotive Works, R. S. Binkerd, repeated claims of speeds up to 111 mph (179 km/h) by an Atlantic locomotive of the Reading Railroad between Camden and Atlantic City in 1907. Binkerd was addressing a meeting in New York, and a member of his audience – an ex-driver on the Reading – joined in the discussion to recall an occasion when a nine-coach Reading train had raced a Pennsylvania on a parallel track, covering 5 miles (8 km) in 2½ minutes. This would have been a speed of 120 mph (193 km/h), and in support of his claim the speaker said it could be vouched for by

C. H. Ewing, President of the Reading, who had been in the despatcher's office at the time. It is surprising to find both episodes quoted without comment by Andre Chapelon in his classic book on the steam locomotive, *La Locomotive a Vapeur*, when discussing the speed potential of steam power.

Scepticism over 'records' such as these must not blur the fact that well-attested runs over longer distances in the United States show start-to-stop average speeds of a level which suggests that maxima in the 90s may have been attained. An average speed of 78·2 mph (125·8 km/h) over a distance of 55·5 miles (89·3 km) by a simple Atlantic of the Reading Railroad was long accepted as a start-to-stop record, but later speed analysts have accepted as possible a time of 41 minutes for the same distance by a slightly larger Atlantic, achieved on 14 June 1907. This gives an average speed of 81·2 mph (130·7 km/h) and gives credence to the claim that in descending a 1 in 137 gradient the locomotive actually touched 100 mph. A speed recorder fitted to an experimental three-cylinder Atlantic running on the same route on another occasion is said to have shown 97 mph (156 km/h).

For many years the classic 'hundred' in railway lore was the achievement of the Great Western Railway locomotive *City of Truro* on 9 May 1904, when it was recorded to have touched 102·3 mph (164·6 km/h) while working a special conveying ocean mails from Plymouth to London. *City of Truro* was an inside cylinder 4-4-0 of a class which appeared while William Dean was still Chief Mechanical Engineer of the Great Western Railway but his assistant, G. J. Churchward, was closely associated with the design. On this occasion the locomotive was hauling an estimated load of 148 tons (150·38 tonnes). The record speed was reached on a down grade approaching Wellington in Somerset. Charles Rous-Marten, a technical journalist and close observer of locomotive performance, rode on the engine. His account published in *The Railway Magazine* of June 1904 confined itself to point-to-point times and spoke only of 'a "hurricane descent" of the Wellington bank, nearly spoiled, however, by a check near the station through some foolish plate-layers calmly staying on the "four-foot" when the "lightning special" was close on them . . .'.

At that time enthusiasm for three-figure speeds was not shared by the public and the Great Western Railway feared that publication of Rous-Marten's recorded maximum of 102·3 mph (164·6 km/h) would cause alarm. Rous-Marten respected the railway's feelings and did not publish the figure until December 1907 when it appeared in a table of maximum speeds recorded by himself with locomotives of various wheel diameters. Even then he did not identify the occasion or the railway although to those who had been pressing him for details there were strong hints in his comment that 'even at the exceptional rate of 102·3 miles an hour the 6ft 8 in

engine had not 'shot her bolt' for her steadier progress towards the higher rates was only interrupted by a special check . . . 'we were running with perfect ease and smoothness and there was nothing to indicate that we had reached our *maximum possible* when we were checked'. Finally, in his article in *The Railway Magazine* of April 1908, Rous-Marten mentioned both the speed and the occasion, amplifying his earlier report by adding that the 'unprecedented rate' of 102·3 miles an hour 'was attained over a single quarter mile and exactly 100 miles an hour for half a mile. . . .'.

In later years analysis of the speeds quoted by Rous-Marten immediately before the maximum led to the conclusion that *City of Truro* may not quite have reached the coveted 'hundred' but undoubtedly Rous-Marten was very much closer to the truth than previous claimants for speeds of that order. The figure of 102·3 mph continues to be quoted and has earned *City of Truro* a resting place in the museum at Swindon, the town where she was built in the nearby works of the Great Western Railway.

The 'Cities' and other 4-4-0s were followed by a brief experiment with Atlantics, both compound and simple, and then Churchward turned to the two-cylinder and four-cylinder 4-6-0s which made him famous. He built one Pacific, *The Great Bear*, which appeared in 1908. This was the first British Pacific and sensational in those days for its size, measuring 74 ft (22·5 m) overall and with a huge boiler and wide firebox. Technically it was an enlarged version of Churchward's four-cylinder Star class. Its size was its undoing for there were clearance problems on the West of England main line and in regular working the engine was confined to the section between London Paddington and Bristol. *The Great Bear* earned some useful publicity for the

No 730 was one of a pair of compound Atlantics built for the North Eastern Railway in 1906, designed by W. M. Smith, Chief Draughtsman of Wilson Worsdell, the North Eastern's CME.

Great Western Railway but its operational usefulness was limited because of the restrictions on where it could work. In 1924 it was rebuilt as a 4-6-0 by Churchward's successor, C. B. Collett. From 1908 to 1922 it was the only Pacific on British metals.

In France the Chemin de fer du Nord launched out in 1911 with two huge four-cylinder compound 4-6-4 locomotives. They had been planned by du Bousquet but appeared after his death and were often referred to as 'the two orphans'. Both presented du Bousquet's successor, Georges Asselin, with numerous problems, particularly No 3.1102 which had a du Temple water-tube firebox. Du Bousquet had already experimented with a du Temple firebox in 1907 when an Atlantic was rebuilt with a trailing bogie as a 4-4-4 so as to carry it. In its origin the du Temple boiler was a water tube boiler for marine use but a locomotive version would have been too heavy and so only the firebox had the characteristic du Temple arrangement of tubes. The boiler steamed well but there were numerous difficulties with cracks and leakage at the firebox tubeplate. A new boiler of the same type but with a combustion chamber was fitted in 1908 but after further trials the locomotive was rebuilt with a Belpaire firebox, Schmidt superheater and piston valves in 1913. In this conversion the trailing bogie was replaced by a third coupled axle and the locomotive survived as a 4-6-0 to be taken into the stock of the French National Railways.

Before the final conversion of the 4-4-4 the two 4-6-4s had been delivered, one from the Nord's own works and the other, with the du Temple boiler, from Schneider at Le Creusot. Some design faults showed up in service. The draughting arrangements were poor and there was a tendency for the bogie axle bearings to overheat because of the heavy load of over 7·38 tons (7·5 tonnes) on each wheel. The du Temple firebox of No 3.1102 had 623 water tubes, contributing nearly a third of the total heating surface, and the water circulation was so vigorous that in spite of superheating there was considerable moisture in the steam entering the cylinders. In 1914 this locomotive was rebuilt with a conventional Belpaire firebox. Both engines continued in service through the war years and after, but apart from the new firebox in 3.1102 no other important modifications were made. Asselin was looking for a Pacific with the performance that had been specified for the 4-6-4s and a lighter axle-load that would give them a wider route-availability. He found a suitable design in some Pacifics built for the Alsace-Lorraine Railways by the SACM Works in Graffenstaden, and ordered 20 similar locomotives but with high-pressure cylinders of larger bore, from the same builder's establishment in Belfort. These were the first of the celebrated 'family' of Nord Pacifics, all of which were four-cylinder compounds on the de Glehn system.

The Nord Pacifics achieved fame for their performance on the expresses between Paris and Calais in connection with the cross-Channel steamers. These days, when French businessmen and women on internal journeys may outnumber the cross-Channel travellers on a Paris-Calais express, it is easy to forget that London to Paris by rail and sea was once an important international travel route and that the boat trains were the pride of the railways serving the Channel Ports. On the French side they conveyed sleeping cars and through coaches serving many parts of Europe as well as a main portion to

Churchward's Pacific locomotive *The Great Bear* was the only 4-6-2 the Great Western Railway ever had. A high axle-loading restricted *The Great Bear* to working on the Paddington-Bristol line. In this illustration it heads a down Cheltenham Spa express.

One of D. E. Marsh's I3 class 4-4-2 superheated tank locomotives passes Balham with a characteristic 'Brighton Fast' of the London Brighton & South Coast Railway. Two clerestory-roofed Pullman Cars in the middle of the train provide refreshment service for passengers paying the Pullman supplement.

and from Paris. The Nord Pacifics became widely known and admired. Later and more powerful versions handled loads up to 590·5–639·73 tons (600–650 tonnes), which they could haul on the level at 75 mph (120 km/h), for a time the maximum speed permitted in France. On one occasion a special train weighing 747·99 tons (760 tonnes) was taken up the long 1 in 200 gradient to Survilliers on the way out of Paris at a steady 53 mph (85 km/h).

While the early Nord Pacifics were settling down to their work before the First World War, the British lines serving Dover and Folkestone had nothing larger for their boat trains than 4-4-0 locomotives. The London, Brighton & South Coast Railway, however, which ran to Newhaven for the Dieppe service, began building Atlantics in 1905 and these were seen regularly at the head of the company's boat trains.

The first decade of the century also saw developments in locomotives for heavy freight service on steeply graded routes. There were many six-coupled and eight-coupled designs for these duties but when more driving axles were required for good adhesion there was a trend in some countries towards articulation, particularly where there was severe curvature. Mallet's system was taken up by the Baltimore & Ohio Railroad in the United States early in the century with an 0-6-6-0 that could exert the very high tractive effort of 71,500 lb (32,432 kg), but the two short wheel-bases proved unstable on the main line and the locomotive was used largely for yard work such as hump shunting.

The forerunner of a series of large Mallet locomotives in the United States was a 2-6-6-2 built by the Baldwin Locomotive Works for the Great Northern Railway in 1906. This soon became a popular wheel arrangement on the US railways but was quickly followed by the 2-8-8-2, the first of which was built for the Southern Pacific in 1909. With a tractive effort of 85,400 lb (38,736 kg) it surpassed the Baltimore & Ohio and the Great Northern engines

and pointed the way to still higher outputs in the future. At this period the US Mallets were compounds in the true Mallet tradition but in 1911 ALCO built a simple-expansion 2-8-8-2 for the Pennsylvania, and after the First World War the ever-larger Mallets in the United States retained the original system of articulation but abandoned compounding.

Articulated designs took some unusual forms. The Santa Fe rebuilt two compound 2-10-2 locomotives as one 2-10-10-0 Mallet, changing from the original Vauclain compound system to the usual Mallet arrangement. The boiler was in two jointed sections, an arrangement seen again in a 2-6-6-2 of the same railroad, of which 40 were built. Overall length of the boiler barrel in the 2-6-6-2 was 56 ft (17 m). It comprised a firebox and a fire tube section with tubes 19 ft 7 in (6 m) long at the rear, and superheater and feedwater heater sections in front, ahead of the high-pressure cylinders. Steam pipes connected the dome with the superheater section, bridging the joint between the two parts of the boiler, which in 38 locomotives had a bolted joint while two had a 'bellows' connection or a ball joint.

By 1912 Mallet locomotives to the number of some 2,000 were in use on every continent except Australia, where the system was never used. No British railway had a Mallet, either, but British manufacturers were active in turning them out for other countries.

South Africa's first Mallet was a 2-6-6-0 built by ALCO for the Natal Government Railways in 1909. After the formation of the Union of South Africa in 1910 the North British Locomotive Company supplied the South African Railways with a simple-expansion 2-6-6-2 and from then until the early 1920s the Mallet type of locomotive, simple or compound, was the mainstay of heavy haulage on the SAR system. In Europe the Maffei company built two Mallets for Switzerland in 1889, one for the Hauenstein line of the former Swiss Central Railway

and one for the Gotthard line. The latter was an 0-6-6-0T and was the heaviest and most powerful locomotive of its day, able to haul 399·59 tons (406 tonnes) up a gradient of 1 in 62 at 12·5 mph (20 km/h). By 1915 there were nearly 300 Mallets of the 2-4-4-0 and 0-6-6-0 wheel arrangements at work on the Trans-Siberian Railway – all were compounds. The Budapest works of the Hungarian State Railways built 60 2-6-6-0 Mallets between 1913 and 1918 for hauling trains of 439·94 tons (447 tonnes) on the long 1 in 40 gradients of the Fiume (Rijeka) line.

In the United States development of the compound Mallet locomotive culminated in 10 huge 2-10-10-2 locomotives built by ALCO in 1918 for banking service on the Virginian Railway on the 11 miles (17·7 km) of 1 in 48 gradient from Elmore Yard to Clark's Gap. Coal trains of 14,999 tons (15,240 tonnes) were worked over this section with a 2-8-8-2 at the head and two of the 2-10-10-2s at the rear, the whole massive convoy making the ascent at a stately but majestic 7 or 8 mph (11–12 km/h).

There were various alternatives to the Mallet system of articulation. The Kitson-Meyer locomotive differed from the Mallet in having two steam bogies, and from the Fairlie in supplying them both from one boiler. Some designs were described as 'semi-articulated', such as the Hagans type in which the same cylinders drove two groups of coupled axles, one in the main frames and the other in a bogie at the rear, with a complicated system of articulated coupling rods and cranks. In 1908 the most important development in the history of the articulated locomotive took place when H. W. Garratt patented his own distinctive system. He used two steam bogies but slung the boiler in a cradle between them so that its dimensions were not restricted by the wheels, cylinders and motion. The patents were acquired by Beyer, Peacock & Co Ltd.

Meanwhile the Tasmanian Government Railways had been having problems with a Hagans semi-articulated locomotive acquired in 1900, the com-

plicated drive system causing numerous breakdowns and high maintenance costs. They called for tenders for a replacement, and Garratt persuaded Beyer, Peacock to offer his new design. The company was not much interested in a small order from a railway with light traffic but agreed to Garratt's suggestion. To their surprise, the Tasmanian Government Railways ordered two Garratt locomotives and there was a flurry of activity to produce the working drawings in time to meet the contract date.

The Garratt design for Tasmania was an 0-4-0+ 0-4-0 four-cylinder compound with the low-pressure cylinders on the leading bogie and the high-pressure on the rear one. Water supplies were carried in a tank of some 500 gallons (2,273 litres) capacity on the leading bogie and a smaller one at the rear, where the fuel bunker was also situated. Further Garratts supplied to Tasmania in 1912 included a 4-4-2+2-4-4 designed specifically for passenger traffic with 5 ft (152·4 cm) diameter wheels for running at 50 mph (80·5 km/h), and Beyer, Peacock were already taking a more optimistic view of Garratt prospects due to an order received from the Darjeeling-Himalayan Railway in 1911.

The later development of the Garratt was as a large freight locomotive for heavy haulage on railways with light permanent way and steeply graded lines, conditions usually associated with severe curvature. The age of the large Garratt can be dated from 1914 when the first of many orders from the South African Railways was received, although because of the First World War delivery had to be postponed until 1920. By the end of the steam era Garratts were at work in many parts of the world both on standard, broad and narrow gauges. The two steam bogies enabled six or more driving axles to contribute to high tractive effort while individual axle-loads remained low, and the locomotive layout allowed large boilers to be carried on lines of less than standard gauge where stability required a low centre of gravity.

C. J. Bowen-Cooke introduced superheating on the LNWR in his 4-4-0 locomotive *George the Fifth* built in 1910. This was the forerunner of a class of 90 locomotives, the first of which had round-topped fireboxes. The 'George V' class engine illustrated, *New Zealand*, working an up Liverpool express near Harrow, is one of the later members of the class with Belpaire fireboxes.

10. LUXURY ON THE RAILS

Previous page: A Pullman dining car on the New York Central in 1902. Interior finish was in Santiago mahogany. Potted ferns decorate the walls between the windows.

Five Pullman dining cars introduced in 1890 for services in the USA were named after famous American hotels. The car illustrated has white silk upholstery, walnut finish, decorative oil lamps and an elaborately painted ceiling. A member of the Pullman Car Company patented a closed connection between the end vestibules of adjacent cars, providing safe and weather-proof communication between vehicles.

BOTH GEORGE PULLMAN in the United States and Georges Nagelmackers in Europe were concerned in the first instance to improve the comfort of overnight travel. For both of them it was a natural step to provide a higher standard of accommodation by day. Others were in the field as well and as we have seen stock for the New York Central's 'Exposition Flyer' of 1893 was supplied by the Wagner Palace Car Company. A correspondent for the *New York Times* who rode the train on its inaugural run on 28 May wrote approvingly that:

The steadiness of the train was particularly noticeable in the beautiful dining car where there was not sufficient oscillation to spill a full glass of water . . . the cars were uncommonly attractive and luxurious, the polished dark woodwork and upholstery being particularly rich. The buffet car was provided with movable easy chairs, a writing desk and reading table. The buffet was well stocked with refreshments.

By 1901 other lines were becoming interested in elegance. A journalist who travelled in that year from Detroit to Chicago by the Michigan Central line described in her coverage the 'parlour car' and also 'a library car with all the principal magazines and plenty of papers, also a good stenographer and typist; in the other end of the car there was a good barber's shop.' The railroad provided an unusual service, but one that captured the heart of this writer. Three times in the eight-hour journey boys came on board and gave each passenger 'either a fine rose or two, or a bunch of flowers'.

Some of the US railroads built magnificent vehicles in their own shops. A dining car put in service by the Chicago, Burlington & Quincy in 1902 was claimed to be 'the finest in existence'. The official description of the car might well have been applied to the apartments in a stately home on the other side of the Atlantic. It ran:

The design of the dining room follows the Italian Renaissance style, the finish being in San Domingo mahogany, with lemon brass trimmings. The deck is designed in full Empire style, with headlining decorations in Gobelin green and gold. At each end of the dining room massive disengaged columns, reaching from the floor to the cornice, support the deck. The window curtain boxes are placed about 10 in below the tops of the windows, and the

intervening space is filled with cathedral art glass, which adds a pleasing touch of colour to the general effect. The car is lighted by electricity, the ceiling fittings being combination electric light and gas, while each table has an electric candelabra.

By the time the Pennsylvania and the New York Central got down to hammer-and-tongs competition for the New York-Chicago traffic they had cut the times to the practicable minimum and offered other inducements to win patronage. Pullman had absorbed the Wagner Palace Car Company and was now meeting the demands from the rival routes for something special. He had already equipped the Pennsylvania with a train hailed as 'the finest in the world'. Its 'Marquetry Room Car' was a wonder of inlaid satinwood and primavera as a setting for potted palms and chaises longues. Patrons of the smoking car sat in two facing rows of padded armchairs under a painted vaulted ceiling. Romanesque arches sprang from pillars with decorated capitals. Judging by contemporary illustrations the effect was highly ecclesiastical with the occupants of the armchairs facing each other across the aisle like church dignitaries in the choir stalls of a cathedral. There was a more mundane sight, however, in two rows of circular objects recessed into the floor that may have been spitoons.

The New York Central went for something less overpowering. With a sidelong glance at the Pennsylvania splendour, the company's publicity for its new trains emphasised 'the absence of all heavy carvings, ornate grilles and metalwork, stuffy hangings etc; the quiet elegance of design, combined with the beauty of the natural wood, being relied upon entirely for decorative effect'. For all that, the NYC could not resist 'Gothic windows and oval lights of stained glass set in metal frames' to embellish the exterior of the cars.

A correspondent of *The Times* of London travelled on the NYC's 'Twentieth Century Limited' in 1903. His impressions were favourable as far as the appointments for daytime travel were concerned:

Here one finds – in addition to the ordinary arrangements of Pullman cars – a barber's shop, an observation car, and a library, while woodwork and decorations are of the most costly style. Besides the open sleeping cars there are drawing

The bridal suite in the Pullman Car *Gladiolus* built for service on the 'Pennsylvania Limited' in 1898. The vestibule connection encouraged the design of cars with special features since passengers could move freely through the train.

The Wagons-Lits Company made relatively little use of Pullman Cars. The 'Fleche d'Or' Pullman Express between Paris and Calais is illustrated. Preserved in the French railway museum at Mulhouse.

Interior of a 'Blue Train' Wagons-Lits car made up for night travel. This vehicle is also at Mulhouse.

rooms and compartment cars, where those who wish for a higher degree of privacy can have it on paying more money. The smoking room is a good-sized compartment, provided with comfortable armchairs, and having the look of a club room rather than that of a railway car. Then there is a shorthand writer and typist who accompanies the train a good part of the distance, and any one can make free use of his services in dictating correspondence, the idea being that a traveller to Chicago or New York shall be able to carry on his business on the train just as if he were in his own office. To this end, also, the closing prices of the New York and Philadelphia exchanges will be received en route and posted up. As for the lady passengers, who may not want either a typewriter or the closing prices, they are furnished with a lady's maid, while their particular needs are studied by the provision for them of electrical appliances on which they can heat their curling tongs.

The same writer was less satisfied with the arrangements for night travel in the ordinary Pullmans, considering that undressing behind the curtains that screened the berths from the central aisle required 'a dexterity worthy almost of an acrobat'. Those who doubted their agility could pay for accommodation in a state room with an upper and a lower berth and its own toilet arrangements; or a drawing room with one upper and two lower berths and a toilet annexe. He put these arrangements on a par for comfort with a sleeping compartment on the London & North Western Railway at home, with the added advantage of being convertible for day use as a private drawing room.

On the transcontinental routes the last vehicle of a train was often an observation car from which passengers could admire the majestic scenery of the

Rockies and other mountain ranges. A typical vehicle of this kind was the 'single room observation car' with a sleeping section of compartments with one bed each; a lounge with wide windows, easy chairs, writing desk and bookshelves, and an end observation platform.

Many of the specially appointed trains in the first decade of the 20th century were named. Several luxury services ran to the resorts of Florida. One of them, the 'Florida Special', ended its run to Palm Beach at the front door of an hotel, having finished its journey on special tracks owned by the hotel company. A train from Chicago to California operated by the Santa Fe in 1911 was succinctly titled the 'De Luxe'. It carried a maximum payload of only 60 passengers, accommodated with room to spare in six Pullman cars, and they were waited on by a valet, lady's maid, barman, librarian, manicurist and barber. Gold-embossed pigskin wallets

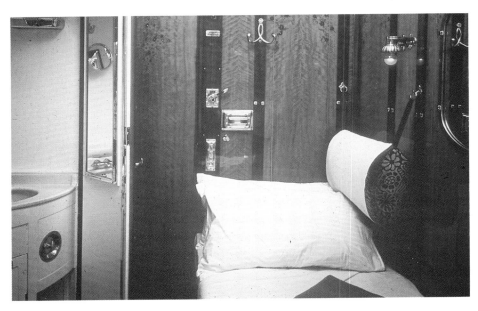

One of the Pullman Cars built for the Midland Railway is the leading vehicle in an express from St Pancras photographed near Elstree. Heading the train is one of the speedy Midland 'Singles' with 7 ft 9 in (2·4 m) wheels.

The interiors of the Pullman Cars built for the Midland Railway were austere compared with more florid examples in the United States. This may have been more in line with British taste, but the seating in individual armchairs proved less popular than had been expected.

were presented to all gentlemen passengers, and when the train reached California all the ladies were presented with orchid corsages.

European luxury trains provided solid comfort without the flourishes sometimes seen on the other side of the Atlantic. Basically the *train de luxe* was a train formed throughout of Wagons-Lits stock – sleeping cars, dining cars, sometimes saloon cars of various kinds, and the Wagons-Lits company's own vans for its express parcels service and passengers' luggage. The sleeping cars were divided into two-berth compartments, convertible to ordinary seating during the day. Single-berth compartments were not introduced until after the First World War. Every compartment had its own wash-basin.

In certain *trains de luxe* that travelled only in the daylight hours all passenger accommodation was in saloons. One such train was the 'Sud Express' running between Paris and the Spanish frontier in connection with another Wagons-Lits service to Madrid and Lisbon. When inaugurated in 1887 the 'Sud Express' was a through train from Calais to the frontier via Paris, and travelled overnight. From 1889 it started from the Gare du Nord in Paris, passengers from Calais by a connecting train changing into it there. Important changes took place in 1900, the Paris departure being transferred to the newly-opened Gare d'Orsay and retimed at midday. Now that it was a day train the 'Sud Express' in France was formed of saloons and a restaurant car. At first the saloons were borrowed from Wagons-Lits stock in Belgium. Two of them were badly damaged on 15 November 1900 when the north-bound express was derailed on a sharp curve between Bayonne and Dax. There were 34 passengers on board, of whom 27 were taking breakfast in the restaurant car; 14 of these were killed and six severely injured. After the accident the railway authorities set a limit on the weight of the train. To keep within it, and still provide enough passenger accommodation, the rear van with its raised lookout

Superheated 4-4-2T of the London Brighton & South Coast Railway speeds through the London suburbs with the 'Southern Belle' all-Pullman express on its 60 minutes non-stop run to Brighton.

for the guard had to be dispensed with. The railway insisted, however, that there should be a lookout position on the last vehicle of the train and so the Wagons-Lits company ordered three saloons and three restaurant cars with this feature. They were the only Wagons-Lits stock so equipped.

There were several series of 'Sud Express' saloons, all with a similar internal layout comprising an open smoking section with twelve armchairs, and five compartments for three or four passengers furnished with armchairs and settees. Decoration was luxurious as can be seen in this description of new stock in 1903:

Although intended for daytime travel, the compartments are veritable mobile boudoirs with seats on which the passenger who so desires can recline at ease. Nothing has been left to chance in building these coaches; the smallest detail has been studied with equal attention to comfort and hygiene. In the woodwork the colours of mahogany and American birch blend harmoniously, and the

grey wall hangings with their embroidered patterns help to create a serene and restful atmosphere in which there is nothing to distract the eye. The thick carpeting is patterned with ferns and briars. At a higher level ivy entwines with honeysuckle, eglantine and rambler roses; and finally the glass in the clerestory is etched with a pattern showing the flowers of the convolvulus — the symbols of light.

The 'Sud Express' was the first of the *trains de luxe* with electric lighting from axle-driven dynamos. As we have seen it was not a heavy train, the formation in France from 1900 to 1910 consisting of one van, a restaurant car, and two or three saloons, the rear one having the obligatory lookout. From 1910 the load was increased to four saloons. The broad-gauge connecting train in Spain was made up of a van, one or two sleeping cars for Lisbon, two sleeping cars for Madrid, and a restaurant car.

The other half of Nagelmackers' unrealised dream of a through train between St Petersburg and

A major development of the 1899–1914 period was the introduction of through coaches from Ostend and Paris to Warsaw. From 1909 they connected at Warsaw with the 'Warsaw-Moscow-Nord Express', a *train de luxe* formed entirely of Wagons-Lits stock. This was the express which provided the connection in Moscow with the Trans-Siberian service mentioned in chapter 7.

The First World War and the Russian Revolution left an aftermath in which the 'Nord Express' as it had been known before 1914 could not be revived. But the service lived on, thrusting in new directions – to the Baltic countries, Scandinavia, and Rumania. In 1936 a connection with Moscow was restored. Suspended in the Second World War, the train ran again in 1946, still serving Berlin but with an important branch for Scandinavia. In later years another service the 'Ost-West Express' conveyed through sleeping cars between Paris and Moscow, with a change of bogies at the frontier as Nagel-mackers had envisaged so many years before.

George Pullman's activities on the Continent were relatively limited and Pullman Cars were not included in the *trains de luxe* until the 1920s. He opened a factory in Turin, building cars which ran in the trains of some Italian railways, but his real success came in 1873 when he visited England and attended the annual general meeting of the Midland Railway Company. The Midland prided itself on the comfort of its rolling stock, which was a useful selling point for the services on its main line to London, opened five years earlier. Pullman Cars would be an additional attraction, and when it was put to the meeting that the company should authorise the building of cars to its particular

Inside a Southern Railway Pullman Car of the mid-1930s. The open door gives a glimpse of the bar counter and stools.

Lisbon was the 'Nord Express'. When introduced in 1896 the main portion of the train ran from Ostend to Berlin and the Russian frontier at Wirballen (Eydtkuhnen) where passengers changed into Russian-gauge Wagons-Lits for the remainder of the journey. Other sections of the train departed from Calais and from Paris, all uniting at Liège. At first the sleeping cars and restaurant car were supplemented by a vehicle with a smoking saloon and a luggage section but experience soon showed that the luggage space on the train was insufficient and the smoking saloon was converted to add to it. There were problems with late running of the Calais section, which was withdrawn, and by 1900 the two points of departure were Ostend and Paris. The Paris section was not a true *train de luxe*, the Wagons-Lits sleepers travelling in company with Paris-Cologne first and second class through coaches of the Chemin de fer du Nord. For a short time this section included a Wagons-Lits restaurant car and saloon for Spa, which were detached at Liège.

Interior of the *Maid of Morven* Pullman car.

requirements the motion was carried. It was agreed that 18 cars should be built in America and shipped to England in sections where they would be assembled in the Midland's works at Derby, where workshop accommodation had been made available. Pullman was permitted to build cars in the workshops for other railways in the United Kingdom.

The Midland wanted its trains with Pullman Cars to be of uniform appearance and so the first order to Pullman included coaches styled externally to match the Pullmans but accessible to passengers without paying a supplement. The Pullman company's own vehicles comprised sleeping cars and parlour cars. The sleeping cars were convertible for day use, when the lower berths were transformed into pairs of seats or sofas. Parlour Cars contained a general saloon with 17 armchairs and two private rooms, each with two armchairs and a sofa. All armchairs were pivoted, so that passengers could face in any direction, and could be tilted into a reclining position.

A train of two Pullman Cars and three Pullman-style coaches began running between Bradford and London St Pancras on 1 June 1874. It travelled to London in the morning and returned north at mid-night, the Pullmans then being used as sleeping cars. When the Midland opened its route to Scotland in 1876 the Pullman Cars were transferred to the Anglo-Scottish expresses.

Pullman also built cars for the Great Northern Railway. In 1879 the Great Northern sent one of its cars back to Derby to be converted into a Pullman Dining Car with a kitchen, a dining saloon, and a smoking saloon. The car went into service between London and Leeds on 1 November 1879 when for the first time travellers in the British Isles could enjoy a full meal on the train with 'soup, fish, entrées, roast joint, puddings and fruits for dessert'.

On the whole, however, the principle of hauling cars operated by a separate company and accessible only on payment of a supplement did not take firm root on the railways running northwards from London. The Midland took over all the Pullman Cars on its system in 1883 and operated them itself, charging lower supplements. Restaurant cars soon became available to all passengers and with the general improvement of passenger rolling stock there was less inducement to pay extra for added comfort. Moreover, the British public showed a preference which lasted for many years for separate compartments rather than saloons or 'parlour cars'.

In the South, however, Pullman Cars became an established feature on trains to the Kent and Sussex coasts. These were short journeys of less than a 100 miles (161 km) and the railways involved did not concern themselves with the design of their ordinary rolling stock to the same extent as those making provision for journeys of several hours. The traveller who wanted something better could pay the supplement and ride in the Pullman, which offered a refreshment service as well as superior comfort.

The London, Brighton & South Coast Railway had been operating Pullmans in certain trains since 1875, and when George Pullman's contract with the Midland Railway ran out in 1888 the company moved its works to Brighton. A train composed entirely of Pullman Cars began running between London and Brighton in 1881. Non-stop runs by all-Pullman trains between London and Brighton, in one hour for the 51 miles (81·6 km), began in 1898. But the pride of the Brighton line was the 'Southern Belle', which made its first journey on 1 November 1908. Formed of a set of entirely new first class Pullmans, it was hailed as 'the most luxurious train in the world' and 'a chain of vestibuled luxury'. Publicity for the service dwelt on mahogany panelling with decorative inlays, delicate mouldings and fluted pillars, soft green carpeting, damask silk blinds and 'cosy chairs and settees in a restful shade of green morocco'. It sounds excessive for a journey of 60 minutes but the 'Southern Belle' and its electric successor, the 'Brighton Belle', had a regular and appreciative patronage for 64 years, the last trips on 30 April 1972 being an occasion of general lamentation. One of the Pullman Car conductors summed it all up in his comment to a Brighton newspaper on the last day: 'More like a club than a train!'

The Pullman Observation Car *Maid of Morven* was one of ten vehicles built for the Caledonian Railway when a contract was signed in 1914 for the railway's catering services to be provided by the Pullman Car Company. The car ran between Glasgow and Oban, outliving the Pullman contract which expired in 1933. *Maid of Morven*, now in LMS colours, was withdrawn in the late 1930s.

II. RAILWAYS
IN WAR

Previous page: Firefly of the US Military Railroad in Virginia during the Civil War, about 1863. Armour-protected gun-carrying trucks were used for the first time in the Civil War.

MILITARY MEN MUST HAVE pricked up their ears when they heard that the Liverpool & Manchester Railway had conveyed a regiment of soldiers 34 miles (54·7 km) in two hours, a distance it would have taken two days to cover on foot. The battle of Waterloo and Blücher's last-minute arrival after arduous marches to support Wellington was still fresh in the memory. A British periodical in 1859 commented that the railways were a means ready to hand for conversion 'from mercantile purposes to engines of war', and soon afterwards an anonymous staff officer outlined proposals for an armoured train in *The Times*. He suggested 'a rail cordon round the metropolis on which there should be Armstrong and Whitworth ordnance mounted on large iron-plated trucks, the trucks and locomotives being protected by shot-proof shields'. His theme was soon taken up by another military man with a suggestion for 'portable batteries' as a means of 'concentrating with unerring certainty a crushing force of artillery, with guns of heavier calibre than even the warships of the invader could command'. His letter mentioned trials of an 81-ton (82·3 tonnes) gun having proved that the heaviest ordnance could be moved and fought on the railway.

Some of these ideas were given practical form in the American Civil War (1861–65), when armour-protected gun-carrying trucks were used for the first time in modern warfare. One of the trucks was formed by heavy timbers built up on a flat wagon, the armour at the sides and front consisting of old rails spiked to the timbers. A gun from a field battery was mounted on the truck and fired through a port-hole at the front. Slits for musketry fire were pierced in the side walls. A second similar truck carried a naval howitzer. These trucks were propelled by a locomotive at the rear, which at first was unprotected because the armouring of the truck in front was considered sufficient. In practice it was found that the cabs were riddled with bullets and the engine-men only escaped injury by lying on the floor. Later in the war the cabs were armour-plated.

During the Franco-Prussian War of 1870–71 the French operated four trucks with armour plating to a total thickness of 2 in (50·8 mm); the engines were also protected. Field gun shells did no more than dent the armour on the trucks. The British used two gun trucks in the Egyptian campaign of 1882. Each carried one Nordenfelt and two Gatling guns, protected by iron plating and sandbags. One truck was also used to transport a 9-pounder gun and was equipped with a crane for unshipping the gun before it was fired. Later in the war a further truck carrying a 40-pounder with iron mantlet protection was added. The locomotive was placed

Between 1917 and 1920, J. G. Robinson built four-cylinder 4-6-0s for the Great Central.

in the middle of the train and protected by sandbags and railway iron.

There was further use of armoured trains by the British in the South African campaign of 1899–1902, for which five armoured trains were built. They were armed with a 6 in (154·2 mm) gun and a 9·2 in (233 mm) gun. As far as possible gun trucks were run in ordinary trains in charge of a military escort, and drivers' cabs were armour-plated. In the meantime international crises were concentrating thoughts on the protection of Britain against invasion. In 1894 a coastal defence train was demonstrated at New-haven on the Sussex coast. The armour-plated gun truck, carrying a heavy gun, was the first to combine armour plating, a turntable, and recoil cylinder. Cross-girders were run out and supported on blocks to provide a firm base when the gun was fired at right angles to the line. On 5 May 1894 a heavy gun was fired broadside for the first time on the perma-nent way of a British railway. In these trials the army had the co-operation of the London Brighton & South Coast Railway and of its Chief Mechanical Engineer, R. J. Billinton.

After the outbreak of the First World War on 4 August 1914 two Naval Brigades were sent from England to support the Belgians in their defence of Antwerp. They took with them several 4·7 in (119 mm) guns which they mounted on Belgian 39·37 ton (40 tonne) flat trucks, protected by armoured bulwarks 3 ft (0·9 m) high. The Belgians themselves had built some light armoured trains. In these the main armament was a 2·2 in (57 mm) gun mounted in a steel-framed bogie wagon which had been protected by 0·71 in (18 mm) ships' plates and a roof of 0·47 in (12 mm) plate, with observation turret. There was a machine-gun and 18 slits for rifle fire on each side.

Two armoured trains were built in Britain for coastal defence. At each end of the trains there was a gun truck converted from a Caledonian Railway vehicle and fitted with a 12-pounder quick-firing gun. The infantry vans were converted Great

US War Department loco-motives gathered at St Nazaire, France, in 1918: in the fore-ground, narrow-gauge 2-6-2 tracks for the light railways of the forward areas, in the rear standard-gauge Baldwin-built 2-8-0s.

Americans newly arrived in France and English Tommies aboard a hospital train.

Below: Wounded being placed on a light railway near Feuchy, in France, on 29 April 1917 following the battle of Arras.

Western Railway bogie wagons built at Swindon in 1906, armoured with 0·5 in (12·7 mm) plating all round in which there were 56 rifle ports for firing, standing or kneeling. The overall roof was of 0·37 in (9·5 mm) steel plate. Maximum headroom inside the vans was 6 ft 9 in (2·05 m). The middle of the vehicle was a magazine, and at the rear there was a Maxim gun compartment. Two Great Northern Railway Class N1 0-6-2 tank engines were armour-plated for hauling the trains.

One of the trains operated in East Anglia for local coastal defence. The other was stationed near the Forth Bridge and patrolled the coast to Aberdeen, as well as visiting the Clyde Coast. Its special task was to safeguard supply routes to the fleet in the northern anchorages where it was based to avoid the submarine threat around the southern coasts of Britain. After the war the two engines were sold back to the LNER in 1923 and with armour-plating removed worked on London suburban services until both were withdrawn in 1956.

From 1916 the British Army built up an extensive network of narrow gauge 23·62 in (60 cm) lines in France. Traffic was worked by numbers of four-wheeled 20 hp petrol locomotives. A smaller number of similar 40 hp units was introduced in 1917. Some of the locomotives were supplied in a completely enclosed armoured version. Others had shrapnel-proof cab doors. Drivers preferred the latter type, the armoured locomotives with their small adjustable lookout slots being uncomfortably hot.

The major task of the railways in war is the transport of men and materials. All the countries involved in the First World War were faced with heavier tasks than ever before both in the theatres of war and in overseas territories from which supplies were drawn. Plans for operating the railways in Britain in a war emergency were ready to hand in 1914, having been drawn up as early as 1871. Management was taken over by a Railway Executive Committee consisting of the General Managers of the principal companies so that government control was exercised through experts in railway operation. In eight days of August 1914 the British

British soldiers leaving Salonika during World War I.

Caledonian Railways' West Coast Anglo-Scottish Route power was the graceful inside cylinder 'Cardean' 4-6-0. Seen here is No 903 *Cardean*, descending Beattock bank with a southbound express.

Expeditionary Force was despatched through the port of Southampton, 334 trains conveying 69,000 men, 22,000 horses, 2,500 guns and all the baggage of an army. In the course of the war soldiers made 9 million journeys through the Channel port of Folkestone and 7 million through Southampton on their way to and from the Continent and overseas. Although plans existed for converting passenger stock into ambulance trains, none had been built by the outbreak of war but by the end of August 1914 12 were ready. During the war 20 ambulance trains were supplied for service in Britain and 49 for overseas railway work.

Heavy tasks fell on the relatively small Highland Railway in the north of Scotland, whose main line, much of it single-track, kept the bases of the Grand Fleet in Cromarty Firth and Scapa Flow supplied with materials and fuel. The heavy coal trains which brought coal from mines in England and Wales were called 'Jellicoe Specials' after the Admiral of the Fleet, Sir John Jellicoe. Much of the material for the Northern Barrage minefield, stretching from Orkney to Norway, was brought to Kyle of Lochalsh on the west coast of Scotland by American ships and conveyed by rail over a steep and winding route through the mountains. In six months during 1918

this work occupied 400 special trains. The effects of the war were world-wide. It lent urgency to completing the rail link between the east and west coasts of Australia on the other side of the globe and on 25 October 1917 the first through train to the east by the Trans-Australian Railway left Kalgoorlie in Western Australia by the new standard gauge line to Port Augusta in South Australia.

British-built locomotives travelled far afield in the war years. A 2-8-0 freight locomotive designed by J. G. Robinson for the Great Central Railway, and put into traffic in 1911, was adopted as a wartime standard and 521 engines of the same design were built for service overseas.

On the outbreak of war both Germany and Russia put 'strategic' timetables into operation for the deployment of their forces. The German system was better prepared for the strain and in the opening fortnight of 1914 a westbound train crossed the Rhine bridge at Cologne once every 10 minutes on average. Russia was hampered by its previous concentration of resources for building railways eastwards into Siberia and Central Asia. The motives for these costly operations were strategic, but lines to the west had been starved of resources and these were the lines which became of unforeseen strategic

importance in 1914. They wilted under the strain, but the deficiency of men and materials to keep them in operation was not realised until too late.

Russian manufacturers sought to profit from the situation by demanding excessive prices for railway equipment. The government did not bow to their demands and placed orders in the United States for 1,000 locomotives and 30,000 wagons. Railwaymen were recruited from the USA to help in reorganising the rail transport system but the decline had gone too far and conditions were aggravated by social unrest. Revolution in 1917 was followed by civil war, with the railways as the principal means of moving troops and consequently military targets. Destruction of lines and bridges by one side or the other was added to the problems of inadequate resources. For a time all passenger traffic was stopped so that food could be sent to starving populations cut off by war from their normal sources of supply. There were no materials to repair engines and rolling stock, and by the end of the civil war in 1921 some two-thirds of the nominal locomotive stock of 19,000 were out of action and almost irreclaimable.

In 1914–18 air power was in its infancy and railways did not receive the battering they were to suffer some 20 years later. They were, however, attacked by other means, and in the campaign against the Turkish armies led by T. E. Lawrence ('Lawrence of Arabia') the destruction of trains by raiding parties on the Medina and Hejaz railways was an essential part of the successful strategy. Lawrence earned the title among the Arabs who fought with him of 'the destroyer of engines'.

Robinson's 2-8-0 design for the Great Central, premiered in 1911, was selected as a standard, war theatre type by the British Ministry of Munitions: over 500 were built.

12. PROGRESS IN THE LEAN YEARS

Previous page: K class Pacific No 231K37, about to depart Brussels Midi with the 18.57 express to Paris Nord.

WAR TENDS TO STIMULATE INVENTION in the cause of national survival. In its aftermath some industries benefit directly from the technical advances achieved. Others simply find that they have acquired a greater adaptability to changing circumstances. By the end of the First World War the internal combustion engine had proved itself on land, at sea and in the air. It was not yet an ally of the railways but it profoundly influenced the new environment in which they had to work and blew away any complacency that may have lingered from pre-war attitudes.

In the immediate post-war years many railways had to adjust themselves to new forms of organisation. At the end of the war Germany had a number of state systems, the largest of which were the Prussian State Railways. All were merged in 1920 to form the German State Railway, better known as the Reichsbahn. Unification on these lines had been advocated many years before by the German Chancellor, Bismarck, but on his dismissal the project lapsed and the individual states continued to develop and operate their systems according to their own ideas. The eventual unification in the troubled post-war years was carried out with characteristic efficiency, and when the Reichsbahn celebrated the centenary of railways in Germany in 1935 its technical achievements in many fields commanded widespread admiration among railway engineers and operators. The ceremonial accompanying the event was conducted in a style similar to that of the political rallies of the period. A British observer recorded the performance of 'the way-builders litany, rendered in recitative solos and anthem-like chorus by a hundred and more black-uniformed men bearing spades'.

Austria was declared a republic on 12 November 1918. The Imperial State Railways of Austria as-sumed the less impressive title of German-Austrian State Railways for a short time but were reorganised as the Austrian State Railways a year later. The extent of the system was about 3,700 miles (5,955 km), roughly a seventh of the former Austro-Hungarian network on about one eighth of the former territory.

The Sudbahn was the last of the large private systems to survive. Its lines within the new frontiers of Austria were taken over in 1923 by the state system, which had been reorganised in 1921 as the Austrian Federal Railways. Yugoslavia and Italy took over the former Sudbahn in their territories but the Hungarian section continued as the independent Danube-Save-Adriatic Railway until 1932. On the annexation of Austria by Germany in 1938 the railways in Austria became part of the Reichsbahn. They resumed their former independence in 1945.

All the French railways had come under state control during the war. Afterwards they reverted to the former organisation of a State Railways system and the private main-line companies operating under concessions from the state. Their situation has been described as that of 'operating tenants of State-owned assets'. Full nationalisation had long been mooted but it did not come about until the French National Railways Company (SNCF) was formed in 1938.

In Britain there had been arguments in favour of nationalising the railways for many years, often on ideological rather than practical grounds. Government control of the railways during the war had enabled things to be done that could not have been contemplated by the individual and rival companies, but these were exceptional conditions and for peace-time a compromise was adopted. Under the Railways Act 1921 the 120 previous railway companies were

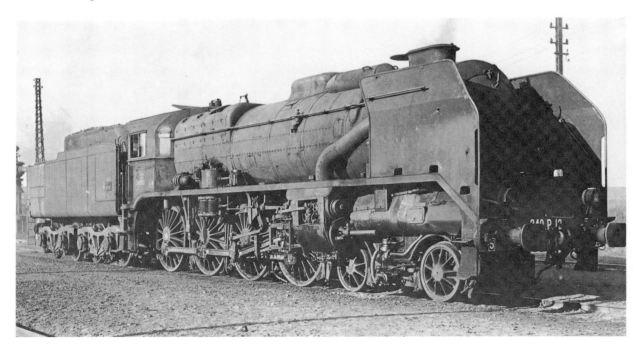

Right: The 4-8-0 class, 240P, was another conversion on Chapelon principles from earlier PLM locomotives and was carried out in wartime in 1940. This engine is No 240P12.

merged into four large groups: London Midland & Scottish, London & North Eastern, Great Western, and Southern. A competitive element was retained. The LMSR and the LNER included the companies which previously had collaborated in the west coast and east coast routes to Scotland respectively. These two Groups also competed for traffic between London, the Midlands and Yorkshire, and on cross-country services. In the south and west of England the Southern Railway and the Great Western both ran fast trains from London to Exeter and Plymouth. Within the Groups there were lines that had previously been in competition with each other, such as the former London & North Western and the Midland routes to Manchester, now absorbed into the LMSR. The least changed system was the Great Western, which retained its 'shape' but now took over a number of smaller lines in its territory, particularly in South Wales, with which it had always worked closely.

The railways in the United States were placed under the control of a United States Railroad Administration soon after the country entered the First World War. Here, too, there was strong pressure from some quarters for nationalisation when the war ended but public opinion was more on the side of the railway companies, who strongly opposed the idea, and in March 1920 the railways were returned to private control. Some useful co-ordination of effort had taken place under the United States Railroad Administration but its effect was soon lost when the companies were free to follow their own policies.

In Canada there had been several private or government-supported railway projects which by the beginning of the First World War had established alternatives to the Canadian Pacific's transcontinental route. Some of the lines got into difficulties

in the war years and were taken over by the government. After the war all went into public ownership to form the Canadian National Railways, a second coast-to-coast system totalling some 24,000 miles (38,620 km). Railway construction continued in various parts of the world. As the turmoil of war and revolution subsided in Russia a new link was forged between isolated systems in the Soviet Union's eastern territories by the building of the Turksib (Turkestan-Siberian) Railway, from Krasnovodsk on the Caspian Sea to Barnaul via Tashkent, Alma Ata, and Semipalatinsk. From Barnaul there was a connection to the Trans-Siberian line at Novosibirsk. The Turksib line, opened in 1930, was 909 miles (1,463 km) in length and the first major railway to be built by the Soviets.

In western Europe a new trans-Alpine route was opened on 30 October 1928. It ran from Cuneo on the Italian State Railways over the Col de Tende in the Alpes Maritimes to Nice, with a branch from Breil to Ventimiglia. Work at both ends of the route was

PO Pacific No 3563 leaves Les Aubrais with the 'Sud Express' to Irun. By 1936, the overhead wiring of the electrification to Tours was already in place.

A Lemaitre blastpipe and smoke deflectors give an unfamiliar look to Atlantic No 221.2659, here battling its way through heavy mist with the Pullmans of the southbound 'Oiseau Bleu' in 1936.

Ex-LNW 0-8-0 No 49344 of
C. J. Bowen-Cooke's design
approaches Tile Hill, between
Birmingham and Coventry,
with a down freight in 1959.
These long-lived locomotives
were in power class 7F.

in progress from the early 1900s onwards but was interrupted by the war. It was a scenic route, clinging to the sides of the mountains with many tunnels and bridges, and for some 12 years carried a considerable tourist traffic. In the Second World War many of the works were destroyed and traffic was not restored until 1978. The line shortens the distance from Turin to Nice via Cuneo to 137·3 miles (221 km) compared with 180·2 miles (290 km) via Savona, but speeds over the route are limited by gradients and curvature. Cuneo to Nice by the new line is 75·2 miles (121 km), and to Ventimiglia 61·5 miles (99 km).

Social changes after 1918 resulting in higher wages and shorter working hours increased the demand for passenger travel but expectations of the standards of comfort the railways should offer were also higher. Four-wheel and six-wheel coaches, some of which had surprisingly long lives, were now considered museum pieces and the bogie vehicle became general for passenger travel. In the old fixed-wheelbase stock, including some eight-wheel coaches with sideplay in the axles to permit negotiation of curves, the springing was between the axleboxes and the body. Bogie vehicles introduced two-stage suspension; there was springing between the axleboxes and the bogie frame, called the primary suspension, but also between the bogie frame and the body – the secondary suspension. The body was therefore not supported directly by the bogie frame but rested on a transverse beam, or 'bolster', which was in turn carried by springs based on a 'spring plank'. The spring plank was hung from the bogie frame by swing links which enabled the whole assembly to be independent of side-to-side movements of the bogie frame. This was necessary because a bogie running on permanent way does not move straight ahead but follows a sinuous course, which would otherwise be transmitted to the coach body.

The bolster was located in the bogie by being placed betweeen two transoms with sufficient clearance to allow for side-to-side movement. The inner faces of the transoms and both bolster faces were protected by wear-resistant material. Tractive effort was transmitted through the transoms to the bolster, and then to the body through the pivot seating and kingpin at the centre of the bolster. Many small improvements were made in this construction over the years, notably in dampers of various kinds to suppress horizontal and vertical oscillations. Rubber stops absorbed shocks if excessive movements brought the bolster and bogie frame into contact. There was little change in these arrangements until after the Second World War when rubber-bushed links were used for anchoring the bolster and transmitting the tractive forces from the bogie frame, dispensing with the rubbing surfaces involved in the transom system, and at a later stage airbag suspension replaced coil springs for supporting the body.

Various forms of gas lighting had begun to replace oil lamps in carriages about the 1860s. Gas remained in use in some areas until after the First World War

but its last stronghold was for cooking in restaurant cars. Its disappearance from lighting was signalled by the development of electric systems at the end of the 19th century. In the widely used Stone system first patented in Britain in 1894 a lighting battery in each coach was kept charged by a dynamo belt-driven from an axle. The dynamo was suspended by a hinge in such a way that its own weight kept tension on the belt. As speed rose, the dynamo output increased, and so did the mechanical load the belt had to transmit. When this was at a certain level, the belt began to slip and so the speed of the dynamo remained steady despite the varying speed of the train. Electrical methods of maintaining a steady voltage from the dynamo over a wide range of train speeds were developed later, with particular emphasis on it being high enough to continue to charge the battery when the train was travelling slowly.

Heating throughout a train by low-pressure steam from the locomotive was a development of the 1880s and by the end of the First World War the old-fashioned foot-warmer was little more than a memory. At one period it had to be hired and was sometimes a privilege of first class passengers. In later years, however, it was available without charge, although the porter who brought it would expect a tip. One of the advantages of the Pullman Car in those days was that it had its own hot water heating system consisting of an oil stove, boiler, and pipes running round the car.

Two methods of train heating were in general use in the years between the world wars. The 'direct' method supplies steam to radiators under the seats. In 'indirect' heating, mainly used in America, air was warmed by steam or hot water coils under the car before entering the compartments, or heated air for the coaches was passed along train pipes from the engine.

The usual system in Europe was to take steam from the engine boiler, pass it through a pressure-reducing valve, and supply it to the train pipe at about 60 lb per sq in (4·2 kg per sq cm). A check valve on the engine released steam from the system if the pressure exceeded the limit allowed.

H. N. Gresley built three 2-8-2 (Mikado) locomotives for heavy coal trains on the East Coast Main Line. No 2394 of class P1 passes a bracket signal with the 'Somersault' arms typical of Great Northern practice.

The train pipe was wrapped in non-conducting material but condensation might take place, particularly towards the end of long trains. Water in the pipe impeded the flow of steam and might freeze in cold weather. To overcome the problem drip valves were fitted to release the water. They were operated automatically by a diaphragm filled with ether. In low temperatures the diaphragm contracted and opened the valve, which remained open until the temperature had risen enough to expand the diaphragm and reclose the valve.

The carriage heater was a metal tube of about 6 in (153 mm) diameter, installed under the seat. Inside it there was a cane rod, one end of which was fixed while the other end bore on a ball valve through which steam was admitted. When the heater became hot it expanded slightly, but the cane rod was not affected. The expansion brought the valve on to its seating, cutting off the steam supply. When the heater cooled it contracted and the ball was pushed off its seating, allowing steam to be admitted again.

In another steam heating system the pipes were exhausted of air so that the steam did not have to force its way against atmospheric pressure. A lower steam pressure could therefore be used, with a saving in steam. Tests with this system in France on the PLM Railway showed that 10 per cent of the steam produced by the locomotive was used for heating.

Through coaches which had begun their journey on a main line train behind a locomotive equipped for steam heating might, after being detached at a junction, be taken on by a locomotive without a steam heating facility. This situation was met by a storage heating system. The heater consisted of a tube filled with sodium acetate which retained the heat supplied by steam circulating through an outer casing surrounding the tube. After the coach was disconnected from the heating system, the heat lasted four or five hours.

Carriage construction passed through several phases. At the beginning of the century the usual form had been a wooden body on a steel underframe, the body taking none of the forces of traction. The next step was steel panelling of the body, which served as protection but did not add to the strength of the structure as a whole. A later stage was part steel construction, the lower portion of the body, to the waistline, being of steel sheet, 0·2 in (5 mm) thick, and forming one unit with the underframe. The wooden uprights and roof were steel-sheathed. From the late 1920s all-steel coaches came into use, the whole structure constituting a beam with all parts carrying load.

While the speed and comfort of railway passenger travel were improved during the difficult years of economic recession between the wars, freight working tended to follow traditional patterns up to the Second World War and after. Wagons picked up from wayside stations by local trains were taken to marshalling yards and formed into longer trains travelling greater distances. At other yards on their routes wagons would be detached and added according to their various destinations. Wagonloads were often made up of small consignments which had to be unloaded at different places along the route of the local freight trains on which many vehicles finished their journey. Most stations had their sidings and goods shed in which these operations took place.

During the 1920s the marshalling of trains in large yards was speeded up by 'hump' shunting. Wagons were propelled by a shunting locomotive up the gradient forming one side of the hump and ran down the other side of the hump by gravity to enter a 'fan' of sidings on level ground at the bottom. Before this operation began they had been uncoupled to form 'cuts' of one or more wagons, and each cut was switched into one or other of the sidings according to its destination. Finally, therefore, each siding contained a complete train ready to leave for a particular route as soon as the train engine backed on. The points by which cuts were directed into the appropriate sidings were con-

trolled by operators in a control tower giving them a view of the yard from the top of the hump.

At first the speed of wagons descending the hump was controlled by shunters running alongisde and operating the wagon brakes with their poles. This was dangerous work and soon replaced by rail brakes operated from the control tower. Most rail brakes were hydraulic and consisted of brake rails inside the running rails which were 'squeezed' by hydraulic power against the wheel flanges of wagons as they ran through the brake. The pressure was controlled by the operators in the tower, and fine judgment was needed to apply just the right amount of retardation so that a cut would come to rest gently against the wagons already standing in the siding into which it was directed.

Alternative types of brake were the eddy current brake and the slipper brake. In the former brake powerful electromagnets set up eddy currents in the wheels passing between their poles, which had a retarding effect. The slipper brake, mainly used in France, acted like the drag on a cartwheel. The shoe was mounted on a carrier attached to a continuous cable driven by an electric motor, and travelled in a guideway between the outer edge of the running rail and a guide rail parallel with it. The shoe was first drawn towards the wagon wheel by the electric motor, and when it had engaged with the wheel allowed the wagon to run down the hump at a controlled speed. At the bottom of the hump the carrier was diverted into a 'layby' formed by the guide rail turning away from the running rail and a second guide rail parallel with it.

Germany, France and the United States made considerable use of hump yards soon after the war but the first of this type in Britain was at Whitemoor, near March (Cambridgeshire) in 1929. Whitemoor yard could accommodate some 10,500 wagons at a time on sidings totalling about 50 miles (80·5 km) of track. On one occasion 357 wagons in 232 cuts were shunted over the hump in an hour.

A characteristic of British freight working at this period was the prevalence of the short-wheelbase four-wheel wagon without continuous brakes. The brakes had to be applied manually from the trackside. Wagons belonging to private owners numbered tens of thousands. There were problems in fitting them with continuous brakes. For one thing they would have to be fitted with both vacuum and Westinghouse equipment if they were to travel all

The six-cylinder Garratt banking locomotive built by the LNER for assisting coal trains on the steeply-graded line from Wath marshalling yard to Penistone and the Woodhead Tunnel.

LNER class P1 Mikado No 2394 was fitted with a booster on the trailing truck. In this view of the locomotive as built the steam pipe to the booster can be seen below the cab.

over the country, and for another the owners might not comply and the railways would be obliged to buy up all the private wagons themselves.

These problems were not resolved until the British railways were nationalised after the Second World War, and then only after long debate on which braking system to use and an eventual *volte face* from the choice of vacuum to adoption of Westinghouse. Railways in Britain also faced difficulties because of their position as 'common carriers' which obliged them to accept all freight offered to them under a cumbersome charging system, while the roads could choose the most lucrative traffic and charge competitive rates. The roads also offered door-to-door transits. When the railways were granted powers to operate road vehicles themselves they were better placed, and door-to-door transport in small containers was being offered in the 1930s, but the common carrier obligation remained and left the problem of handling numerous miscellaneous small consignments which were difficult to consolidate into full wagon-loads.

For many years the 0-6-0 locomotive held sway for miscellaneous freight duties in Britain. Heavier work was done by 0-8-0 and 2-8-0 classes, while the LNER had a 2-8-2 class of three engines. The 1930s saw further development of mixed traffic locomotives able to work both fast freight and express passenger services. Notable examples were Stanier's Class 5 4-6-0s for the LMS (affectionately known as 'Black Fives' in the closing years of steam), and Gresley's 2-6-2 'Green Arrow' class.

In countries with long stretches of single track the ability to move heavier loads at higher speeds brought an increase in line capacity. Often single lines had severe gradients and axle-load restrictions, and in order to provide the necessary motive power the number of coupled axles was increased in fixed-wheelbase designs while the Mallet and Garratt systems were further developed. In 1926 the prototype of a series of 4-12-2 locomotives appeared on the Union Pacific Railroad in the USA for working heavy freight trains between Ogden and Cheyenne on the transcontinental line. These locomotives were the largest three-cylinder engines ever built, and the largest with a single group of driving wheels in a rigid frame. With a driving wheelbase of 30 ft 8 in (9·3 m), a side-play of 1 in (25·4 mm) each way had to be allowed for the first and sixth coupled axles, which had a spring-controlled centering device. On the 176 miles (283·2 km) from Ogden to Green River, where the gradient eastbound through the Wahsatch Mountains was 1 in 88, the class took loads of 3,996 tons (4,060 tonnes) with pusher assistance on the banks and cruised on the level at speeds between 35 and 40 mph (56 and 64 km/h). Between Green River and Laramie, where the ruling gradient was 1 in 125, they showed a 44 per cent increase in traffic handling capacity compared with their 2-10-2 predecessors. This was also the period of the big Mallets in the United States, and in 1936–37 the 4-12-2s by then numbering 88, were supplemented by the first of the 'Challenger' class Mallet 4-6-6-4s.

Meanwhile, exports of Garratt articulated locomotives from Britain had been building up. Among many notable designs delivered to Africa and elsewhere where three classes supplied to the Kenya &

Haymarket shed, Edinburgh, stables three famous LNER locomotives. Streamlined Pacific No 2511 *Silver King* is in the foreground, in front of 2-8-2 No 2001 *Cock o' the North*.

Uganda Railways (later merged as the East African Railways) between 1926 and 1939. The Class EC3 of 1939 were the first Garratts with the 4-8-4+4-8-4 wheel arrangement and the largest and heaviest engines to work on 50 lb (22·7 kg) rails, yet the load on each driving axle was less than 11·8 tons (12 tonnes). Two Garratt designs worked on British lines in the 1920s and 30s. One was the 'one-off' 2-8-0+0-8-2 banking engine of the LNER which was used for assisting coal trains from the Wath marshalling yard on the heavy gradients between Wath and Penistone, where the trains joined the main line to Manchester via the Woodhead Tunnel. The other Garratts were the 33 2-6-0+0-6-2 engines built for the LMS for working coal trains from Toton marshalling yard to Cricklewood. They eliminated the double-heading previously necessary with two 0-6-0 locomotives and with loads up to 1,400 tons (1,422 tonnes) raised the average speed of the loaded southbound traffic fron 18 to 21 mph (29 to 32 km/h) with a fuel saving of some 15 per cent.

Towards the end of the 1920s a development of lasting influence on railway permanent way was taking place. Several administrations had begun to weld rails in long continuous lengths to reduce the number of rail joints. Maintenance of joints was estimated to account for about one-half the expenditure on labour and materials involved in the upkeep of permanent way as a whole. In 1936 the Delaware & Hudson Railroad in the USA took the decision to abolish joints altogether except through switch and crossing work or at track circuits. Rails were welded in the depot into lengths of 1,400 ft (426·7 m) and transported on flat wagons to site, where the lengths themselves were welded together. The longest stretch without joints was 6,970 ft (2,124·5 m), which was claimed as a record. Experience had shown that if the rails were held immovably on the sleepers, the tendency to expand with heat acted as a stress which could be confined within the rail, making the usual gaps at rail ends unnecessary.

In the same period electric relays were beginning to take over the functions of mechanical interlocking in signalling, usually in association with colour-light signals rather than semaphores. The system was soon extended to enable all the points and signals involved in a traffic movement to be set by operating one small lever or switch. This was known as 'route relay interlocking' and is the basis of modern signalling controls. A 'route' in this sense extends from one main running signal to the next, whether straight ahead on the main line or crossing on to other tracks.

These technical developments took place against a background of economic and political uncertainty. The railways responded to growing competition from private motoring by inducements to travel such as special fare offers and accelerated services. Local trains were speeded up to compete more effectively with buses. In Belgium superannuated main-line

locomotives were given an extended life hauling short-distance trains called *trottinettes* (scooters) which with their light loads and rapid acceleration improved appreciably on previous journey times. The excursionist no longer had to put up with slow and uncomfortable journeys for cheap-fare trains were scheduled at express speeds and often included buffet cars serving refreshments. Sometimes, the excursion fare to a tourist spot included a tour by motor-coach of nearby places of interest.

Retaining or winning freight traffic, however, became an increasing problem, its severity varying according to the restrictions under which the railways operated. In Britain the ability of road hauliers to choose the most lucrative traffic and leave the rest to the railways, which – as we have seen – were obliged to accept it by their 'common carrier' status, was particularly frustrating. A 'Square Deal' campaign was mounted to exert pressure for changing the rules, but this came on the eve of the Second World War in which all means of transport were united in a common cause.

An LMS 2-6-0 + 0-6-2 Garratt hauls a heavy load of coal out of the sidings at Toton marshalling yard bound for Cricklewood.

13. STEAM BETWEEN THE WARS

Previous page: The first Pacifics on the former London & North Western main line were W. A. Stanier's 'Princess' class, which were put on through workings between Euston and Glasgow. No 6207 seen here is one on the later engines with a higher degree of superheat than the first two of the class.

Below: Recording locomotive performance 'on the road' in a dynamometer car.
Above right: BR 2-10-0 No 92013 'at speed' on the rollers of a stationary test plant.
Below right: Opening day of the short-lived Rugby test plant with Pacific No 60007 *Sir Nigel Gresley* in position on the rollers.

IF THERE WERE PROBLEMS for all railways in the years after the First World War there were also opportunities and the period was one of noteworthy progress in many directions. Locomotive engineers had always sought efficiency in terms of work done for fuel consumed, but over the years they had acquired a better understanding of the conversion process. Measurements of tractive effort were made early in the history of the steam locomotive. A method of doing so was devised as early as 1818 by George Stephenson and Nicholas Wood. A dynamometer car in which time and distance travelled were recorded as well as tractive effort was built in Britain towards the end of the 1830s. At that time the measurements were made when the car was attached to an ordinary train, and the constant variations of speed inevitable on a normal journey prevented precise measurements of fuel and water consumption for given power outputs at various specified speeds.

The idea of running a train in controlled conditions was first proposed in Russia in the early 1880s and put into practice by Dr G. V. Lomonossoff. At the same period the first step towards running a locomotive on a stationary test plant was taken in the Kiev workshops of the Russian South Western Railway. A locomotive was jacked up clear of the rails and its driving wheels were connected by a belt to the overhead shafting in the shop. Various measurements were taken while the engine was driving the machinery.

The first true test plant, in which a locomotive runs on rollers connected to brakes to absorb the power, was installed at Purdue University, Indiana in 1891. Its functions were both academic and commercial, and various types of locomotives were tested on it up to the 1920s, by which time US locomotives were becoming too large for it to handle. The plant had a considerable influence on locomotive design in America.

Other test plants followed in the United States, Germany, Russia and Britain. G. J. Churchward built a test plant for the Great Western Railway at Swindon in 1904 and it survived until 1959, doing valuable work for British Railways in its later years. Almost as long-lived was the Altoona test plant of the Pennsylvania Railroad in the United States which operated from 1906 to 1955. Valuable information was made available to the locomotive engineering profession in test bulletins. Horsepowers recorded at the plant reflect the development of the US locomotive. In 1914 a K4s Pacific put out 3,200 hp; by 1922 a large 2-10-0 had produced 3,700 hp, and in 1927 a high-pressure three-cylinder compound 4-10-2 gave 4,500 hp. The highest output recorded in the inter-war years was over 4,650 hp from a 4-8-2 in the early 1930s. The trend continued upwards, and the maximum of 8,000 hp from a Pennsylvania 'duplex' 4-4-6-4 in 1945 is believed to be the highest output ever from a steam locomotive on a test plant. The driving wheels were revolving at a speed equivalent to 56·5 mph (91 km/h) on the track, and the regulator was full open, with cut-off at 40 per cent.

In France a testing station available to all major railways was opened at Vitry-sur-Seine in 1933. Over the next ten years 68 steam locomotives were tested, including the British 2-8-2 *Cock o' the North* in 1935. The need for a testing station in Britain available to all railways was urged as early as 1919 and in 1927 the idea of a national establishment was put forward. No action could be taken in the current economic conditions but in 1936 the London, Midland & Scottish and the London & North Eastern Railways jointly decided to build a locomotive testing station at Rugby. Work was delayed by the outbreak of the Second World War, and Rugby was finally inaugurated officially on 10 October 1948.

Some alternatives to conventional steam locomotive design made appearances, though mostly brief, in the years between the wars. Several were

Top: Stanier turbine-powered Pacific No 6202 ('Turbomotive') passed Edge Hill with the 5.25 pm Liverpool to Euston express in LMS days. *Above:* A Swedish-built Ljungstrom turbine locomotive heads a St Pancras-Manchester express during the short period in 1928 when it was on trial on the Midland main line of the LMS.

attempts to apply the steam turbine to railway traction. A step in this direction had been taken in Britain by the North British Locomotive Company in 1910 with a turbo-electric locomotive but the experiment was abandoned during the war.

Another British company, Armstrong Whitworth, built a twin-unit turbo-electric locomotive in 1922. Wheel arrangement was 2-6-0+0-6-2. One unit carried the boiler and the main and auxiliary turbines, with their generators; the second unit carried the condenser and fuel. In each unit a traction motor drove the three coupled axles through a layshaft and side rods. It was difficult to keep the flexible steam and vacuum connections between the two units leakproof and the experiment was short-lived.

In 1924 another turbine locomotive emerged from North British, this time with mechanical drive. A high-pressure turbine drove the leading bogie and exhausted steam to a low-pressure turbine on the rear bogie. Both machines carried forward and reverse rotors on the same shaft. It was an uneconomic arrangement because the turbine running light in either direction of travel absorbed energy to no purpose. This experiment, too, was abandoned by the builders.

The next move came from Sweden where the Ljüngstrom company built four turbine locomotives with mechanical drive which were accepted for trial in Sweden, Britain, and Argentina. The locomotive sent to Britain worked experimentally on the London Midland & Scottish Railway, working expresses between London and Manchester in 1928. There was no immediate reaction, but when a simpler, non-condensing turbine locomotive was put to work on the Grangesberg-Oxelosund Railway in Sweden in 1932 it attracted the interest of W. A. Stanier, Chief Mechanical Engineer of the LMS. He visited Sweden to see the locomotive in service and the figures of saving in coal and water impressed him enough for a start to be made on designing a locomotive with similar Ljüngstrom turbines for the LMS.

The LMS 'Turbomotive' was a 4-6-2 with gear drive from separate forward and reverse turbines. It began work in June 1935, mainly on London-

Liverpool expresses, and by the outbreak of the Second World War in 1939 had averaged 54,205 miles (87,234 km) a year compared with about 80,000 miles (128,747 km) by conventional Pacific locomotives. This was a satisfactory performance by a new and untried type of locomotive. During the war, however, there were problems in maintaining a locomotive that needed many non-standard spare parts, some of them from abroad, and shortly after the end of the war the Turbomotive was converted into a standard Pacific.

High boiler pressures were also tested as a path to improved efficiency in the steam locomotive. In 1925 a 4-6-0 locomotive with a boiler pressure of 870 lb per sq in (60 bar) was exhibited at the Munich Transport Exhibition as 'the first high-pressure locomotive in the world'. At this period H. N. (later Sir Nigel) Gresley, Chief Mechanical Engineer of the London & North Eastern Railway in Britain, was looking at the possibilities of marine boilers for locomotives. Deciding to use a pressure of 450 lb per sq in (31 bar), he commissioned a marine engineering firm to build a water tube boiler for a four-cylinder compound Pacific locomotive. On completion, the locomotive made trial runs surrounded by some secrecy, to the extent that the press called it 'Gresley's hush-hush locomotive', but in 1930 it worked normal public services for a time

from its base in the north of England, and made one run to-and-from London on the 'Flying Scotsman' express. There was much trouble with the boiler, however, and the 'hush-hush' locomotive was virtually scrapped in 1938, although the mechanical portion was converted into a 4-6-4 (actually a 4-6-2-2, because the trailing wheels were not in a bogie) with a conventional boiler. There were other experiments in Germany, France and Canada with high-pressure boilers of various types but often they were complicated and difficult to maintain. The Canadian example was a huge 2-10-4 for freight traffic with a working pressure of about 870 lb per sq in (60 bar). It went into service in 1931 but boiler troubles requiring long and costly repairs began after running 4,600 miles (2,858 km). The locomotive was withdrawn from regular working in 1936 but appeared from time to time as a substitute for conventional locomotives of the same class. The outbreak of the Second World War sealed its fate and it was broken up in 1940.

More serious consequences attended the second British experiment with high-pressure steam. A three-cylinder compound locomotive working at 900 lb per sq in (62 bar) was built for the London Midland & Scottish Railway in the early 1930s. It never entered regular service. On one of its trial runs a small tube failed and a member of the testing staff

An express unofficially named the 'Cornishman' was introduced by the Great Western Railway between Paddington and Penzance in 1890. From 1904 its fame was dimmed by the new 'Cornish Riviera Limited Express' but, in 1935, the name was given officially, to a new West of England departure from Paddington.

was killed. The experiment did not continue and the boiler and cylinders were scrapped in 1935 but the frames were retained for building a standard locomotive with the same 4-6-0 wheel arrangement.

Early applications of the diesel engine to rail traction highlighted the losses that occurred in the cooling system. Experiments in making use of the waste heat for steam generation took place in Britain and Russia, resulting in locomotives that combined steam and diesel power in one engine. Steam acted on one side of the pistons, and combustion of diesel fuel provided the driving force on the other side. In the Still system tested in Britain, boiler feedwater from a condenser passed through a heat exchanger in which its temperature was raised by the diesel exhaust, and then entered the cooling jacket at the diesel end of the cylinder, already partly vaporised. The jacket was connected directly to the steam space in the boiler and so the extra heat gained in it from the combustion process contributed to steam generation. Steam from the boiler was fed to the 'steam' side of the piston through a slide valve controlling admission and exhaust in the usual way.

The principle was applied in the Kitson-Still locomotive of 1927, in which an eight-cylinder engine under the high-pitched boiler drove the coupled axles through reduction gearing. Wheel arrangement was 2-6-2. The locomotive started with steam power, which overcame a transmission problem inherent in diesel traction – a diesel engine produces no power until its crankshaft is turning. When speed had reached 5 to 7·5 mph (8 to 12 km/h) full diesel power was available and steam admission could be progressively reduced. The steam boiler was oil-fired but the burners were only needed for start-ing or to meet high power demands, steam generation with heat recovered from the diesel being sufficient for normal running. Trials of the Kitson-Still locomotive took place between York and Hull in 1928 but the system proved complicated to operate and maintain and the experiments were not taken further.

Russian engineers were working on similar lines in the 1930s but proposed to increase the role of steam, diesel power only coming into action above about 18·6 mph (30 km/h). The engine cylinder was divided into three sections, with pistons working in opposition in each outer section. At first steam was admitted to all sections but after 30 km/h had been attained it was cut off from the centre section, between the pistons. This section now formed the combustion chamber of a two-stroke diesel engine, the fuel being compressed and ignited by the two pistons as they travelled towards each other. Steam working continued on the other side of the pistons but a greater proportion of the power came from the diesel. Two locomotives working on this system were tested in 1939, and a third in 1948, but the economies hoped for were not attained and the experiments lapsed.

Steam engineers seem to have concluded from these interesting but unproductive experiments that the way ahead lay along traditional lines, increasing some of the design parameters to meet growing demands for power and speed. In Britain the Great Western Railway followed this policy with much success. When C. B. Collett succeeded G. J. Churchward as Chief Mechanical Engineer in 1921 he provided the new motive power that was being asked for in his 'Castle' class 4-6-0, which carried on the principles adopted by Churchward

With the LNER streamlined Pacifics holding the limelight on the 'Silver Jubilee' express in 1935, the Great Western Railway Board decided that their railway needed a streamlined image too. The 'King', No 6014 *King Henry VII* is seen here on a trial run with a train of new 'Centenary' stock built for the 'Cornish Riviera' service.

The 'Claughton' *Alfred Fletcher* hurries northwards with a Belfast boat express in the London suburban area. The electric lines are in the foreground.

in his four-cylinder Star class, but enlarged the cylinder bore and increased the grate area and firebox heating surface. Similar measures were applied successfully when only three years after the first Castle came out in 1923, a larger engine was again called for to work the increasingly heavy west of England traffic. The new design was the 4-6-0 'King' class, again in direct descent from the Churchward classes but with the biggest boiler yet fitted to a Great Western engine. Apart from the short-lived *Great Bear* the Great Western Railway had no Pacifics. After nationalisation in 1948, when the railway became the Western Region of British Railways, it was allocated Pacifics of a new standard design.

Up to the 1920s, indeed, the 4-4-0, 4-6-0 and Atlantic worked the bulk of British express traffic. The Pacific era in the country began in 1922 with Pacifics on the North Eastern and Great Northern Railways. There were only five in the North Eastern class and they were short-lived, but the Great Northern engines were the first in a long series designed and later improved by H. N. Gresley which culminated in his streamlined series of the middle 1930s. On its formation in 1923 the London Midland & Scottish Railway numbered the former Midland Railway among its possessions. This had relied on 4-4-0s for express traffic, double-heading when necessary. The London & North Western also had some redoubtable 4-4-0s but its most recent 4-6-0s, the 'Sir Gilbert Claughton' class, were under-boilered, the boiler originally planned for them having been rejected to keep within weight limits laid down by the civil engineers. A new 4-6-0 was

The Stanier 'Duchess' class Pacifics for the LMS were a development of the earlier 'Princess Royal' Pacifics and similar to the streamlined engines built for working the 'Coronation Scot' Euston-Glasgow express. No 6232 *Duchess of Montrose* is just leaving Bushey troughs with the up 'Royal Scot'.

therefore built for the LMS, coming into service in 1927. This was the 'Royal Scot' class, and its total heating surface of 2,497 sq ft (232 sq m) compared with 2,232 sq ft (208·2 sq m) in the Claughtons. The grate areas were: Royal Scots 31·2 sq ft (2·9 sq m), Claughtons 30·5 sq ft (2·8 sq m).

The LNER Pacifics and the LMSR Royal Scots began what came to be regarded as the 'big engine' era in British practice. They were joined by R. E. L. Maunsell's 'Lord Nelson' 4-6-0 for the Southern Railway, built in 1926 with the increasingly heavy boat train traffic to Dover and Folkestone particularly in view. This was a four-cylinder locomotive with the cranks set so as to give eight exhaust beats per revolution. The softer exhaust obtained in this manner reduced the fluctuations in smokebox vacuum and had a beneficial effect on coal consumption. Maunsell also held to his principles of achieving short and direct passages for live and exhaust steam by placing the four cylinders in line. This was an aspect of 'front end design', of which more was soon to be heard as designers stepped up their pursuit of efficiency.

Maunsell reverted to the 4-4-0 wheel arrangement in his 'Schools' class of 1930 but this was dictated by the loading gauge restrictions and curvature of the route from Tonbridge to the Sussex coast at Hastings for which the new motive power was required. As far as possible components standard with the Lord Nelsons were used. There were three cylinders because there was insufficient clearance in tunnels for two outside cylinders of adequate size. The Schools class was highly successful and used on all non-electrified main lines of the Southern

Experiments with blastpipes were a feature of locomotive development in the late 1930s, with unfortunate results on their appearance. Southern Railway 'Schools' class 4-4-0 No 924 *Hailebury* with Lemaitre blastpipe seen working a Folkestone express.

In France the 4-8-0 locomotive set new standards of performance after Andre Chapelon had transformed the more traditional Pacific. SNCF No 240-P-10 is at Laroche on the PLM main line in April 1947.

A Chapelon H class Pacific leaves St Germain des Fosses with an express from Nimes to Paris Austerlitz.

Railway. In the official *History of the Southern Railway* published in 1936 it was described as 'the most powerful 4-4-0 engine in Europe'. The nominal tractive effort of 25,130 lb (11,399 kg) was certainly higher than that of any 4-4-0 built in Great Britain.

On their introduction the LMS Royal Scots had shown well on coal consumption but their performance in this respect deteriorated after a period in service. The trouble was found to lie in steam leakage past the piston valves. It was cured by a new design of valve head, and when this was applied also to the Claughtons it reduced their basic coal consumption by some 20 per cent, extending their useful life in main-line service and demonstrating the importance of apparently minor details in determining the efficiency of a steam locomotive.

It could now be seen that the future of the steam locomotive lay with refining traditional design rather than with startling innovation. This was demonstrated by the work in France of André Chapelon, an engineer with a profound faith in the potential of steam whose work was curtailed by the emergence of other forms of traction which made less exacting demands on manpower. In 1929 Chapelon was commissioned to examine the reasons for the disappointing performance of a Pacific locomotive class of the Paris–Orléans Railway. Among other weaknesses, it was seen from indicator diagrams that the low-pressure cylinders were not doing their share of the work. Chapelon's investigation of the defects and his treatment of them have become classics of steam locomotive engineering. He redesigned the steam circuit, enlarging and streamlining the steam passages and providing free entry and exit at the valves. Superheat was raised, the draughting arrangements improved, and the frames strengthened to accommodate an anticipated increase in tractive effort. When the locomotive was tested on the track after being rebuilt as Chapelon had prescribed, maximum output on heavy express work was found to be improved by no less than 50 percent, while thermal efficiency was also increased.

Chapelon's influence was felt far outside the PO and PO-Midi system, for engines to his design were built for other railways, and locomotive engineers abroad acknowledged their indebtedness to him.

After his work on the Pacifics, Chapelon turned his attention to a 4-8-0 class with equally successful results. After the formation of the French National Railways in 1938 the Sud-Est Region (former PLM) had 25 similar locomotives built, but of slightly greater power and with mechanical stokers. One of these 240P class locomotives achieved fame when it hauled a train of 787 tons (800 tonnes) up the 1 in 125 gradients from Les Laumes to Blaisy Bas, approaching Dijon, with a minimum speed at the summit of 61 mph (98 km/h), after developing a peak output of 4,320 hp (3,221 kW).

At an earlier date the Chemin de fer du Nord had bought 20 Chapelon Pacifics from the PO company

Streamlined A4 Pacific No 2509 *Silver Link* heads the 'Coronation' London-Edinburgh service of 1937 out of Kings Cross.

Quicksilver on the 'Silver Jubilee' contrasts with the style of Ivatt large-boilered Atlantic No 4449.

and then built 28 more. Together they formed Class 231E, known as *Les Chapelons Nords*. Chapelon's last design for the SNCF was a 2-12-0 for freight traffic. Here the requirement was high tractive effort at low speeds and Chapelon chose a six-cylinder compound arrangement. To achieve maximum expansion of steam without inordinately large low-pressure cylinders, there were four cylinders in the low-pressure stage. They were in line across

the frames between the leading carrying axle and the first coupled axle, with the two larger ones, of 25·2 in (640 mm) diameter on the outside. The two high-pressure cylinders were between the frames in front of the third coupled axle. The drive was divided, the inside low-pressure cylinders driving the second coupled axle, the outside cylinders the third, and the high-pressure cylinders the fourth coupled axle. Boiler pressure was 261 lb per sq in (18 bar).

To reduce losses by condensation and radiation there was a second stage of superheating between the high-pressure and low-pressure cylinders, and the cylinders were steam-jacketed. Steam pipes to and from the high-pressure cylinders were duplicated and fully enclosed, with one group on each side of the boiler. Nominally, the locomotive was a conversion of an earlier 2-10-0 but to all practical purposes it was a new machine.

Building was overtaken by the Second World War and the locomotive was not turned out from the works at Tours until 1940. Tests could not begin until 1948, by which time France had embarked on a wholesale programme of main-line electrification. The test results showed that tractive effort remained continuously between 45,000 and 49,500 lb (20,411 and 22,453 kg) in the speed range 12 to 18 mph (20 to 30 km/h), equivalent to outputs of between 1,775 and 2,278 hp. In the speed range 28 to 40 mph (45 to 60 km/h) tractive effort varied between 37,125 and 29,400 lb (16,838 and 13,336 kg), the equivalent power outputs being between 2,713 and 2,647 hp. From results such as these, many saw a continuing and important future for the steam

locomotive in rail traction, discounting the labour involved in servicing it before and after a turn of duty, and the high degree of skill called for in achieving the best performance from it.

Chapelon recognised that the improvements he had made in the locomotive steam circuit, feed-water heating, and other refinements had produced machines that might be sometimes more than adequate for the duties they had to perform. In his book *La Locomotive à Vapeur* he advised drivers to be ready to counteract a tendency for a locomotive to accelerate more rapidly and climb gradients faster than the schedule required. Obviously power in hand was an asset; what mattered was how it was used. 'Do not be misled by high speeds' said Chapelon, and emphasising his views with italics he continued: 'Remember that the best way *to regain time* is to do so at low speeds, for example *on up-grades* and *while accelerating*.' Both driver and fireman should be expert in interpreting instrument readings. Back pressure in the exhaust and smokebox vacuum were particularly significant in guiding the fireman in his firing rate. Once these indications were understood he would be able to take maximum advantage of the line profile whatever the nature and severity of the duty. Chapelon urged that all modern locomotives should be equipped with the necessary instruments.

H. N. Gresley acknowledged his indebtedness to some of Chapelon's principles in the design of his own Pacific locomotives for the high-speed London–Newcastle service, the 'Silver Jubilee' of 1935. The locomotives were streamlined externally, but there

was also 'internal streamlining' of the steam circuit. In 1932 the German State Railway had introduced its high-speed 'Flying Hamburger' diesel service, and with acceleration of schedules between London and the north-east in view a party of LNER officers, Gresley among them, visited Germany to study the new trains. Gresley concluded that the two-car 'Flying Hamburger' sets did not provide the amount or standard of accommodation the British business

No 6220 *Coronation* poses alongside the ex-LNWR 4-4-0 *Coronation* of 1911 and a replica of a Liverpool & Manchester locomotive.

The 'Coronation Scot' in service. Note the 'speed whiskers' on the streamlined 'nose'.

Above: For six miles after Englewood the 'Twentieth Century Limited' and the 'Broadway Limited' ran side by side, providing a daily spectacle which has captured the imagination of the artist.
Below: A representative of the Pacific classes of the Pennsylvania Railroad.
Above right: The streamlined 'Hudsons' worked all the principal New York Central expresses.
Right: One of the 'Hudson' class stands in La Salle Street station, Chicago.
Below right: NYC 'Hudson' No 5448 approaches Chicago with a passenger train.

traveller would expect, and he was not convinced of the reliability of the diesel engines at that period. He therefore undertook the design of a high-speed steam train to be headed by a streamlined version of his Class A3 Pacifics.

In the streamlined engines the boiler pressure was raised from 220 lb per sq in (15·47 kg per sq cm) to 250 lb per sq in (17·58 kg per sq cm). Cylinder diameter was reduced from 19 in (482.6 mm) to 18½ in (470 mm) but 9 in (228·6 mm) diameter piston valves were used, increasing the proportion of valve area to cylinder diameter compared with the previous Pacifics. Gresley again chose a twin-orifice blastpipe, as he had done after consultation

with French engineers for his earlier 2-8-2 'Cock o' the North' class locomotives built for heavy express trains on the hilly main line between Edinburgh and Aberdeen. The front end profile of the streamlined Pacifics was based on the contours of the Bugatti railcars then beginning to work high-speed services in France, and was extremely effective in lifting the exhaust clear of the cab.

More LNER streamlined Pacifics were ready in 1937 for the inauguration of the 'Coronation' express between London and Edinburgh. This was a chal-

lenge to the Anglo-Scottish services of the London Midland and Scottish Railway on the other side of the country. When W. A. (later Sir William) Stanier took over locomotive engineering on the LMS he gave the railway its first Pacifics in 1933. Two were built at first, and more followed in 1935 incorporating various improvements. In 1937 the LMS riposte to the 'Coronation' was its 'Coronation Scot' express between London and Glasgow. A streamlined version of the Stanier Pacifics was built for this service. As Gresley had done, Stanier increased the valve diameter and did everything possible to ensure a free flow of steam, but the major technical step was the increase of 670 sq ft (62·2 sq m) in heating surface for an increase of only three-quarters of a ton in the total weight of the locomotive. This was achieved by using thinner boiler plates made of a nickel steel equal in strength to the usual mild steel.

After the first batch of Pacifics built specifically for working the 'Coronation Scot' a further series was built, some streamlined and some not. One of the non-streamlined engines, No 6234 *Duchess of Abercorn*, put up a classic performance on 26 February 1939 by working a train weighing 604 tons (613 tonnes) from Crewe to Glasgow and back at an average speed of 55·2 mph (88·8 km/h) for the round trip of 487·2 miles (784 km). The output of 3,333 hp (2,483 kW) at the summit of an ascent of 17·28 miles (29 km) taken at an average speed of 63·4 mph (102 km/h) has been acclaimed as the peak of British steam locomotive performance.

Stanier's Pacifics were part of the standardisation of motive power he had undertaken on the LMS. In Germany Dr R. P. Wagner had been pursuing a

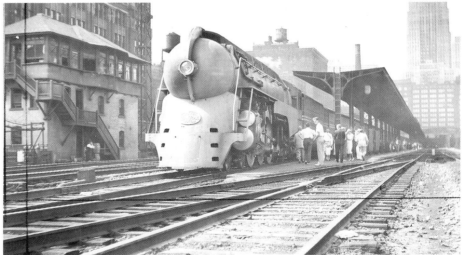

Below: During a Royal Visit to the United States, an NYC 'Hudson' heads a Special near Paskill.
Middle: A Milwaukee 'Hiawatha' service headed out of Chicago by a 4-6-4.
Bottom: Streamlined 4-6-4 locomotives built for the Milwaukee Road by Alco took over from the high-speed Atlantics as loads increased.

similar policy on the Reichsbahn. He, too, produced some noteworthy Pacifics but his response to the high-speed diesels was a streamlined 4-6-4, two of which were built. In 1936 No 05.002 of this class reached a world record speed for steam of 124·5 mph (200·4 km/h) with a special test train of 300 tons (305 tonnes) running between Berlin and Hamburg. Two years later, on 3 July 1938, Gresley's stream-lined Pacific No 4468 *Mallard* touched 126 mph (202·7 km/h) while descending the 1 in 200 gradient

of Stoke bank, between Grantham and Peterborough, with a train carrying out brake tests. This has remained a world record for steam, but the Germans were not slow to point out that their maximum speed had been attained on level track, and a respected British commentator on locomotive affairs is said to have conceded that they deserved the palm in terms of performance.

The roots of the K4s Pacifics on the Pennsylvania went back further than those of Gresley's or Stanier's engines but they served that railroad well right up to the age of the high-speed steam train that began in the second half of the 1930s. Although by that time they worked in pairs on the steepest section of the New York–Chicago line, and were being super-seded on many trains by 4-8-2s, they made the then fastest steam run in the world in 1934 — 75·6 mph (121·6 km/h) over the 40·3 miles (69·2 km) be-tween Valparaiso and Plymouth (Indiana) with the 'Union' express. With the 'Broadway Limited' they ran between Englewood and Fort Wayne in each direction at an average speed of 68·9 mph (110·7 km/h). In 1936 the Pennsylvania had seven daily steam-hauled runs at above 72·5 mph (116·7 km/h) all worked by the K4s class.

The New York Central changed from Pacifics to 4-6-4 (Hudson) locomotives on its 'Twentieth Century Limited' in 1927. There were several series of NYC Hudsons. One of the J1-e series was stream-lined in 1934 and named *Commodore Vanderbilt*. It was the first streamlined US locomotive. Ten of the later J-3a series were built as streamliners in 1938, and in that year the schedule of the 'Twentieth Century Limited' was cut by 30 minutes to 16 hours, giving an average speed of 59·0 mph (96·4 km/h) for the New York–Chicago journey. The train often weighed 1,000 tons (1,016 tonnes). Seven stops *en route*, including the change between steam and electric power at Harmon, occupied 26 minutes.

Speed competition between the Pennsylvania and the New York Central on the New York–Chicago run was traditional. In 1935 similar rivalry began between the railways serving the twin cities of Minneapolis and St Paul from Chicago. The first challenge came in July 1934 when the Chicago

Milwaukee St Paul & Pacific (the Milwaukee Road) made a fast experimental run on the route in the course of which the 85 miles (136·8 km) from Chicago to Milwaukee were covered in 67 min 35 sec. Scenting what was in store, the Chicago & North Western introduced an express called the '400' on 4 January 1935 which ran the 408·6 miles (657·5 km) from Chicago to St Paul in 7 hours with three intermediate stops, and covered the initial 85 miles (136·8 km) to Milwaukee in 80 minutes, compared with a best time of 85 minutes by the CMStP&P. With an average speed from Chicago to Milwaukee of 63·8 mph (102·7 km/h), and again from Milwaukee to Adams, 124·5 miles (200·3 km), the '400' was the fastest train in the United States over such a distance. It was hauled by oil-burning Pacific locomotives which were standard with other classes except for driving wheels of 6 ft 7 in (200.7 cm) diameter instead of 6 ft 3 in (190·5 cm).

There was swift response from the Milwaukee Road which reduced its Chicago–Milwaukee time to 80 minutes as well and gave the first hints of more to come from new locomotives and trains under construction. The new equipment formed the 'Hiawatha' express with timings of 1 hr 15 min between Chicago and Milwaukee, and 6 hr 30 min between Chicago and St Paul. The 'Hiawatha' was streamlined from locomotive to the curved end of the rear coach.

Its first locomotives were Atlantics with 7 ft (213·4 cm) diameter driving wheels and 300 lb per sq in (21·1 kg per sq cm) working pressure. It was surprising at that period to see a return to the Atlantic wheel arrangement for first class express work, and the Atlantics were in fact joined in 1938 by streamlined 4-6-4 locomotives which worked other and heavier trains as well as their 'Hiawatha' duties. But the 'Hiawatha' Atlantics were not alone. In the summer of 1939 the Belgian National Railways put streamlined Atlantics into service on a high-speed train between Brussels and Ostend which covered the 70·8 miles (114 km) in one hour exactly, with a stop at Bruges. On the journey to the coast the 57·7 miles (92·8 km) from Brussels to Bruges had to be covered at an average speed of 75·3 mph

(121·2 km/h) which outdid the fastest point-to-point time of the 'Hiawatha' and gave Belgium the fastest steam-hauled run in the world. The six Atlantics built for the service were two-cylinder engines with poppet valves, double-chimney and all the other refinements of contemporary steam practice. Wheel diameter was 6 ft 10½ in (209·6 cm). They worked the high-speed service for only a few months before it was overtaken by the Second World War. In the post-war years the rapid spread of 3,000V DC electrification in Belgium progressively reduced

Below: One of the original high-speed Atlantics of 1935 heads the Milwaukee Road's 'Hiawatha'.
Bottom: A streamlined Pennsylvania Pacific gives a new look to the front end of the 'Broadway Limited'.

Passengers in the 'Hiawatha' enjoy the amenities of the spacious dining car.

The rear parlour car of the 'Hiawatha' had a 'beaver tail' end with observation windows.

Opposite above : An aerial view of the 'Silver Jubilee' at speed shows how effectively the front-end streamlining lifts the exhaust clear of the cab windows and carriage roofs. *Opposite below :* Radio entertainment for passengers in the 'headphone' period.

Following the success of the A4s on the streamlined expresses, more were built for other top-rank services. No 4486 *Merlin* of the later series passes Woolmer Green with the up 'Flying Scotsman' in 1938.

space and a corridor connection to the train at the rear so that on a long run a spare engine crew could travel in the front compartment of the train and walk through to the footplate to relieve their colleagues at the half-way point. Armed with this facility the LNER was able to schedule a genuine non-stop journey from London to Edinburgh in the summer timetable of 1928, the distance of 392·9 miles (632·3 km) constituting a new world record.

The LMSR was at a competitive disadvantage, for the 'Royal Scot' served both Glasgow and Edinburgh, and had to stop at Symington to detach the Edinburgh coaches. As a gesture, however, it ran the train in two separate portions, non-stop to Glasgow and to Edinburgh respectively, a few days before the new LNER timetable came into force. The feat was not repeated.

Still observing the 8 hr 15 min minimum limit, the 'Flying Scotsman' ambled rather than flew in order to fill out the time. The restaurant car, a cocktail bar, a barber's shop for the men and retiring room for the ladies helped to relieve the tedium, and a kindly critic described the journey as 'relaxing', but there was little to quicken the pulse. In 1932 the two railways agreed to abolish the 8 hr 15 min agreement and there were accelerations on both routes. At its best before 1939 the 'Flying Scotsman' reached Edinburgh in 7 hours and the 'Royal Scot' was also a 7-hour train on its journey to Glasgow.

Long non-stop runs were useful material for railway publicity departments, but speed was better

still, particularly with the prospect of claiming 'the fastest train in the world'. Surprisingly, this distinction went to a train which started as a run-of-the-mill service from Cheltenham to Swindon, and then made a brilliant dash over the 77·3 miles (124·4 km) from Swindon to London Paddington. As a first step the Great Western Railway simply seized the 'fastest train in Britain' title in 1923 by scheduling the Swindon–Paddington run in 75 minutes, the resultant average speed of 61·8 mph (99·4 km/h) toppling a long-held record of the North Eastern and LNER Railways which had a run at 61·5 mph (99 km/h) from Darlington to York. In 1929 the Swindon–Paddington time was cut to 70 minutes and the resulting average speed of 66·2 mph (106·5 km/h) earned the coveted 'fastest train in the world' accolade. It was lost again by a whisker to the Canadian Pacific Railway in 1931, but regained later in the same year by reducing the time to 67 minutes and increasing the average to 69·2 mph (111·3 km/h). A final acceleration to 65 minutes and 71·4 mph (114·9 km/h) came in 1932. At first the 'Cheltenham Flyer' was still the fastest train in the world but by this time the German high-speed railcar sets were on the horizon and in May 1933 the 'Flying Hamburger' took over the title with its speed of 77·4 mph (124·5 km/h) over the 178·1 miles (286·6 km) between Berlin and Hamburg. A speed revolution both with steam and other forms of traction had begun, and by 1939 the 'Cheltenham Flyer', with its timing still unchanged was only

eighth in the list of fastest steam trains and eightieth in the table of fastest runs by all forms of traction.

It used to be said that the passengers who most appreciated the 'Cheltenham Flyer' were Great Western officials visiting the railway works at Swindon who wanted a quick run back to London to be in time for dinner and a theatre. They got what they wanted, together with a considerable bonus in publicity for their railway. Most business travellers, however, ask for a fast journey at convenient times in both directions, and this is what the LNER provided with its London–Newcastle streamlined train, the 'Silver Jubilee', which from 30 September 1935 made the journey of 258·3 miles (415·7 km) between the two cities in 4 hours flat each way, with one intermediate stop. With its streamlined locomotive and coaches, finished externally in silver grey from end to end, the 'Silver Jubilee' gave the steam express a new image and was at once rewarded with full loads. Its evening departures from Kings Cross were often attended by a

A streamlined two-cylinder
4-6-4 built by Henschel for the
Deutsche Reichsbahn in 1934.
It was designed for a top speed
of 109 mph (175 km/h).

smokebox, and was furnished as an observation car with armchair seating. The 'Coronation' was also the first British train to have an automatic pressure ventilation system that gave a change of air every three minutes.

The London Midland & Scottish Railway replied to the 'Coronation' with the 'Coronation Scot' and a 6½-hour schedule between London Euston and Glasgow. As already mentioned, streamlined Pacific locomotives were built to work the nine-coach train which was formed of standard coaching stock adapted for this special service. Locomotive and coaches were painted blue with two horizontal white lines which started on the locomotive smokebox and were continued on all the vehicles.

The British streamlined trains of the mid-1930s onwards were only one aspect of a general upward trend in railway speed both in Britain and elsewhere. By 1938 the distance covered daily at 70 mph (112·6 km/h) and over, taking the world's railways as a whole, had reached 10,169 miles (16,356 km), 76 per cent with diesel, 21 per cent with steam and 3 per cent with electric haulage.

On the Continent the immediate years after the First World War saw earlier service patterns changed by political events and new frontiers. The 'Nord Express' on its restoration in 1923 lost its links with

small crowd of interested sightseers. In 1937 a similar formula was followed in the 'Coronation' express which gave a 6-hour journey, with one stop, between London Kings Cross and Edinburgh. This time the colour scheme was garter blue and all coaches were open saloons so that meals could be served from the kitchen car to every seat. The last vehicle had a sloping rear, reflecting the slope of the streamlined casing that concealed the locomotive

The LNER 'Coronation' stock
was designed for meal service
at seats throughout the train.
These are first class saloons
with swivelling armchair seats.

St Petersburg (now Leningrad), Moscow and the Trans-Siberian, but it now served the Baltic States. In 1932 a section for Scandinavia was added, and in 1934 the service was extended to Rumania. There was a brief interruption to points east of Berlin in 1926–27 during fighting between Poland and Russia. During the 1930s there was a thaw in relations between the Soviet Union and the West which enabled connections with Moscow to be resumed in 1936. Meanwhile the train had adjusted itself to post-war social patterns by including second class sleeping cars from 1931.

The itinerary of the original 'Orient Express' through Germany and Austria was disrupted by the war and not resumed until 1932. In order to provide a similar service the Allied Governments charged the Wagons-Lits company with providing a new through train to Eastern Europe to travel via France, Switzerland and Italy. The result was the 'Simplon-Orient Express', inaugurated on 11 April 1919, which departed from the Gare de Lyon in Paris and was routed via Dijon and Vallorbe to Lausanne. Continuing along the Rhône Valley, the train entered Italy through the Simplon Tunnel. After Milan the route was eastwards across northern Italy via Mestre (for Venice) to Trieste and so into Yugoslavia. At Vinkovci a portion was detached for Bucharest,

and at Nis there was another division, one portion proceeding to Istanbul and the other to Athens.

There was now a 'family' of 'Orient' trains for in 1901 the 'Ostend–Vienna Express' had been extended to Bucharest, changing its name to 'Ostend–Vienna–Orient Express'. And in 1932 there was an addition when a Paris–Vienna service which had been introduced in 1924 was extended from Vienna to Bucharest. The train travelled via Switzerland

The down 'Coronation Scot' at Queens Park, LMS 4-6-2 locomotive No 6221.

The interior of the 'Coronation' observation car with the sloping rear window.

The 'Orient Express' in its early years. The three sleeping car and two luggage vans with their characteristic Guard's lookouts are all Wagons-Lits vehicles, qualifying the train for the description *train de luxe*.

and Austria, crossing the frontier at Buchs and continuing through the Arlberg Tunnel. It was therefore named the 'Arlberg–Orient Express'. By now the original 'Orient Express' was running again and so there were four international trains with 'Orient' in their titles. They did not run en bloc to their ultimate destinations, cars being detached and worked forward in other trains as convenient. A traveller by the westbound 'Arlberg–Orient' from Athens in 1938 began his or her journey in a train of ordinary coaches with a Wagons-Lits

restaurant car and two sleeping cars attached, one to travel by the Arlberg and one by the Simplon route. They separated at Beograd. The 'Arlberg–Orient' coaches from Bucharest came on at Budapest, consisting of one for Paris and one for Boulogne, and a new restaurant car was attached. From there until Chaumont in France the 'Arlberg–Orient Express' consisted of a brake van, three sleeping cars (Athens–Paris, Bucharest–Paris, and Bucharest–Boulogne) and a restaurant car. At Chaumont the Boulogne sleeper was detached and assembled

The Russian 5 ft (1·5 m) gauge gives exceptional spaciousness to the interior of this Wagons-Lits restaurant car for the Trans-Siberian service in 1900.

with a brake van and a restaurant car to form a mini *train de luxe* which was hustled to the Channel coast first by an Est 4-6-0 and then by a Nord Pacific. It arrived dead on time.

By 1938 air travel was making inroads into long-distance traffic by rail. The 'Simplon–Orient' service captured the imagination of writers and film producers who made it a setting for skulduggery and intrigue of various kinds, possibly because they knew of the spell cast on less adventurous travellers by the sight of the through sleeping car to Istanbul on the boat train at Calais. Until 22 May 1977 a through service between Paris, Athens and Istanbul, corresponding in its route but little else to the 'Simplon–Orient', continued to run under the name 'Direct Orient'. Even before it was withdrawn memories of its distinguished predecessors had been revived by running a special train of vintage rolling stock from Zurich to Istanbul, and similar excursions took place later. In 1982 a British travel

Inside the diner on the 'Oriental Limited', of the Great Northern Railroad.

The observation platform on the rear coach of the 'Oriental Limited' was a moving grand-stand for viewing the grandeur of the Cascade Mountains.

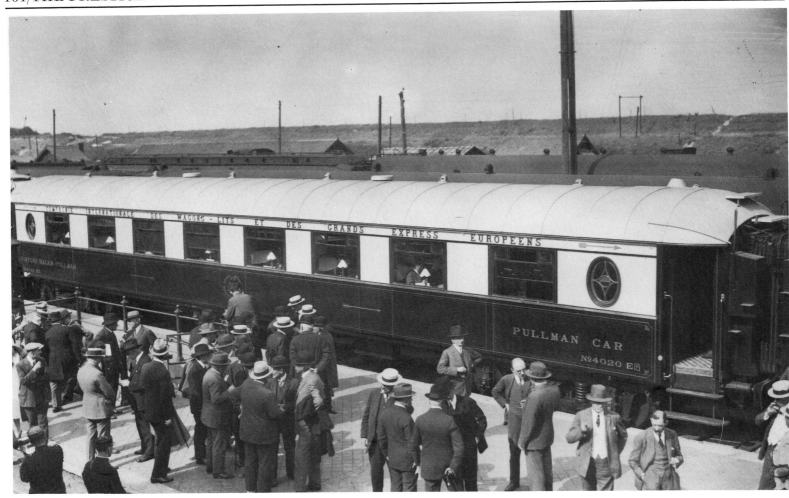

The all white Pullman train named the Golden Arrow Express which ran between Calais and Paris was considered the last word in modern comfort in 1926. The photograph shows passengers leaving the train after its inaugural run to Calais.

Travellers enjoy the pleasures of the table in a restaurant car of the International Sleeping Car Company.

company launched a 'Venice Simplon–Orient Express' running to a fixed schedule throughout the year between London, Paris and Venice. From London to Folkestone the train was formed of Pullman Cars which had been withdrawn when British Railways dropped all but one of their Pullman services and were now refurnished throughout. The continental train not only reconstructed its forerunner with genuine Wagons-Lits stock but improved on its luxury and elegance in the interior furnishing and decoration, while introducing features the original 'Simplon–Orient' had never known, such as a cocktail bar and public address system relaying announcements and music. The organisers claimed to have 'restored the art of travel'. What they had in fact done was to transfer the atmosphere of cruising in a luxury liner to a railway train.

Trains gain romance from their destinations, and this was certainly true of the 'Simplon–Orient' with its mental pictures of the Mosque of Saint Sophia and the Golden Horn. The 'Calais–Mediterrannée Express' was similarly evocative, whisking the traveller from the often grey shores of the English Channel to the brilliance, both climatic and social, of the French Riviera. Probably even more people had heard of the 'Blue Train' than of the 'Simplon–Orient'. That name was not given officially to the 'Calais–Mediterrannée' until 1949 although it was generally current from 1922. The origins of the 'Blue Train' went back to 8 December 1883 when a service called the 'Calais–Nice–Rome Express' was put on. Three years later the Rome portion was separated and ran as an independent train, the 'Rome Express' via Modane and the Mont Cenis Tunnel. Thereupon the Riviera section became the 'Calais–Mediterrannée Express'. After suspension during the First World War, the service was resumed on 16 November 1920, at first running three times a week between Paris and Menton. The next summer it was restored as a through train between Calais and Vintimille. At the same time the Wagons-Lits company ordered new steel rolling stock to replace the varnished teak vehicles of the original formation. The new vehicles were coloured blue, but the reason for the choice is not certain. It may have been to symbolise the Côte d'Azur, or perhaps to distinguish them from the rolling stock of the Paris Lyons & Mediterranean Railway which was then painted red.

An inaugural run with the new stock was made on 9 December 1922. There were 100 guests in the

The British Pullman Car Company was headed by Lord Dalziell of Wooler, here seen about to board one of his company's vehicles.

Opposite : The hotel-room atmosphere in a private sleeping compartment.

Two British-built electric locomotives head an express of the South African Railways on one of the main routes electrified at 3000V DC.

two portions of the train, one starting from Calais and the other from Paris. The Calais portion skirted Paris on the Petite Ceinture line to enter the Gare de Lyon, and left the terminus five minutes after the portion starting from Paris. The respective departure times were 7.25 pm and 7.30 pm; through the night the Calais coaches were hard on the heels of the Paris portion, and the two arrived at Nice at 11 am and 11.10 am. A four-course dinner was served *en route*, rounded off with dessert and accompanied by three wines of a 1911 vintage. At Nice 30 limousines were waiting to convey the guests to their hotels.

The press comment on the event echoed the paeans written by journalists in the United States after being the guests of George Pullman in one of his new 'Palace Car' trains. The correspondent of *Le Petit Parisien* wrote:

It's just the finest train in the world; and it doesn't run in China, or the United States, but here at home; it is comfortable, elegant, and *French* . . . This *train de luxe* concerns everybody, even those who will never ride in it because it is a

symbol of progress. Today the beneficiaries of progress are the wealthy patrons of the sleeping cars, but tomorrow, without a doubt, they will be travellers of more modest means. Progress is like the sun; it brings comfort to the poor man and the millionaire alike.

These first 'Blue Train' coaches had eight single-berth compartments with washstands, and four double-berth compartments with a shared toilet compartment for each pair. They were panelled in mahogany with decorative motifs in marquetry. At first the new stock ran in company with older teak vehicles. The train was not composed entirely of the blue-coloured steel stock until 1926. The peak of 'Blue Train' luxury was not attained until 1929 when new cars with ten single-berth compartments were put on the train. The beds were wider, 2 ft 7 in (80 cm), and folding doors concealed the ample washstand and its accessories when the compartment was made up for day use. Four famous designers were responsible for the interior decorations in marquetry, lacquer or coloured woods. From the introduction of these new coaches

in 1929 the train was normally hauled by new PLM 4-8-2 locomotives and with ten vehicles in all weighed 470·45 tons (478 tonnes). With deepening economic recession some of these cars were converted in 1932 to four single-berth and six double-berth compartments, while others were made double-berth throughout.

The 'Blue Train' was restored in 1946 after the Second World War, and in 1950 acquired new amenities in the shape of converted Pullman Cars with a 24-seat dining section to relieve pressure on the restaurant car, and a lounge section with bar. From 1958 it lost its uniform blue livery with the introduction of new stainless steel coaches and in 1976 began to include first and second class couchettes. The final break with the past came on 1 June 1980 when the train was divided into two portions, the first leaving Paris an hour before the second and still carrying the 'Blue Train' name, this was primarily for passengers to Nice and beyond; and the second for travellers to Toulon, St Raphael, Cannes and Antibes, for whom the later start gave a more convenient arrival time in the morning.

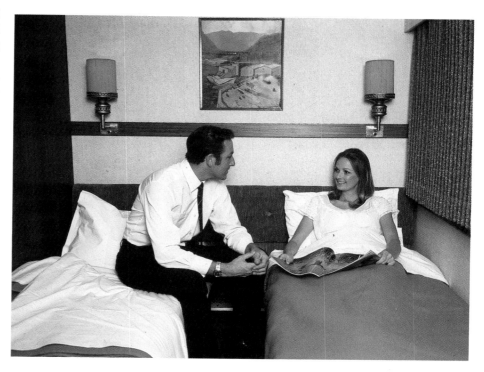

Rolling stock of the South African Railways 'Blue Train' (Cape Town, Johannesburg).

Pullman Cars did not appear in the Wagon-Lits company's *trains de luxe* until 1925 by which time it was linked with the Pullman Car Company (British) through Lord Dalziell, who was Chairman of both organisations. It was during his regime, in 1929. that the all-Pullman 'Flèche d'Or' began running between Calais and Paris, connecting with Southern Railway's 'Golden Arrow' Pullman train between London and Dover, the cross-Channel link being provided by the steamer *Canterbury* built specially for the service.

The 'Blue Train' of South Africa has become almost as well known as the 'Blue Train' of France and is remarkable for the luxurious accommodation provided on a gauge of only 3 ft 6 in (1·067 m). It originated as a first class only service between Cape Town and Johannesburg, connecting at Cape Town with the Union Castle liners from Southampton. This developed into the 'Union Limited' when special stock was built for it. The new formation consisted of three day and three sleeping cars, a dining and kitchen car, an observation car, and a vehicle form-

ing a private suite comprising bedroom, sitting room and bathroom. In the 1920s the train ran on two days a week, making the journey of 955·7 miles (1,539 km) in $29\frac{3}{4}$ hours. Several classes of Pacific locomotive worked the train on the easier sections of the route but the large 4-8-2s of Class 15A were used on the severe gradients in the Hex River Pass where a gradient of 1 in 40 extended for 16 miles (25·7 km). Even with these large locomotives assistance was often needed and was sometimes provided by powerful Mallet 2-6-6-0 compounds. Occasionally the train needed two locomotives at the head on this section as well as a banker at the rear.

In 1940 a new series of blue-coloured vehicles came into service on the 'Union Limited' and the name 'Blue Train' began. Two new 16-car trainsets built in 1972 enhanced the luxury with refinements such as independent air-conditioning for each compartment, tinted heat-reflecting glass in the windows, and electrically-operated venetian blinds. There were three categories of cars classified as Luxury, Semi-Luxury and Standard. The first two cate-

gories offered suites for two passengers with bedroom, lounge and bathroom; and a coupé similarly equipped for one. In the Standard cars the berths folded away to form a sofa in the daytime, supplemented by an easy chair. A lounge car with a bar, armchairs grouped round tables, and corner settees was marshalled next to the restaurant car. The 'Blue Train' continued to run after the withdrawal of liner sailings between Cape Town and Southampton in the 1970s and was extended to Pretoria, the whole journey of 999·2 miles (1,608 km) taking 26 hours in each direction. By that time all but 311·3 miles (501 km) of the route had been electrified.

During the First World War the Mitropa organisation was formed under German control for operating restaurant and sleeping cars in Central Europe. In 1927 the European Timetable Conference in Prague approved proposals by the German State Railway (Reichsbahn) and Mitropa for a new service to provide an improved link between England, Germany, Holland and Switzerland. It was to provide first class and second class accommodation, but both

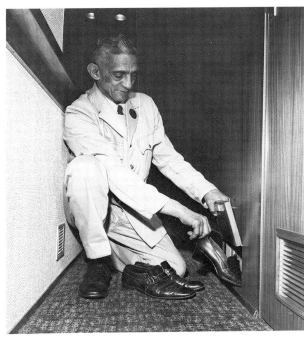

Dinner is served in the SAR 'Blue Train'.
Shoes shined while passengers sleep, another 'Blue Train' amenity.

A lounge area in one of the cars on the Pennsylvania's 'Broadway Limited'. As well as three such areas in each car there was a bar (seen at rear), secretary's office, barber shop, shower bath and two double bedrooms.

Opposite left: A double bedroom on the Great Northern's 'Empire Builder' express between Chicago and the Pacific Northwest.
Opposite right: Daytime in a 'Slumbercoach' of the 'Burlington Zephyr'.
Opposite below: The 'Slumbercoach' at night.

A standard sleeping car interior. On the right the upper berths are folded away and the lower ones converted into seats.

would be of a higher standard than usual in those categories. The service began on 15 May 1928. Separate portions starting from Hook of Holland (connecting with LNER steamships from Harwich) and Amsterdam united at Utrecht and travelled via Cologne and Mannheim to Basle. With its long itinerary following the course of the Rhine, the train was named the 'Rheingold', evoking romantic visions of the secret treasure of the Nibelungs and promising views of the Rhine castles, islands and ancient towns along its banks. At the height of the summer season the train was extended from Basle to Lucerne.

The 'Rheingold' was formed of new Pullman-style coaches, with first class accommodation in open saloons or coupés with armchair seating, and second class in open saloons. The windows, up to 5 ft 11 in (1·5 m) wide, were hung with heavy curtains and a table lamp glowed in every bay. It was a colourful train externally, with silver roofs, cream upper panels, violet below and gold lining and lettering.

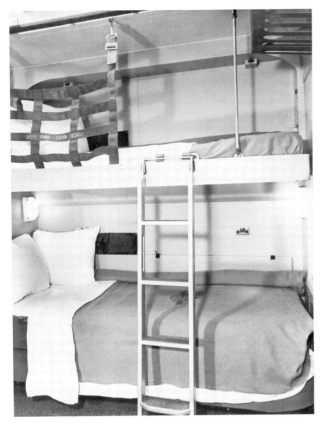

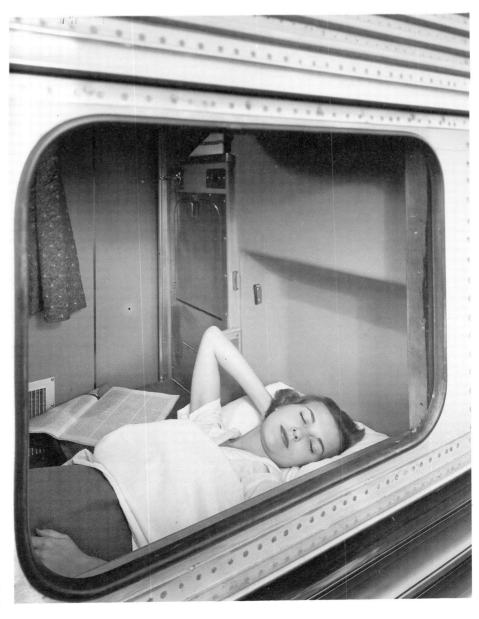

Traditionally, in the early years it was hauled by one of the Maffei S 3/6 class Pacifics.

From the winter of 1932–33 the 'Rheingold' conveyed through coaches for Zurich, which together with the Lucerne portion were taken on from Basle by the 'Edelweiss' Pullman train of the Wagons-Lits company. This was in a sense a rival to the 'Rheingold' in providing a luxury service from Amsterdam to Switzerland, with connections from England at Antwerp by the LNER Harwich–Antwerp sailings and the 'Antwerp Continental' express from London Liverpool Street. From Antwerp the 'Edelweiss' travelled to Basle via Brussels, Luxembourg, and Strasbourg.

The last change in the 'Rheingold' schedule before the Second World War was the extension of the Lucerne portion to Milan as from 15 May 1939. At the same time a high-speed diesel train was put on between Berlin and Basle, enabling a passenger who changed into the Milan portion of the 'Rheingold' at Basle to make the whole journey from Berlin without a night in the train, although the Milan arrival at five minutes past midnight could sometimes be an inconvenient alternative.

The 'Rheingold' first ran again after the war on 17 December 1946, restoring the through service between The Hook and Basle. In 1962 it was re-equipped with new air-conditioned rolling stock, including an observation car and a buffet-bar car. The external colour scheme was now fawn and blue, changed in 1965 to fawn and ruby red when the train was included in the Trans-Europ Express

(TEE) network. In 1983 the rolling stock was re-furbished and the 'Rheingold' offered an additional service in the shape of a through portion for Munich. This was detached at Mannheim and travelled via Heidelberg and the Neckar Valley to Stuttgart, from where it followed a secondary line of scenic and historical interest to Augsburg via Nordlingen and Donauworth. The new facility was aimed par-ticularly at tourist business. A hostess in the special 'Club-Car' pointed out features of interest along the route, and passengers could examine exhibits in the car representing local products, crafts and traditions.

In the United States the 'Broadway Limited' and the 'Twentieth Century Limited' maintained their prestige among many more extravagantly named rivals, of which the 'Overnite Denverite' was a sample. By 1939 the 'Broadway Limited' was elec-trically hauled between New York and Harrisburg and was second in the list of fast electric runs with an average speed of 70·2 mph (112·9 km/h) over the 76 miles (122·3 km) from Newark to North Philadelphia. The New York Central route between Toledo (at the western end of Lake Erie) and Elkhart had become a steam racing ground with the 'Twentieth Century Limited' heading the list over this section of 113 miles (181·8 km) with an average speed of 70·6 mph (113·6 km/h).

By 1939 a variety of accommodation was avail-able for travellers on overnight trains in the USA. For those who did not wish to pay a supplement there was the 'coach', a vehicle with adjustable reclining chairs. The standard Pullman was a car with two-berth sections on each side of a central

gangway, from which they were screened by curtains. Passengers could have a section to themselves on payment of an extra charge. From this arrangement the 'Roomette' car was developed, the roomettes being completely partitioned off from the gangway. A bed was lowered from the wall at night, and by day the roomette was a small private room, with its own washing and toilet arrangements.

The 'Duplex' car had a side corridor with the beds in the compartments arranged transversely instead of longitudinally as in the roomette. The compartments were on two levels, dovetailed into each other to save space. In the 'Double Bedroom' there was a wide settee across the compartment by day, with a second bed let down above it from the compartment wall at night. This corresponded to the second class Pullman sleeper on the Continent. One passenger could occupy a compartment on payment of a fare slightly less than that for two. Some compartments were still more roomy; a transverse settee was made up into the lower bed at night and a longitudinal upper berth was let down from the wall. A loose armchair was provided for day use.

Even more spacious accommodation was offered by the 'Drawing Room' which slept up to three passengers and provided a settee and two armchairs for daytime travel. Only a few crack services included the luxurious 'master car' which provided four movable armchairs by day, two beds by night, and a small communicating compartment with toilet arrangements and a shower bath. Some US services provided a 'mix' of these various types of accommodation.

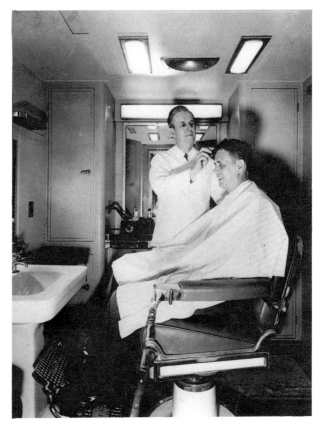

Opposite top: Pullman vestibuled parlour car of the Boston & Maine's 'Boston & Mount Desert Limited Express'. Foot cushions for the armchairs and a tea service are displayed in a glass case at the rear.
Opposite below: The tea room in the observation car of the 'Alton Limited' (Chicago-St Louis).
Centre: A 4000 hp twin-unit diesel heads the 'Golden Gate' express (Bakersfield-San Francisco) of the Santa Fe.
Above: Lounge section of new observation car for the New York Central's 'Twentieth Century Limited' in 1930.
Left: One of the two barber shops in the 'Twentieth Century Limited'.

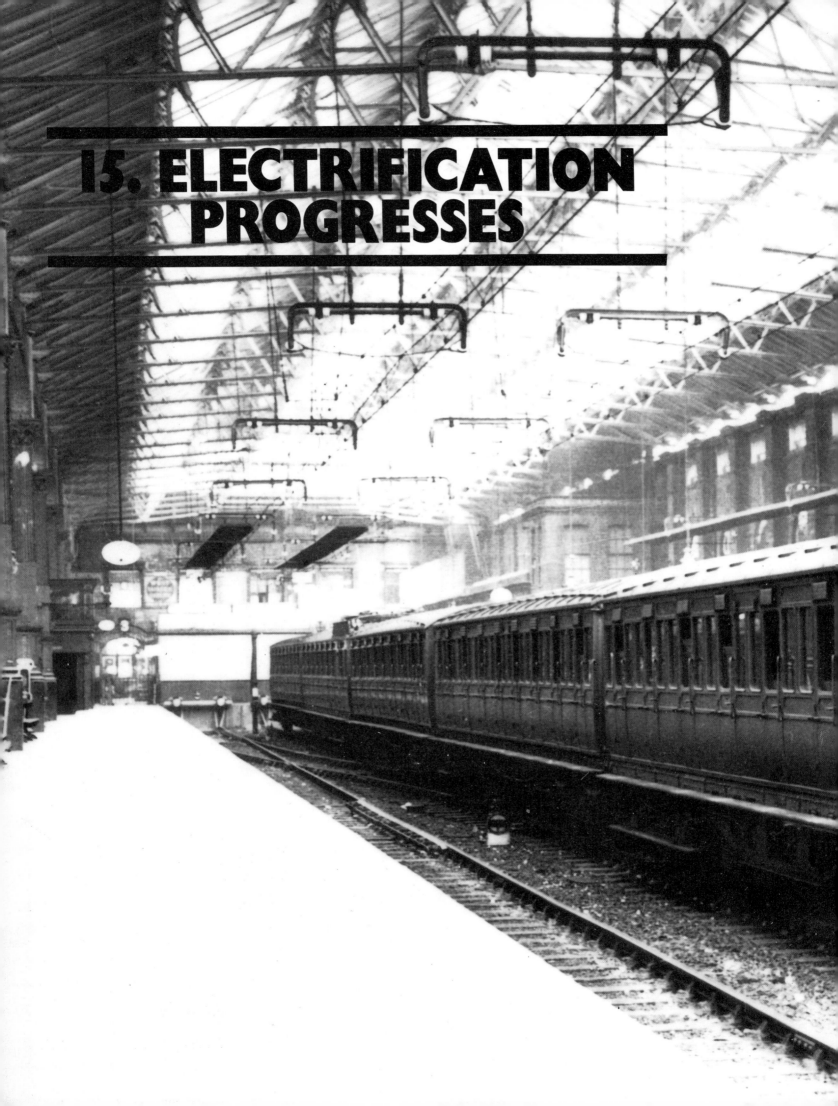

15. ELECTRIFICATION PROGRESSES

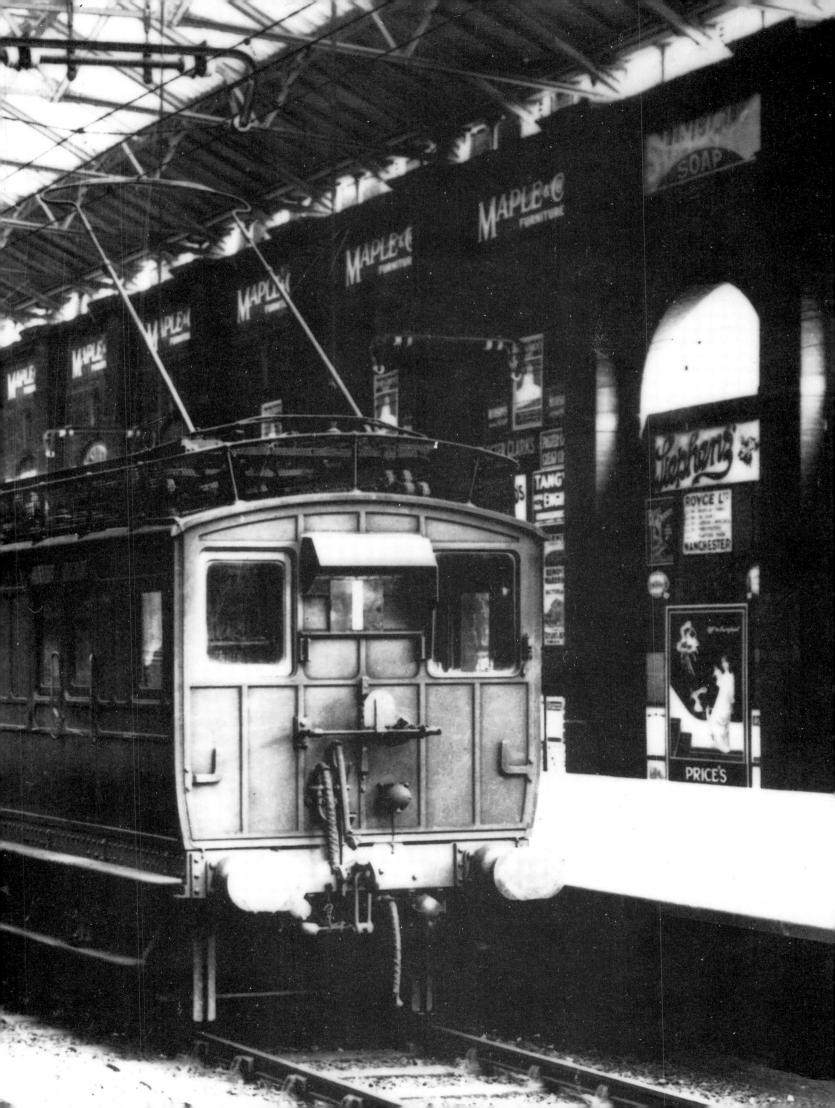

Previous page : London, Brighton and South East Railways overhead AC electric suburban train of 1910 at Victoria Station, London.

ALTHOUGH THE CONVENTIONAL forms of AC and DC electrification were well established by the 1920s, engineers continued to look for improvements. The need for a low-frequency supply continued to be a drawback of AC traction, and there was still a strong feeling in favour of the induction motor if its characteristics could be brought more into line with other traction machines.

When the Norfolk & Western Railroad in the United States decided to electrify 27 miles (43·5 km) through the Appalachian Mountains in 1914, the company's consultants recommended the use of induction motors on the grounds of the punishing work involved in hauling heavy coal trains up a continuous gradient against eastbound traffic, steepening to 1 in 50 at the summit. Steam locomotives had reached their limit in 1910 when three Mallets were needed to maintain no more than 8 mph (12·8 km/h) with trains of 3,199 tons (3,250 tonnes), and on the single track through the Elkhorn Tunnel speed had to drop to 6 mph (9·6 km/h) to reduce the emission of smoke and gas.

To avoid the complication of the two overhead contact wires required by a three-phase system, the Norfolk & Western decided on a single-phase supply to the locomotives, which would be equipped with rotary converters providing a three-phase input to the motors. The first section of the electrification, from Bluefield to Vivian, West Virginia, was opened in 1915. The locomotives were 1,600 hp units semi-permanently coupled in pairs. A unit comprised two two-axle motor bogies and a non-motored carrying axle at each end, corresponding to a 2-4-4-2 wheel arrangement in steam or 1-B-B-1 in electric notation. A complete two-unit locomotive, of 3,200 hp output, was therefore described as a 2(1-B-B-1). Two traction motors carried on each motor bogie were geared to a jackshaft from which the drive was transmitted to the wheels by side rods.

Single-phase current at 16,000V, 25Hz was collected from the overhead wire and conducted to a transformer in the locomotive where it was stepped down to 750V for driving the single-phase/three-phase rotary converter. The converter frequency being fixed, motor speeds were controlled by pole-changing and switching the interconnections of the machines. By this method track speeds of 7, 14 and 28 mph (11, 22·5 and 45 km/h) could be selected. On the down grade the motors worked automatically as generators, returning power to the supply, providing a retarding force sufficient to hold a train of 3,199 tons (3,250 tonnes) at 14 mph (22·5 km/h) on the steepest stretch of the descent east of the Elkhorn Tunnel. Several extensions were made to this electrification, which by 1925 totalled nearly 56 miles (90 km).

The Virginian Railway was a neighbour of the Norfolk & Western (the two later amalgamated) and had similar problems with steam in the Appalachians. In 1925 it electrified 134·5 miles (216·4 km) from Mullens to Roanoke using the same system of single-phase supply and converter locomotives with three-phase motors. Unit wheel arrangements were similar to the Norfolk & Western design but the units operated in sets of three. A triple-unit locomotive provided 7,125 hp, enabling the Virginian to claim 'the most powerful locomotives in the world'.

Both these American railroads generated their own power at 25Hz, which was a convenient frequency for the low-speed heavy freight operations of their lines. In Europe Kalman Kandó of the Ganz company in Budapest was studying electric traction at 50Hz so that railways could take power from public electricity undertakings. In 1917 he was made Director with responsibility for the development of single-phase traction at the industrial frequency. The Ganz company had already gained experience of three-phase traction motors and control systems from their work in Italy and Switzerland, and Kandó therefore decided to use motors of that type in conjunction with a single-phase/three-phase converter in the locomotive. His conversion system differed from the one used in the United States both in the 50Hz frequency and in a converter designed to run on the line voltage of 16,000V, saving the weight of the transformer necessary with the 750V converters in the American locomotives.

By 1923 he had completed an experimental 0-10-0 locomotive powered by two 1,300 hp induction motors, with a control system providing four running speeds in the range from 15·5 to 42·8 mph (25 to 69 km/h). Trial running on 9·3 miles (15 km) of test track near Budapest proved the soundness of Kandó's ideas but it also showed the need for modifications and the locomotive was not ready for further trials until 1928. It then proved a complete success and in November of the same year it was decided to electrify the busy main line from Budapest to the Austrian frontier at Hegyeshalom with single-phase AC at 16,000V, 50Hz. In September 1932 the first section of 64·6 miles (104 km) to Komaron was opened, and the whole electrification to the Austrian frontier, totalling 116·8 miles (188 km) was ceremonially inaugurated on 24 July 1935.

The locomotives for this first main-line electrification at the industrial frequency were of distinctive design. Technically the phase converter was the significant feature but the huge single traction motor was equally noteworthy in its way. With an overall diameter of 10 ft 5½ in (3·14 m), it occupied the centre of the body, the upper half reaching roof level, while to make room for the lower half, which extended far below the floor, the second and third axles of the four-axle driving group were spaced 9 ft 6 in (2·90 m) apart compared with the 5 ft 8 in (1·73 m) spacing between them and the two outer axles. Most of the remainder of the body was occupied by the phase-converter at one end and the

Early experimental AC locomotives in Switzerland.

The 14½ miles (23 km) of the Swiss Federal Railways between Seebach and Wettingen were electrified with single-phase AC in 1904. Seebach-Wettingen No 1, illustrated, was equipped at first with a rotary-converter supplying DC traction motors.

Many inter-city services on the Austrian Federal Railways are worked by multiple-unit electric trains. The Class 4010 stock illustrated was introduced for this traffic in the 1980s.

control equipment at the other. Driven at a steady 1,500 rpm by a synchronous motor, the phase converter provided three-phase and six-phase outputs at the input frequency of 50Hz but in the range between 900 and 1,200V. In conjunction with pole-changing in the traction motor this gave the locomotive four economical running speeds of 10·3, 21·4, 32 and 42·4 mph (16·6, 34·4, 51·5 and 68·3 km/h).

The traction motor was rated at 2,500 hp and drove the four coupled axles through a system of side rods incorporating the linkage known as the 'Kandó triangle'. This provided continuous turning effort during vertical movements of the axles, without the use of sliding components, which in other drives of the period were subject to considerable wear.

It had been planned to build two classes of locomotive with similar electrical equipment and drives, one with four driving axles and a carrying axle front and rear, and the other with six driving axles and no separate carrying axles. The latter were intended for heavy freight work but in practice it was found that the average load of freight trains remained well

below that which had been foreseen and only three locomotives with six driving axles were built. The 1-D-1 (2-8-2) class proved adequate for freight and passenger trains and by 1937 there were 29 of them in service. These two locomotive types worked all traffic on the Budapest-Hegyeshalom line for two decades and were not withdrawn until they had been in service for some 30 years. New locomotives introduced after the Second World War still used the Kandó principle of a rotary phase converter, but the axles were driven individually by smaller, higher-speed motors and speed was controlled by converting the 50Hz input to the converter into a range of frequencies so that five economical running speeds were obtained without the complication and larger size of pole-changing motors.

Rotary converting machinery in a locomotive introduces extra losses, and in spite of the successful application of Kandó's principles alternative methods of using industrial frequency current for traction continued to be sought. As public power systems increased in extent and capacity it seemed increasingly unreasonable for railways to have to generate their own supplies. In the past it had been justified on the grounds that a public supply might not be able to cope with the railway load, but as high-voltage distribution systems spread across the industrialised countries such misgivings had little foundation.

The logical goal was a traction motor similar to the ordinary single-phase machine but able to accept the 50Hz frequency without severe sparking. This was hard to achieve. One requirement was a lower magnetic flux at each pole of the magnet system, but this meant that the number of poles for a given motor output had to be increased, leading to extra brushgear, more closely spaced round a larger commutator, with a corresponding increase in the overall size of the motor. Greater precautions against flashover were necessary, and maintenance was heavier.

It was considered in some quarters that the AC traction motor would never equal the DC machine in reliability and low maintenance. Some large locomotives were built in the United States which converted AC into DC in a motor-generator set. In the 1930s this idea became more attractive because the motor-generator might be replaced with a static mercury-arc rectifier. When the German State Railway began experiments with traction at 50Hz in 1936 the four prototype locomotives represented both the AC motor and the converter system solutions to the problem.

The section chosen for the experiment was the so-called Höllental line in the Black Forest, from Freiburg to Neustadt, a distance of 22·4 miles (36 km). It was steeply graded, and from its opening in 1887 until 1933 had been worked on a rack system. The specification of the 50Hz locomotives required them to haul trains of 177·16 tons (180 tonnes) up 1 in 20 at 37·3 mph (60 km/h) and up 1 in 40 at 52·8 mph (85 km/h). Current was switched on to the new catenary for the first time in the autumn of 1935 and the first prototype was delivered to the Freiburg motive power depot in January 1936. All locomotives had to be similar in mechanical construction to the Reichsbahn E44 class, of which series production had begun in 1932. This was a double-bogie locomotive with all axles motor-driven (Bo-Bo) and in many respects laid the foundations for future electric locomotive design in Germany.

The 50Hz version of the E44 class was classified E244. The first example was a converter locomotive using the Schön system for producing a three-phase supply. Each axle was driven by its own converter/ motor group mounted with it in the bogie. During starting the converter contributed to the tractive effort, but at higher speeds the three-phase motor took over completely. With three rotors in each group there was little room to spare in the bogies and accessibility was a problem, but in making maximum use of adhesion and in emergency braking with its motors the locomotive was outstanding. When the Höllental line was converted in 1960 from

20,000V, 50Hz, to the standard 15,000V, $16\frac{2}{3}$Hz, system of the German Federal Railway (Deutsche Bundesbahn) the locomotive was preserved by the joint efforts of the Deutsche Museum and the Karlsruhe Technical College, and given into the care of the German Railway Historical Association.

Two of the prototypes which followed were rectifier locomotives with DC motors, foreshadowing a system that was to become general in later years but with the then novel feature that the mercury-arc rectifiers were fitted with control grids so that in addition to converting AC into DC they could control the DC voltage applied to the traction motors. The fourth prototype had eight AC motors, two geared to each axle. With eight magnetic field systems, individual pole strengths were low and the transformer effect, which was the root of the commutation problem in the AC series traction motor, was reduced. As the armature of a motor revolves, the coils of the winding are short-circuited briefly by the brushes. In an AC motor a short-circuited coil behaves like the secondary of a transformer, a voltage being induced in it by the pulsating magnetic flux. A heavy current circulates in the coil, and when it is interrupted violent sparking may occur. When the future electrification system for British Railways was under consideration in 1950 a committee of engineers watched the AC motor of a German Federal Railway locomotive while starting a train of 556 tons (565 tonnes) on a 1 in 70 gradient between Munich and Stuttgart. They reported that: 'At first the sparking at the brushes was severe; it gradually diminished as the speed increased, but had not completely ceased by the time the train was running at about 10 miles per hour'.

The installation of mercury-arc rectifiers in two of the Höllental locomotives was exceptional, but

Other main-line trains in Austria, particularly those with through coaches to and from neighbouring countries, are locomotive-hauled as seen here.

The first train on London's underground Golders Green to Hendon extension in November 1923.

Right: A Victoria-Brighton electric express train from the late 1930's.

this type of rectifier was beginning to displace motor-generator sets in DC railway substations. It had the advantage of higher efficiency, and substations could work unattended, only being visited periodically for inspection and routine maintenance. Substations with motor-generator sets had been remote controlled on a limited scale, but with mercury-arc rectifiers this practice became general. When the Southern Railway in England opened its electrification to the Sussex coast in 1932, a central control room supervised the operation of the rectifiers and associated switchgear at 18 substations. These developments favoured the spread of DC railway electrification in countries not already committed to an AC system.

Outside Britain, where voltages in the 600–700V range continued to be used for the most part, DC main lines were generally electrified at 1,500 or 3,000V. In France the 1,500V DC system had its origins on the Midi Railway in the south-west and by 1938 extended from Paris to the Spanish frontier. The Midi had begun to electrify certain lines in the Pyrenees with single-phase AC at 12,000V, $16\frac{2}{3}$Hz, in 1911 and by 1917 had 70·2 miles (113 km) in service. After the First World War several committees studied existing electrifications in other countries and it was decided in 1920 that future main-line electrification in France should be at 1,500V DC. In particular, emphasis was laid on the need to use power generated at 50Hz rather than a lower frequency so that the electrified lines could be served by the interconnected distribution networks of the principal power undertakings. This was the end of the Midi's AC venture, and ironically the railway which had chosen the low-frequency AC system became the first in France to operate a main line at 1,500V DC. All the AC lines were converted except the branch from Perpignan to Villefranche, which continued to be operated at 12,000V until

1969. In only 26 months the work of conversion was far enough advanced for electric traction at 1,500V DC to be formally inaugurated from Pau to Lourdes on 30 October 1922. Public services with DC traction between Pau and Tarbes began on 1 May 1923, and in the following years were extended over the whole of the east-west main line from Toulouse to Dax. In 1926–27 electrification was completed from Bordeaux to Dax and Hendaye. The Midi amalgamated with the Paris-Orléans Railway on 1 January 1934, forming the PO-Midi Railway, and when the

PO catenary was extended southwards from Tours to Bordeaux in 1938 the route from Paris to the Spanish frontier was all-electric.

The Midi company had commercial and financial links with Great Britain. Its first DC locomotives were closely based on those operating on the North Eastern Railway's freight line from Shildon to Newport in County Durham, conveying coal from collieries to the Newport marshalling yard. Although the centre cab layout of the Newport-Shildon locomotives was not followed, the same arrangement of two motor bogies carrying the buffing and drawgear, and coupled by an articulated joint through which the tractive effort was transmitted, was adopted in the Midi design. Motors, and control gear were supplied by the British manufacturer who had equipped the Newport-Shildon locomotives. These were the forerunners of a long 'family' of Midi locomotives with the same four-axle wheel arrangement, the last of which were still in service 60 years later.

The influence of the North Eastern Railway's 1,500V DC electrification was seen further afield. Although the proposed electrification of the main line from York to Newcastle did not take place, the 4-6-4 express locomotive built with it in mind ran trials on the Newport-Shildon line and provided data for the locomotives supplied to the Great Indian Peninsula Railway for its 1,500V DC electrification in 1929. The GIP had already carried out suburban electrification round Bombay in 1925. It then started work on the main lines out of Bombay to Igatpuri and Poona, which crossed the steep mountain barrier of the Western Ghats with gradients as steep as 1 in 37. Three prototype locomotives with a wheel arrangement corresponding to a steam 4-6-2 were supplied for passenger services initially, one of which was selected as the pattern for the 21 which followed. They were rated at 2,160 hp (1,610 kW), and on a trial run with the 'Punjab Mail' one of them averaged 54 mph (87 km/h) from Bombay to Karjat. In regular service the crack train was the 'Deccan Queen' from Bombay to Poona which made the journey of 119 miles (181·5 km) including the ascent of the Bhore Ghat in 2¾ hours. The train was assisted on the Ghat section by one of the electric freight locomotives. On the more level running of the first 62 miles (99·8 km) out of Bombay the 'Deccan Queen' was scheduled to average 52 mph (83·7 km/h).

An ore train on the Kiruna-Narvik line is headed by an articulated locomotive of 9750 hp. Locomotives with side rod drive continued to be built for this service after individual gear drives were generally used elsewhere.

40 locomotives of 2,600 hp (1,940 kW) were built for freight traffic. They were double-bogie machines with all axles motor-driven. All the motive power for the GIP electrification came from Great Britain, which had a flourishing export trade in main-line electric locomotives in spite of its own use of electric locomotives being very limited at that time. Both 1,500V and 3,000V DC systems were catered for, the most numerous 3,000V locomotives being for the South African Railways, where electrification in Natal began in the 1920s.

In Europe the 3,000V DC system was adopted by Italy for its wholesale programme of electrifying main lines, begun in the inter-war years, with eventual elimination of the three-phase system in view. By 1938, 1,850 miles (2,977 km) of the Italian State Railways were operating at 3,000V compared with 1,080 miles (1,738 km) still using three-phase AC. Most DC services were worked by electric locomotives but some streamlined high-speed three-car

sets and single-unit streamlined railcars had become a characteristic feature of the Italian DC lines. Where a through route was electrified on both systems, a 'dead' section of overhead line separated them at points where they met. The incoming electric locomotive coasted through this section with lowered pantographs, coming to rest at a point where it could be shunted by a locomotive of the other system, or by a steam locomotive.

Electrification in Belgium at 3,000V DC was inaugurated on 23 April 1935 with a service of fast multiple-unit trains between Brussels and Antwerp. On 5 May the King of the Belgians made a ceremonial journey over the line to mark the day on which the Belgian National Railways attained their centenary. On the same date 100 years earlier the line from Brussels to Malines had been the first on the Continent of Europe to use steam traction.

A study group set up in Switzerland to examine alternative electrification systems found in favour of single-phase AC at 15,000V, 16⅔Hz and this conclusion was accepted by the Swiss Federal Railways. The Swiss Federal line from Berne to Scherlizgen was electrified on that system in 1919 and connected with the Berne-Lötschberg-Simplon Railway, which was already operating with single-phase AC. Electrification of the Gotthard line followed in 1921–22, and by the outbreak of war in 1939 electric traction had taken over on 74·2 per cent of the Swiss Federal network.

Early main-line electrifications in Germany were with single-phase AC at 15,000 volts, 16⅔Hz. The States of Prussia, Baden, Bavaria and Silesia had agreed to standardise this system in 1912 but the First World War prevented extensions that might have linked their networks together. When the German State Railway (Deutsche Reichsbahn) was formed in 1920, therefore, it acquired several unconnected groups of electrified lines and a variety of locomotive types. In central Germany there were lines from Leipzig to Halle and Magdeburg; in Silesia from Görlitz to Breslau; and in the south from Regensburg to Munich and the Austrian frontier, and from Basle to Zell and Sackingen. Early plans for standardising a small number of locomotive types were postponed by the economic difficulties of the 1920s, but in the early 1930s a new programme was put in hand. Further electrification to connect the widely separated electrified systems made progress in the same period, and in May 1939 the 113 miles (182 km) from Nürnberg to Saalfeld were electrified. The work continued in the early war years, reaching Leipzig in 1942. It completed the most important undertaking of the period, totalling 217·5 miles (350 km) and connecting the electrified

networks of southern and central Germany. In the post-war years this route crossed the frontier from West to East Germany between Ludwigstadt and Probstzella, 97·5 miles (157 km) from Nürnberg.

Austria dates its electrification history from 1880 when a line 984 ft (300 m) long was demonstrated at an exhibition in Vienna. There were similarities with Werner von Siemens' demonstration in Berlin a year earlier but by now the locomotive could be reversed electrically instead of through gears. There were several short electrifications with DC and AC before the First World War, but between 1912 and 1913 the State Railways of Austria, Germany, Norway, Sweden, and Switzerland agreed to standardise 15kV, 16⅔Hz. The first main-line electrification on this system in Austria was in 1912 from Innsbruck to Scharnitz on the Bavarian frontier, a distance of some 40 miles (64 km).

After the First World War Austria was cut off by its new frontiers from its former sources of coal so that electrification became a necessity. The country was fortunate in having ample hydro-electric power. A study group had been set up as early as 1905 to investigate railway electrification with power generated by this means and several power stations were working, so that a basis for expansion already existed. In 1919 the State Railways established an Electrification Department, and in 1920 an Act of Parliament authorised electrification of the Arlberg and Tauern routes, and of the Salzkammergutbahn (Stainach-Irding to Attnang-Pucheim). By 1937 the State Railways had electrified 570 miles (918 km).

Austrian locomotives in the inter-war years were mostly powered by conventional series commutator AC motors, although the alternative Winter-Eich-

The Great Northern and Milwaukee Railroads had substantial electrified sections. The GN's 41-mile scheme was brought into operation in 1929, and used 11,000 Volts AC current to power Baldwin-Westinghouse locomotives.

berg repulsion type had been developed by two engineers in Vienna and used in motor-coaches of the Stubaitalbahn (Innsbruck-Fulpmes), opened in 1904. This short line, 11 miles (18 km) long, was supplied at 2,500V, 42Hz, single-phase, foreshadowing the 50Hz electrifications of 50 years later. In 1925 the State Railways tested two locomotives of the Kandó converter type but they were not taken into stock. Another form of converter locomotive underwent trials in 1930 and was at work until the early years of the Second World War. Rotary machines converted the single-phase AC into DC for the traction motors, with stepless control of voltage on the Ward-Leonard system by varying the DC generator excitation. With its rotaries in a cylindrical housing and a cab at the rear, it closely resembled a steam locomotive with pantographs perched on boiler and firebox, a likeness increased by the coupling rods between the five driving axles, only three of which were motored. In its short career it hauled heavy loads on the Arlberg line, but when the Deutsche Reichsbahn took charge its days were numbered because it was uneconomic to keep a locomotive in running order which required its own stock of spares and specialised expertise.

In the United States the 1930s saw completion of the biggest single-phase AC electrification undertaken in the country. The Pennsylvania Railroad decided in 1923 to electrify its network of lines centred on Philadelphia. When the work was completed in 1930 the catenary extended to Trenton on the main line to New York, to Paoli on the main line to the west, and southwards towards Washington as far as Wilmington. These lines and others in the electrified network were busy suburban routes worked by multiple-unit trains, but the Pennsylvania had main-line electrification in view and announced its plans in 1928. By 1933 the gap between New York and Trenton was closed, and in 1935 electrification was extended southwards to Washington. With the whole of its New York-Washington main line electrified the railroad began work on its route to Chicago, reaching Harrisburg from Trenton in 1938. It was then operating 656 route-miles (1,056 km) at 11,000V, 25Hz, and had introduced the celebrated Class GG1 electric locomotives. A GG1 measured 79 ft 6 in (24·08 m) overall and could develop 4,620 hp (3,445 kW) continuously. The six driving axles, each driven by two motors, were grouped in two articulated sub-frames, and there was a four-wheel bogie at each end. This impressive array of axles carried a streamlined body, which in the production version of the class was refined from its less elegant original appearance by the work of the industrial designer, Raymond Loewy. The prototype GG1 attained 115 mph (185 km/h) on test runs.

The classic image of the GG1s is at the head of the 'Congressional Limited' express between New York and Washington. In 1939 the northbound train headed the list of fast runs with electric traction in the United States with an average of 71·3 mph (114·7 km/h) over the 76 miles (122·3 km) from North Philadelphia to Newark. The southbound train averaged 70·2 mph (113 km/h) over the same stretch, and the same average was maintained on this section by the westbound 'Broadway Limited' *en route* to Harrisburg and Chicago. Pennsylvania plans to extend electrification from Harrisburg to the Middle West were frustrated by the Second World War, but the work that had been done proved invaluable with electric locomotives of all classes coping with the greatly increased traffic, both passenger and freight, of the war years. It has been said of the GG1 class that, 'if the GG1 was the greatest locomotive of American electrification, World War II was its finest hour'.

As already mentioned, in northern Europe both Sweden and Norway had adopted single-phase AC electrification at 15,000V, $16\frac{2}{3}$Hz for main lines. Swedish electrification originated with 74·5 miles (120 km) of line from Kiruna to the Norwegian border at Riksgransen in Lapland, the principal traffic being iron ore. Operations began in 1911. The railway was then privately owned but it was later taken over by the Swedish State Railways, which extended the electrification from Kiruna to Lulea on the Gulf of Bothnia. Norway electrified its own

section of line from Riksgransen to the port of Narvik in 1923, completing an electric main line from the Gulf of Bothnia to the Atlantic Ocean. The whole route is known as the Lapland Iron Ore Railway and for many years was noted for its massive double-unit locomotives with side-rod drive – a feature continued here after its obsolescence elsewhere.

In southern Sweden the 285·8 miles (460 km) from Stockholm to Goteborg were electrified in 1925. Main-line electrification in Norway also dates from the 1920s. Practice in both countries was similar, much of the equipment coming from the same supplier.

Important changes in electric locomotive construction took place in the years between the world wars. Large, slow-running motors driving the axles through side rods generally gave way to smaller, faster and therefore lighter machines with gear drives. These motors might be mounted on the main frames of the locomotives or attached to the bogie frames. In either case they could not be geared directly to the axles because the action of the springs caused constant small changes in the distance between the axles and the motor shafts. The motor pinion therefore drove a large gear-wheel mounted on a hollow shaft enclosing the axle, which had freedom to move vertically and laterally, and some form of flexible coupling was provided between the hollow shaft, or quill, and the axle; or between the shaft and the driving wheels.

When motors were mounted on the main frames the driving wheelbase was fixed as in a steam locomotive. Large express locomotives were built to this pattern up to the end of the Second World War, after which bogie-mounted motors became universal. Flexible drives took many forms, not often easy to detect in looking at a locomotive, but the Buchli system could be recognised by the circular casings outside the driving wheels on one side of the locomotive which enclosed the mechanism.

In motor-coaches and low-speed locomotives the complications of a flexible drive could be avoided by the axle-hung system of motor suspension. Here, one side of the motor was attached by a resilient support to a transom in the bogie; the other side was equipped with suspension bearings through which the axle passed, carrying half the weight. Therefore, the distance between the axle and the motor shaft was fixed. The resilient mounting of the motor 'nose' allowed some movement with the springs without the centre-to-centre distance changing. It was a simple arrangement, but with the penalty that half the motor weight was unsprung.

The Brighton Belle about to leave Victoria Station, London.

16. THE RISE OF
THE DIESEL

Previous page : Diesel haulage for the Chicago & North Western's '400', which with standard steam power triggered the speed competition between Chicago and the Twin Cities in the 1930s. The train is leaving Chicago.

EARLY EXPERIMENTS in the use of internal combustion engines for rail traction were usually based on the petrol engine. Drawbacks of petrol as a fuel were the large tanks necessary to give vehicles a useful range, and the risks of storing so much highly inflammable fuel on a public vehicle. Several workers experimented with engines using heavy oil fuel towards the end of the 19th century but the first successfully to use the principle of compression ignition was Dr Rudolf Diesel in 1897. His name is now generally given to engines of this kind, although some of their features come from other inventors of earlier date. In the petrol engine the fuel in the cylinder is ignited by an electric spark, but in the diesel the fuel ignites by the heat generated by the high degree of compression. For this reason it is often called a compression ignition (ci) engine.

The diesel engine extracts more power than the petrol engine from the same amount of energy in the fuel, and its fuel cost per mile is only about half that for petrol. On the other hand it must be of heavier and more robust construction and larger for a given power output because its maximum running speed is about 1,500 rpm compared with 5,000 rpm or more for the petrol engine. The power delivered depends on the amount of fuel burned in the cylinders on each power stroke, and the number of such strokes per minute.

A problem of using any kind of internal combustion engine for rail traction is that it develops no tractive effort until it is running, unlike the steam engine where tractive effort is effective as soon as steam is admitted to the cylinders and exerts pressure on the pistons, or the electric motor, in which the flow of current through the windings immediately produces a turning force or torque. Therefore, the diesel engine has to be started 'off load' and connected with the wheels after it is running. In the early experimental years this was a problem because the conventional type of motorcar clutch and gearbox could only handle a limited power input.

An electrical system was an alternative to mechanical transmission, the engine driving a generator which supplied current to traction motors geared to the axles as in an electric locomotive. Some of the earliest practical diesel units were in fact described as 'electric power houses'. They ran on the Buenos Aires Great Southern Railway in Argentina in 1929, attached to suburban trains with motors taking current from the 'power house' travelling with them. This was not an economic way of converting diesel power to electric power and then to mechanical power. There had to be 'feedback' between the diesel engine and the generator or in some circumstances the current demand would overload the generator, and in others the power produced by the diesel engine would not be fully utilised.

Electrical power (kilowatts) is the product of volts and amperes. When a diesel locomotive is travelling

The two-car diesel-electric 'Fliegender Hamburger' high-speed unit leaving Berlin.

fast, the current (amperes) is relatively low, being restrained by the reverse voltage developed by the motors. The generator voltage must therefore be high to keep current flowing against the opposition. On reaching an adverse gradient the locomotive will be slowed (assuming the diesel engine is already giving its full power) and the motors will take more current. The generator voltage must therefore be reduced so that the electrical power demand remains equivalent to the mechanical power at the engine shaft. In all modern diesel motive power the adjustments necessary all the time the locomotive is at work are made automatically. When power demand changes it is sensed by the engine governor, and the governor is linked with the electrical system so that when the delivery of fuel is adjusted there is a corresponding adjustment in the generator output.

The first dramatic impact of diesel power on railway working came from the German Reichsbahn. Early in 1932 the Reichsbahn announced details of a new high-speed diesel train and later in the year the new unit made a demonstration run from Berlin to Hamburg at an average speed of 75 mph (120·7 km/h) for the journey of 178 miles (286·5 km). The train was a two-car articulated unit powered by two 410 hp diesel engines, each mounted on one end bogie. Each diesel engine drove a diesel generator supplying current to the two traction motors in the central bogie of the set. The design of the coach bodies was based on wind tunnel tests in the Zeppelin works at Friedrichshafen, resulting in the choice of a low-pitched outline with the roofs rounded at the end to minimise wind resistance. Internally, the

train seated 102 passengers; there was a small buffet and luggage compartments.

Up to 1932 the best steam expresses in Germany had been limited to a top speed of 62 mph (100 km/h) in normal running, or 68 mph (109·4 km/h) when making up time. To maintain its 75 mph (120·7 km/h) average the diesel train would have to travel much faster than this. Before it went into service on the Berlin–Hamburg line the signalling was altered to increase the braking distance from a warning signal to a stop signal from 765·5 yd (700 m) to 1,312 yd (1,200 m), which was safe for a speed of 93 mph (150 km/h). A general move to higher speeds was afoot, and the maximum permitted speed

Streamlined 4-6-4 No 05.001 of the Deutsche Reichsbahn, began service in 1935.

The first of the Reichsbahn high-speed tank engines with streamlining partly removed. No 61.001, illustrated, was a 4-6-4; its sister engine, 61.002, a 4-6-6.

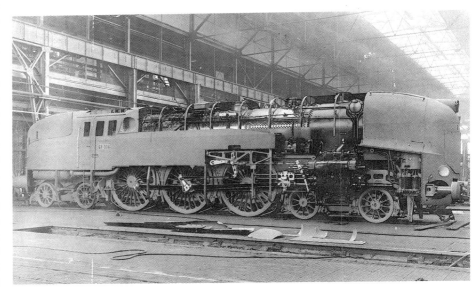

The Kruckenberg 'Rail Zeppelin' on a trial run from Hannover.

The Great Western Railway used some of its AEC diesel railcars to accelerate cross-country services. The car illustrated has arrived at Cardiff after a fast run from Birmingham. There is a buffet compartment at the rear.

for steam locomotives was raised to 75 mph (120·7 km/h).

Announcement of the schedule for the new Hamburg–Berlin diesel service in 1933 brought a new sensation for the speed of the demonstration run was to be improved on, the unit being required to cover the distance from Hamburg to Berlin in 2 hr 18 min, an average speed of 77·5 mph (124·7 km/h). Two minutes more were allowed for the northbound journey. The new service began on 15 May 1933 and was named the 'Fliegende Hamburger' ('Flying Hamburger'). A businessman or woman could now leave Berlin at 8.02 am, spend nearly five hours in Hamburg, and be home again at 5.36 pm. For the first time in railway history a train was required to run at speeds up to 100 mph (160·9 km/h) on parts of its journey in order to keep time.

In promoting the new service the Reichsbahn sought among its 1,140 railcar drivers for one whose appearance would suggest special competence and reliability, to reassure passengers that the 'Flying Hamburger' would bring them punctually and safely to their destination. When located, a portrait of him seated at the controls with a suitably de-termined expression was reproduced in the Reichs-bahn Calendar. A now familiar photograph of the train in a woodland setting was sold as a postcard on board with the words 'At 160 kilometres an hour' printed next to the dateline.

The success of the 'Flying Hamburger' encouraged the railway to introduce more services of this kind in 1935 and to improve the vehicles. There had been some complaints of restricted space in the original 'Flying Hamburger' cars, in which the seats were

arranged three on one side of the aisle and one on the other. The new sets for this service had a two-plus-one seating plan, and the seats had armrests. The overall length of a unit was increased from 133 ft (40.54 m) to 145 ft 3 in (45 m) but its seating capacity was reduced. However, the new units could be operated in pairs when more seats were required. Steam services were being accelerated at the same time, giving rise to friendly rivalry between the two branches of engineering. A cartoon of the period showed one of Dr Wagner's streamlined steam locomotives, its casing looking like the business end of a shark, opening its jaws to swallow the 'Flying Hamburger'. The motive for the drawing was prob-ably the occasion when a relief 'Flying Hamburger' service was insufficient to carry all the traffic and a

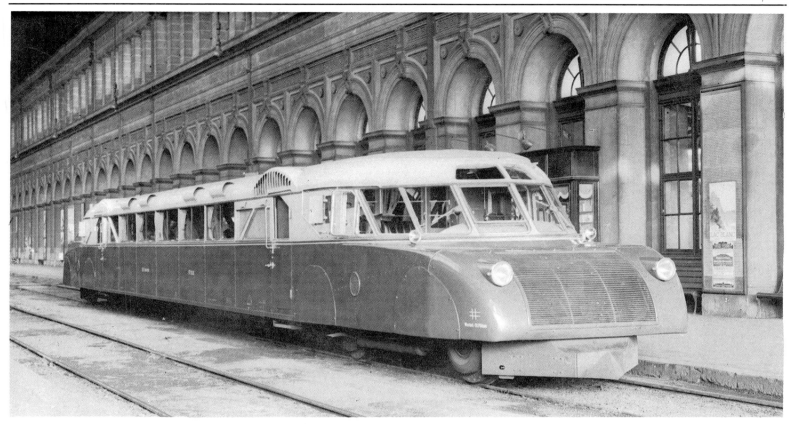

Railcars also appeared in Austria in the 1930s. This Daimler vehicle stands in the Sudbahnhof at Vienna.

steam train had to be substituted. Dr Wagner had a print of the drawing on the wall of his office.

Taking advantage of the new units at its disposal in 1935, the Reichsbahn introduced more and even faster diesel services. It could now claim the fastest scheduled run on rails in the world with the 82·3 mph (132·4 km/h) of its 'Fliegende Kölner' (Flying Cologner') over the 157·8 miles (254 km) from the Tiergarten station in Berlin to Hannover. This service was for Cologne business people visiting Berlin. Departure from Cologne was at 7 am and after stops at Dusseldorf, Essen, Duisberg, Dortmund, Hamm and Hannover the train reached Tiergarten at 12.10 pm, and the Friedrichstrasse station at 12.20. Even with these six stops the train averaged 69·6 mph (112 km/h) for the whole distance of 359·5 miles (578·5

km). The return train in the evening left Tiergarten at 7.21 pm and, omitting the Duisberg stop but serving the other stations as before, reached Cologne at 12.18 am. The diesel cut the best time by steam train between Berlin and Cologne by 1 hr 22 min.

A long day, from 6.40 am to 11.29 pm, was ahead of the Frankfurt businessman or woman using the 'Fliegende Frankfurter' ('Flying Frankfurter') service but they would have plenty of time in Berlin. The journey of 335·3 miles (539·6 km) was made at an average speed eastbound of 65·7 mph (105·6 km/h) inclusive of stops at Erfurt and Leipzig; and 65·9 mph (106 km/h) westbound with an additional stop at Weissenfeld. Much of this route was hilly but good use was made of the level stretch between Leipzig and the Anhalter station in Berlin, the 102·2 miles (164·47 km) being covered at an average speed of 80·7 mph (130 km/h) westbound and 79·6 mph (128·1 km/h) eastbound.

Among the new stock ordered for the 1935 programme were four three-car units with two 600 hp engines. Two of them had electric transmission as in the earlier sets, and two had an hydraulic system. The hydraulic transmission consisted of a device called a torque-converter in which there were two turbine wheels, one driven by the engine and the other connected by cardan shafts to the axles of the power bogie. The converter casing contained oil and was fitted internally with blades similar to those on the turbine wheels. When the wheel driven by the engine revolved, the oil circulated inside the casing and was deflected by the fixed blades back to the blades of the second turbine, causing this to revolve as well and transmit power to the axles. The angle of the fixed blades was chosen so that at starting the

Some PLM Paris-Lyons services were worked by Bugatti railcars. The driver's 'conning tower' above the engine room was characteristic of the Bugatti design. Due to vision problems when shunting, there was a lookout man's position on the 'ground floor'.

transmission turbine revolved slowly but with a strong turning force, which was translated into high tractive effort at the wheels. As the car accelerated, the speed of the transmission turbine approached that of the engine-driven turbine, the effect of which was to reduce the tractive effort progressively as the speed increased. The result was similar to that of electric transmission, giving automatic protection against the engine being overloaded, or operating wastefully by consuming fuel without the power developed being fully used. In later years torque-converter transmissions of this type were used in large diesel locomotives. The power they could handle was less than that of an electric system and so for powers of 2,000 hp and above two diesel engines and two transmissions were installed.

Before the hydraulic transmission was installed in the Reichsbahn railcar sets it had been tested in the so-called 'Rail Zeppelin' of Carl Kruckenberg,

a high-speed propeller-driven vehicle. A practical machine of this kind had been built by German airmen in Palestine for transporting stores by rail when no orthodox motive power was available. After the Armistice of 1918 a prototype machine of a similar type was built for repatriating German troops. At that time the German railways were disorganised and short of motive power but thousands of aircraft engines were available. Tests of the propeller-driven machine were disappointing, however, and no use was made of it. During the war the Aeronautical Research Institute in Germany had tested aircraft propellers by mounting them with an engine on a trolley running on a special track. Speeds up to 87 mph (140 km/h) were attained. These experiments were to test the propeller rather than the vehicle, but the engineer responsible, Carl Geissen, continued them after the war with a rail transport application in view. In the report of the

Two early types of diesel railcar on the Union Pacific. Motor Car 4 in the foreground is coupled to a baggage trailer.

A Great Western three-car diesel train formed of two AEC diesel cars with a standard passenger coach between them.

Aeronautical Research Institute of 1918–19 he declared that:

For the first time the propeller-driven rail vehicle has become a reality, and at the same time there has been a demonstration of the advantage offered to rail transport by lightweight construction techniques developed in the aircraft and power generation industries, using small components made of high-quality materials, ball bearings for powered axles, well-designed vertical and lateral suspension, and designs which minimise wind resistance.

Geissen made preliminary drawings of a three-car

propeller-driven train some 230 ft (70 m) in length which would seat 224 passengers and weigh only 44·29 tons (45 tonnes). He put his plans before the Prussian-Hessian State Railway on 27 October 1919 but his idea was not followed up.

In the 1920s the Aeronautical Research Institute wished to carry on propeller research using Geissen's original vehicle and approached the Reichsbahn seeking a suitable section of track. The Reichsbahn was already having discussions with Kruckenberg whose Air-Rail Company was planning a high-speed overhead railway. It could offer 5 miles (8 km) of track where Fritz von Opel had been experiment-

The Burlington 'Pioneer Zephyr' and the Union Pacific's M-10000 in Kansas City station.

Opposite above : The 'Denver Zephyr' leaves Denver behind a twin-unit diesel-electric locomotive totalling 4000 hp. *Opposite below :* The three-car 'Burlington Zephyr' (later renamed 'Pioneer Zephyr') was the progenitor of a fleet of diesel trains with the 'Zephyr' title on the Burlington Route.

ing with rocket propulsion and suggested that Geissen and Kruckenberg should get together. Kruckenberg by now had decided that his overhead system was too costly. He saw the final phase of von Opel's rocket-propulsion experiments, during which the car had reached 157·2 mph (253 km/h), and had been impressed by the stability of the vehicle at speed in spite of its light weight. While collaborating in Geissen's aeronautical research when the test track became vacant, he pursued his own idea of a propeller-driven high-speed passenger-carrying rail vehicle. According to his memoirs, he thought of a suitable design while out for a walk with his dog and sketched it on the back of an envelope. The building of a prototype lightweight steel body began in February 1929. On completion the vehicle underwent trials on a high-speed test section which is now part of the line from Hannover to Celle. Kruckenberg's work reached its climax on 21 June 1930 when his 'Rail Zeppelin' covered 159·75 miles (257 km) of the Hamburg–Berlin main

line in 98 minutes, and for 6·25 miles (10 km) maintained 143 mph (230·1 km/h).

It is hard to imagine a propeller-driven vehicle running through the stations on an ordinary line, possibly creating havoc with its slipstream, but such a thing might be possible on one of the special high-speed lines that are being built today. But there was another drawback to adopting a propeller system at that time. The railways were not looking for speeds much above 93 mph (150 km/h) which would have meant that for much of the time the propeller would be working at below its maximum efficiency. The Rail Zeppelin was later rebuilt for testing the Fottinger hydraulic transmission which was used in some of the high-speed railcar sets, and Kruckenberg's participation in this work gives him an honoured place among the pioneers of high-speed rail transport in Germany.

In France in the 1930s there was a period when some fast railcar services were worked by Bugatti vehicles with engines using a petrol-alcohol-benzol

mixture as fuel, fired by magneto ignition. There were single, double, and three-car units, all powered by two or four 200 hp engines. In all versions the engine room was central, with the driving position in a 'conning tower' above it. From this position the driver could only see the track some way ahead and so for use in shunting and when very careful running was necessary, as in fog, there were seats for a look-out man at each end of the car. He could communicate with the driver and also stop the train himself in an emergency. One of his tasks was to listen for fog signals, which the driver might not be able to hear, and he was therefore known to the staff as 'the banger man'.

All the Bugattis had mechanical transmission with fluid couplings between engine and propeller shaft. A fluid coupling acts as a clutch, transmitting the drive when the engine is accelerated, but it does not multiply torque in the manner of a torque-converter. Three-car units and certain 'twins' working on services with frequent stops were fitted

Top: The Santa Fe's 'Super Chief' on the double-horseshoe curve near Ribera, New Mexico, on the Chicago-Los Angeles run.
Above: The 'Super Chief' approaches Chicago at the end of its run of 41¾ hours.

The Bugattis worked on such important routes as Paris–Strasbourg, Paris–Cherbourg and Le Havre, Paris–Trouville, and Paris–Lyons. Full meals or light refreshments were available on some services. All the cars were stored during the war but a number were returned to traffic from 1945 onwards and some remained at work until the late 1950s.

High-speed diesel services in Germany reached their climax in 1939. At that time the 'Fliegende Kölner' was the fastest train in the world with an average speed of 83·3 mph (134 km/h) from Hamm to Hannover. From 1938 the German high-speed fleet included the non-articulated three-car sets ordered in 1935 with a 600 hp engine and electric transmission in each power car. Passenger accommodation was divided between the central trailer and one power car. The other power car incorporated a kitchen and a restaurant section. All these services were withdrawn on the outbreak of the Second World War and were not restored subsequently.

There was a less dramatic but significant application of diesel power in England in 1933 when the Great Western Railway began to operate diesel railcars with mechanical transmission on local services. The bodies were streamlined on the basis of wind tunnel tests, which were said to have shown that the wind resistance at high speed was only one-fifth of that of a square-ended car. After the first 230 hp single-unit cars, the GWR ordered some 260 hp cars with buffet accommodation and put them to work on the cross-country journey between Birmingham and Cardiff. On this route the average speed was a not very impressive 50 mph (80·5 km/h) but was a useful improvement over the previous steam schedules. Top speed of the cars was between 75 and 80 mph (120·7 and 128·7 km/h). Where the route allowed fast running they could put up good performances and one of them was timed to average 68 mph (109·4 km/h) over a 40-mile (64·3 km) stretch of the line from Oxford to Paddington. These cars foreshadowed the widespread use of diesel multiple-unit trains by British Railways from the 1950s onwards.

Also in the 1930s the London Midland & Scottish Railway experimented with diesel locomotives for shunting, choosing a diesel-electric system after comparative trials with other types. When British Railways began building diesel shunters in large numbers after the Second World War the standard 0-6-0 type adopted was derived with only minor modifications from the 450 hp shunter which had been at work on the LMS.

In the United States as in Europe there were early experiments with petrol engines for rail traction. The Chicago, Burlington & Quincy operated petrol railcars, which were virtually buses on rails, as early as 1922, and although the Central Railroad of New Jersey had introduced a 300 hp diesel-electric shunter in 1925, the Chicago Great Western chose a petrol-electric system for its 'Blue Bird' service in

with two-speed gearboxes but in the rest the proportion of power to weight was such that gearboxes were considered unnecessary. It was also a characteristic of the engines that they developed a high torque at low revolutions.

Between 1933 and 1938 Bugatti supplied 76 railcars of different types to the Etat, PLM and Alsace-Lorraine Railways. All versions had four-axle bogies, either one or two axles being driven. The body weight was carried by large longitudinal laminated springs. No load was taken by the centre pivot, which was for guidance only and was constructed as an hydraulic vertical shock absorber.

During trials of an 800 hp unit on the Etat system in October 1934 a speed of 115 mph (185 km/h) was averaged over a distance of 3·7 miles (6 km) and a top speed of 119·3 mph (192 km/h) was attained – a record in France for speed on rails.

1929. This was a three-car train running between the Twin Cities (St Paul and Minneapolis) and Rochester, Minnesota. A six-cylinder engine developing 300 hp at 900 rpm drove a generator supplying current to two traction motors in the leading bogie of the first vehicle, which was a combined power, baggage, and mail car. The other vehicles were a day coach with 74 seats and a parlour-club-cafe car seating 57. In this vehicle there were also four Pullman sections for invalids travelling to a sanatorium at Rochester, and a 'well-stocked buffet serving meals at any time'. The parlour section was furnished 'with the same luxury as the best-equipped steam trains', having seats and tables for parties of four, armchairs, carpets, smokers' companions, lighters and table lamps. Externally the train was coloured blue, with gilt lettering. These amenities

did not survive the slump of 1930 and memories of the 'Blue Bird' were soon submerged by the rising diesel tide.

Metallurgical progress was greatly improving the power/weight ratio of diesel engines, while new and strong light alloys enabled lightweight rolling stock to be built. A new 600 hp diesel engine designed by General Motors in 1932 weighed only 20 lb (9 kg) per horsepower. It caught the attention of Ralph Budd, President of the Chicago Burlington & Quincy, who realised its potential as the power unit of a high-speed train. In 1933 he ordered one of these engines and at the same time commissioned the E. G. Budd Manufacturing Company of Philadelphia to build a lightweight streamlined train of three cars.

As soon as the train was delivered in 1934, General Motors began work on installing the power plant.

The 'City of Denver' streamliner, a ten-car train, was the Union Pacific's answer to the Burlington's 'Denver Zephyr'. *Inset*: The power of the 'City of Denver' comes from a three-unit diesel totalling 3600 hp.

Evidently the task was full of problems, for when the engineer-in-charge was questioned about them he replied diplomatically: 'I don't remember any trouble with the dipstick'. In April 1934 the train was ready for a trial run, and a maximum of 104 mph (167·4 km/h) at once made it a focus of attention. The Chicago World Fair was being held in May, with a 'Wings of the Century' pageant as a high point. Budd announced that he would run the train from the foot of the Rockies at Denver to the show ground in Chicago in 14 hours for the distance of 1,015 miles (1633·5 km), timing its arrival to coincide with the climax of the pageant. In fact he improved on the promise, for the train left Denver at 7.05 am and broke the timing tape in Halstead Street, Chicago in 13 hr 5 min from the start. Budd demonstrated the smoothness of the ride by shaving himself with a cut-throat razor *en route*, repeating an experiment said to have been conducted by some of the passengers in the transcontinental theatrical special of 1876. There were no casualties on either occasion.

By the time of its record Denver–Chicago run the diesel train had become known as the 'Burlington Zephyr'. It is said that Budd chose the name himself after re-reading Chaucer's *Canterbury Tales*, but his train and those which followed swept across the West at somewhat higher velocity than the sweet breath of Zephyrus that encouraged the Canterbury Pilgrims to mount horse and amble towards their goal. An episode on the 'Zephyr's' journey to Chicago has found its place in diesel lore. At one point a steel door was slammed and cut a cable. The engined faltered but Roy Baer, a General Motors mechanic, seized the severed ends and held them together until the engine was running smoothly again. His hands were burned but he earned a place in history.

The 'Burlington Zephyr' went into regular service between Lincoln (Nebraska), Omaha and Kansas City on 11 November 1934. It was the prelude to new Zephyr trains on the Burlington system and was later renamed the 'Pioneer Zephyr'. The train remained in service for 25 years before being retired in 1960 to a permanent place in the Chicago Museum of Science & Industry, having carried over a million passengers and travelled more than 3 million miles (4,828,030 km).

Another three-car diesel had been on show at the Chicago World's Fair in 1934. This was the Union Pacific's M-10000 streamliner, fresh from a demonstration tour of the country from coast to coast. It was unusual in that although the engine ran on diesel fuel it had electric ignition. After the Fair it went into revenue-earning service between Kansas City and Salina, under the name 'City of Salina'.

On the wall of the 'Super Chief's' Turquoise Room (a private dining room) is a valuable turquoise and silver medallion made by Navajo Indians of New Mexico.

Union Pacific followed its M10000 with the six-car M10001 illustrated here. It was later renamed 'City of Portland'.

The first and second 'City of San Francisco' streamliners at Southern Pacific's Oakland Pier station in 1940.

A six-car train, M-10001, was also built and in October 1934 made a demonstration run from Los Angeles to New York in 56 hr 55 min. The time of 38 hr 47 min from Los Angeles to Chicago was 6 hr 6 min shorter than the previous record between the cities which had been set up as long ago as 1905 on the Atchison Topeka & Santa Fe route. M-10001 went to work between Chicago and Portland in 1935 as the 'City of Portland'. The time of 39¾ hours for the 2,272 miles (3,656 km) was 18 hours less than the fastest steam service of the time.

From these beginnings there sprouted a family of Zephyrs on the Burlington and Cities on the Union Pacific serving various routes of the two companies. Among them was Chicago to the Twin Cities (St Paul and Minneapolis) where the Burlington began a Super Zephyr service in 1935. The diesels equalled the 6½-hour timing of the steam '400' and 'Hiawatha' although the Burlington route was 34 miles (54·7 km) longer than that of the '400' and 21 miles (32·2 km) longer than the 'Hiawatha's'. The success of all these fast long-distance trains was such that the original short formations soon proved inadequate for the traffic. When the Burlington started a 'Denver Zephyr' service in 1936 the trains were of 12 cars and had a total installed power of

3,000 hp, of which 1,800 hp was in the main articulated power car and 1,200 hp in the booster unit coupled next to it. In effect these were separate locomotives, but they continued to be styled similarly to the original Zephyr sets up to 1939. The 'Denver Zephyr' was an overnight service between Chicago and Denver with all the amenities of the crack steam expresses plus novelties such as a soda fountain, a radiogram, and sockets for electric razors. The diesels were now entering the luxury class. The Union Pacific replied to the Burlington with the 'City of Denver', a 10-car train comprising three Pullman sleeping cars, a Pullman observation car, two reclining chair cars, and three cars carrying the power plant, baggage and mail.

Another diesel launch of 1936 was the 'Super Chief' of the Atchison Topeka & Santa Fe, a successor to the company's long-established 'Chief' express between Chicago and Los Angeles. Covering the 2,228 miles (3,585·6 km) in 39¾ hours, the 'Super Chief' merited its title by cutting the steam train's time by 11¼ hours. This was an all-Pullman service headed by a separate twin-unit diesel locomotive aggregating 3,600 hp. This was to be the future pattern of US diesel locomotives. General Motors had developed the idea of a 'modular' diesel-electric

Below: An eastbound local train of the Erie Railroad at Howles, New York, passes box cars on a siding.
Centre: A baggage car with auxiliary power plant and dormitory accommodation for the crew is marshalled between three diesel units and the passenger cars of the 'City of Los Angeles'.
Top right: The 'Royal Gorge' of the Denver & Rio Grande Western Railroad threads the stupendous scenery in the canyon after which the train is named.
Below right: Erie Railroad diesels head 9,000 tons (9,144 tonnes) of freight crossing the State borderline in New Jersey and entering Pennsylvania.

locomotive made up of units each powered by a 1,800 hp diesel engine; the leading unit, with a driving position, was the 'cab' unit, and additional 'booster' units with similar power equipment could be added as necessary. When the demand for diesel power grew after the entry of the United States into the Second World War, the War Production Board decided to give all orders for diesels other than shunting locomotives to General Motors as the most experienced builders, thus fixing the pattern of the large US diesel for years to come.

The diesel locomotive had now penetrated the heartlands of American history. The Union Pacific's 'Cities' swept across the great plains where once 'the plumed hereditary lord of all America heard in this last fastness the scream of the "bad medicine wagon" charioting his foes'. Then the trains plunged into the fifteen tunnels that took them through the High Sierras and into California. Passengers in the Pullmans of the 'Super Chief' sipped their drinks as they sped south along the trail where in earlier times stage coaches 'gotten up in elegant style' had rumbled behind teams of eight mules from Independence to Santa Fe, each guarded by eight armed men 'ready, in case of attack, to discharge 136 shots without having to reload'.

17. WAR AND RETRENCHMENT

IN THE WAR OF 1939–45 tanks and armoured fighting vehicles played the part once foreseen for the armoured train or rail gun. Railways were targets for the heavy bomber in the effort to disrupt supply routes. For home defence in Britain, however, twelve armoured trains were built early in the war when the island was under the threat of invasion. They patrolled seven zones, covering coastal and inland areas where landings might be made from the sea or by parachute. The main armament was a Hotchkiss Mk II gun carried on a 20-ton (20·32-tonne) coal wagon with armour protection. Six Bren light machine-guns were shared between two armoured fighting trucks, between which the loco-motive was coupled. This was an ex-Great Eastern Railway 2-4-2 tank engine with its side tanks and bunker protected by armour plate.

The low and flat area of Romney Marsh, with the Dungeness peninsula, were seen as particularly vulnerable. The Southern Railway skirted the area but the 15 in (38·1 cm) gauge Romney Hythe & Dymchurch Light Railway ran across the marsh to the tip of the peninsula. It had been built as a tourist attraction and to serve holiday camps but now military importance was thrust upon it. The 4-8-2 locomotive *Hercules* and two wagons were armoured, and the wagons equipped with ring mountings for Lewis guns and anti-tank rifles. With this armament the train could provide extra fire power for coastal defence troops in an emergency.

Wartime transport demands in Britain had to be met by the railways with depleted staffs and reduced maintenance services. Their tasks began with the evacuation of children from London and other cities, for which nearly 4,000 special trains were run. Then came the transport of expeditionary forces to France, and in 1940 to Norway, followed by a masterstroke of last-minute improvisation when at short notice Dunkirk was evacuated and 319,000 men arriving from France had to be con-veyed to destinations throughout the country. The climax came in 1944 when the transport of forces and material to the coast for the invasion of Europe was by far the biggest undertaking of the kind the railways in Britain had ever faced.

War conditions in Britain and Germany produced a new breed of 'austerity' locomotives of functional simplicity. O. V. S. Bulleid's Q1 class 0-6-0 for the Southern Railway is often considered to have earned the palm for the ugliest locomotive to come from a country where once elegance of design had been an inspiration to engineers abroad. The same designer's 'Merchant Navy' class Pacifics had an 'air-smoothed' casing that earned them the nick-name of 'Spam cans'. This was ostensibly a mixed traffic design, or construction in wartime would not have been sanc-

Two 2-8-2 + 2-8-2 Mallet locomotives give rear-end assistance to a heavy freight on the Denver & Rio Grande Western.

A 'Big Boy' 4-8-8-4 of the Union Pacific rolls freight eastwards from California in the 1940s.

tioned, and it would have been indiscreet to call it 'streamlined'.

The German 'Austerities' had their origin in the severe drain on motive power caused by the invasion of Russia. To resolve the situation Albert Speer, Minister for Armaments and War Production, was instructed to take a hand, and recorded in his memoirs how the introduction of assembly line methods and standardisation increased production from 1,918 locomotives in 1941 to 2,367 in 1942, while in 1943 the output was up to 5,243. These were the *Kriegslokomotiven* (War Locomotives), a 2-10-0 design produced in four varieties with small differences in dimensions and weight, one of which had a condensing tender for use in Russia where watering facilities were limited.

In spite of the growing dominance of the diesel, steam development continued in the United States during the war. In the early war years the Pennsylvania adopted a 'duplex' design in which two two-cylinder steam engines were carried in one rigid frame, each driving its own set of coupled wheels. The first 'duplex' of 1939, a 6-4-4-6, was the largest rigid-frame passenger locomotive ever built. This prototype was followed by a 4-4-4-4 class, and then by wheel arrangements of 4-6-4-4 and 4-4-6-4 for freight traffic. A more successful venture into the steam super power class was the Union Pacific's articulated 4-8-8-4 of 1941. These engines, popularly called the 'Big Boys', could develop 3,000 hp at the drawbar at a speed of 10 mph (16 km/h) and maintain this output for an hour or more on a continuously rising gradient of 1 in 85.

At the end of the war, countries on the mainland of Europe faced with reconstructing shattered railway systems embarked on large-scale programmes

The Union Pacific also used massive 4-6-6-4s for heavy freight work. No X3999 was photographed at a crossing in Utah.

Western Region diesel-hydraulic B-B No 807 *Caradoc* of the 'Warship' class rounds the Noss curve beside the River Dart on the descent to Kingswear.
Below: The 'Western' class C-C locomotives were the most powerful diesel-hydraulics on the Western Region. No 1035 *Western Yeoman* pulls away from Bristol Temple Meads with an express to Paignton.

Class 221, was similar except for having two engines of 1,350 hp (1,007kW). Some 50 locomotives of this class were built between 1962 and 1965. Both classes bore the brunt of main-line traffic on non-electrified routes but from the middle 1960s the spread of electrification progressively reduced their sphere of action. At the same time the power-handling capacity of hydraulic transmissions was being increased so that in 1968 the Bundesbahn was able to introduce the Class 218 diesel with one 2,500 hp (1,864 kW) diesel engine and a single torque-converter system from which the drive was taken to both bogies. Two series of these locomotives were built and eventually 250 were in service.

The British Railways modernisation plan of 1955 provided for diesel traction on non-electrified main lines. A variety of prototypes were ordered, mainly diesel-electric, but hydraulic transmission was chosen for the Western Region. The three main diesel-hydraulic types on this Region were the B-B 'Warships' of 2,200 hp (1,640 kW), the C-C 'Western' class of 2,700 hp (2,013 kW) and the 1,700 hp (1,267 kW) 'Hymek' class. The Warships and Westerns had two engines and two hydraulic transmissions, each with three torque converters. A single con-

French National Railways two-car diesel units, Class ETG.

BR 'Warship' No D845 *Sprightly* stands at Exeter St Davids with a train for Bristol.

verter could not provide the required tractive effort/speed characteristic over the range required and so the three converters operated in an automatic sequence. The Hymek was a single-engined locomotive with one torque converter operating in conjunction with an automatic gearbox. After a comparative study of hydraulic and electric transmissions, British Railways decided that the balance was in favour of the electric system. The Western class diesels outlived the other two but the last were withdrawn in 1976.

The replacement of steam with diesel power which gathered pace worldwide after the Second World War had begun in the war years in the United States. By 1948 production of steam locomotives had all but ceased. In that year diesel orders reached a peak of 2,850 units, and by 1950 only 12 steam locomotives were ordered against 2,400 diesels. The pattern in the United States was soon followed in

Canada. The Canadian National had, in fact, two 1,300 hp (969 kW) diesel main-line units as early as 1928. They were able to work individually or coupled as a 2,600 hp (1,938 kW) locomotive but the economic depression of the 1930s put a stop to further development. One of the units was in service throughout the war, however, and not withdrawn until 1946. From 1954 diesel-electric locomotives worked over the whole length of the CPR and CNR transcontinental routes. In 1955 the transcontinental services were further accelerated with the introduction of the 'Canadian' express on the CPR and the 'Super-Continental' on the Canadian National. By that time the timetables showed gains of between 14 and 16 hours compared with steam working.

Wartime development of the gas turbine suggested that this might be an economic power unit for railways. It was adopted in the USA by the

Erecting the overhead 25 kV catenaries outside Liverpool Street station for the electrification to Hertford and Bishops Stortford in 1960.

A heavy goods vehicle and trailer mounted on a low-floor wagon for transport by rail on the German Federal Railway.

Union Pacific for heavy freight service as a successor to the steam 'Big Boys' and by 1957 a fleet of 25 was in operation. In Britain the Western Region of British Railways purchased a 2,500 hp (1,864 kW) gas turbine locomotive from Switzerland in 1950 and ordered a 3,000 hp (2,237 kW) unit from a British manufacturer, which went into service in 1952. None of these locomotives proved as satisfactory in railway operating terms as the diesels and their working lives were relatively short. The British-built locomotive was eventually converted into a 25kV electric unit for driver training preparatory to the opening in 1960 of the Manchester-Crewe section of the London Midland Region's Manchester and Liverpool to London electrification. Canada adopted gas turbines for its CNR Montreal-Toronto Turbotrains in 1968. The French National Railways has also used the gas turbine in trainsets on routes where a light and fast unit meets the traffic requirements. Experience has shown gas turbine propulsion to be more suitable for services of that kind than for the varied duties that must be undertaken by a locomotive. From 1970 the SNCF gas turbine units of Classes ETG and RTG were providing non-electrified lines with services comparable in speed with those on the electrified sections of the system.

Railways as a whole showed an unsuspected inventiveness in meeting the increasingly severe competition from road and air transport in the post-war years. Before they were nationalised in 1948 some of the British companies had tackled the problems of handling small freight consignments by introducing zonal schemes. Each zone had a railhead to which traffic was brought in the railways' own road vehicles. Here it was possible to make up complete wagonloads for other railheads from which the individual consignments were delivered to the addressees by road. Trunk rail freight services travelled between railheads. Under these schemes many small stations at which previously local freight trains had called became simply collecting points from which traffic was despatched to railheads. Similar schemes were continued and extended by British Railways. They foreshadowed the general move which was to come later towards handling freight in full wagonloads or in complete trains with all wagons for the same destination.

Containers for door-to-door transport without transhipment of their contents had been introduced on a small scale before the war. Since 1948 it has become an international activity conducted by specialist organisations. The railways provide the

train services between container terminals and there are various arrangements between them and the container companies regarding the terminal sites and their equipment with cranage for transferring containers between road vehicles and the rail wagons, or 'container flats' as they are often called. The British container organisation is Freightliners Ltd, a wholly owned subsidiary of British Rail but operating as an independent company. In 1983 it owned 5,800 containers, vehicles and 25 of the 35 terminals it served. Freightliner trains normally consist of 20 wagons in four sets of five. At certain points on their routes the sets of wagons are exchanged between trains according to their destinations. The longest through working in 1983 was Coatbridge (Glasgow) to Southampton, 470 miles (756·4 km).

Several other types of door-to-door service by combining rail and road transport without transhipment of goods have been developed. They stem in the main from the 'piggyback' system introduced in the USA by the Southern Pacific Railroad in 1953 in which road trailers were loaded on to flat wagons to travel by rail for the major part of their journeys. Similar schemes were adopted in Europe under a variety of names. In the *Rollende Landstrasse* system operated by the German Federal Railway complete road vehicles, comprising tractor and

Three levels of track on the descent through the Biaschina ravine, south of the Gotthard tunnel, are seen in this picture. In the foreground two Re 4/4 locomotives of the Swiss Federal Railways have negotiated the two upper levels with their train of containers.

Right: 'Cisalpin' Trans-Europ Express (Paris-Venice) in the Rhône Valley. Here the train is operating on 15000V AC but the motor-coaches are equipped for three other forms of supply.
Opposite page: Combined road/ rail transport was developed in the United States after the Second World War under the name 'piggyback'. The road trailers on these piggyback trains of the Santa Fe provide industry with door-to-door service.

trailer, are loaded on to a train for long overnight journeys and their crews travel in the same train in a coach fitted up as sleeping quarters.

In passenger traffic air competition was first felt on international routes which involved a sea crossing. Soon the growing network of airlines began taking traffic from other international rail services. Seven European countries collaborated in 1957 to set up a system of fast daytime trains between their principal cities, scheduled for the convenience of business travellers so that they could spend a useful time in their offices before starting a journey and still be at their destination in time for staying in an hotel overnight. These 'Trans-Europe Expresses' (TEEs) were first class only and charged a supplementary fare. Frontier stops were brief, or eliminated by Customs examination on the train. At first the trains were diesel sets so as to be independent of different electrification systems where these existed on their routes, but from July 1961 electric sets capable of running on any of the four main-line electrification systems in Europe came into service between Zurich and Milan, and between Milan and Paris. Traffic on the TEE network increased and it became necessary on some routes to substitute locomotive-hauled trains for the earlier sets. The first of these came into operation between Paris, Brussels and Amsterdam in the summer of 1964. After 1979 none of the original TEE sets survived and since that year the TEE label has been applied only to certain trains providing the fastest service on their particular routes, whether international or internal, which are first class only and charge a supplementary fare. In 1983 there were still 22 TEE services in operation.

In spite of their efforts the railways found their costs outstripping their revenues and their dependence on subsidies and assistance in various forms was growing. While some services might lose less than others, or perhaps do a little better than breaking even, the overall result after meeting all charges was a deficit. In these circumstances there was a general pruning of railway systems by closure of the worst-hit lines and stations. Other lines were worked more economically by introducing diesel trains and railcars. Further economies could be made by concentrating control of traffic in a smaller number of signalboxes, each controlling a greater area, but all these measures were costly to put into effect. The responsibility of the railways for maintaining their permanent way and works, and for safe operation of their trains, was an expense without a parallel in the costs of their competitors.

The British experience is widely known from being associated with the operation melodramatically described as the 'Beeching Axe'. Dr (later Lord) Beeching was Technical Director of Imperial Chemical Industries Ltd (ICI). In 1961 he was appointed Chairman of the British Transport Commission, an organisation replaced in 1963 for management of the railways by the British Railways Board, again headed by Dr Beeching. He had already initiated detailed studies of the railway business, the results of which were published in the first Beeching Report in 1963. After an analysis of traffic and receipts which showed a serious imbalance between the extent of the system and the proportion which was producing commercially satisfactory results, the 'axe' came in the Appendix, which suggested the withdrawal of 245 train services and closure of over 2,000 passenger stations.

A further report in 1965 studied traffic flows between centres of population and industry. Duplication of routes was identified and proposals were made for concentrating traffic on selected major trunk routes. Both reports caused considerable debate and anxiety and the axe was blunted to some extent, but between 1962 and 1968 the British Railways system was reduced from 17,500 route-miles (28,163 route-km) to 12,100 route-miles (19,473 route-km). It later stabilised at around

A Class 6500 Co-Co of the French National Railways hauls an 18-coach train of Corail stock near Ste Genevieve du Bois on a Paris-Bordeaux service.

The 'Edelweiss' (Amsterdam-Zurich) Trans-Europ Express was introduced in 1957 jointly by the Netherlands Railways and Swiss Federal Railways. This picture shows the original formation of a Dutch-built 2,000 hp diesel locomotive and three Swiss-built coaches comprising two trailers and a driving trailer.

The first TEE sets were powered by motor-coaches but as loads increased many services were locomotive-hauled. One of these was the Paris-Bordeaux 'Etendard' of the French National Railways, seen at Bordeaux with a Class 6500 Co-Co locomotive.

11,500 route-miles (18,507 route-km). In the same 1962–68 period the annual deficits oscillated between a maximum of £159 million in 1962 and a minimum of £125 million in 1964.

It now had to be accepted in Britain and elsewhere that the goal must be a railway that would meet social and economic needs at minimum cost to the taxpayer. Sir Richard Marsh, who became Chairman of the British Railways Board in 1971, told the government of the day that further contraction of the system would lead to further loss, and that the social benefit to the community as a whole of keeping the system intact would easily outweigh the book-keeping deficit.

Retrenchment in the USA took a far more drastic turn. Bankruptcies began in the 1960s, the first victim being the New Haven Railroad in 1961. In 1968 those old rivals, the Pennsylvania and the New York Central, were forced to merge in an effort to keep their operations going, forming the Penn Central. Hopes were pinned on a joint Pennsylvania and government project initiated in 1965 for a service of high-speed electric multiple-unit trains on the Pennsylvania's electrified New York-Washington main line, with 150 mph (241·4 km/h) running in view. The new 'Metroliner' trains went into service after many technical problems in

The massive 2-C-C-2 Class GG1 electric locomotives of the Pennsylvania Railroad survived to take service under Amtrak. A GG1 in its new colours is illustrated.

New motive power was built for the Amtrak services. This Class 900 Bo-Bo electric locomotive and the leading coach display the Amtrak livery to advantage.

January 1969. Only 12 months later, on 21 January 1970, the railroad was obliged to file a petition for bankruptcy. Railroad operations in the United States are regulated by the Interstate Commerce Commission, a body set up in 1887 to block any attempts to impose transport monopolies. In the financially disastrous 1960s they were reluctant to allow railroads in difficulty to abandon passenger working but by the end of the decade the situation was so serious that the government set up the National Railroad Passenger Corporation to take over the operation of long-distance services. Companies which handed over suitable equipment were allowed to drop that side of their operations. The NRPC began to operate trains under the name Amtrak on 1 January 1970. Amtrak later acquired its own locomotives and rolling stock, but the lines over which its trains ran still belonged at first to the railroads.

The situation of the railroads continued to decline. ICC regulations delayed proposed mergers and were inflexible over the adjustment of freight rates. Services deteriorated because of poor maintenance, tarnishing the railroads' image and accelerating the decline in receipts. In 1975 the government took action, setting up a Consolidated Rail Corporation to take over bankrupt lines. The new organisation, Conrail, got to work on 1 April 1976, taking over 15,000 miles (24,140 km) of track, 3,800 locomotives and 140,000 vehicles. A quarter of the system which

The Pennsylvania electrification did not go west of Harrisburg on the New York-Chicago main line. Diesel power takes the 'Broadway Limited' round the curve at Bennington in winter after Amtrak took over operation of this classic service.

had the least traffic was abandoned. Amtrak became the owner of the North East Corridor rail route from Washington to Boston via New York, where previously it had operated a service over metals belonging to the railroad companies.

The North East Corridor is the only predominantly passenger main line in the USA. It is formed by the Pennsylvania's electrification from Washington to New York, and the New York, New Haven & Hartford's line from New York to Boston, which is electrified as far as New Haven. Although most

New Haven trains used the Grand Central terminal in New York, the railroad built a connection to the Pennsylvania's station, crossing the Hudson River on the massive Hell Gate bridge. This link was opened in 1917 and has provided Amtrak with a through route from Washington to Boston, electrified for some 300 miles (483 km) on the 11kV, 25Hz system. A massive investment programme to upgrade this important route, which has the best growth potential of the US long-distance rail routes, was under way in 1980. Elsewhere in the United States Amtrak operates a number of long-distance and transcontinental trains which keep some of the famous names of US railroading alive and have added new ones. A new generation of rolling stock known as 'Superliners' began to be introduced with the Amtrak winter timetable of 1979. In these bi-level vehicles the lower level is generally occupied by restrooms, baggage areas, kitchens in the dining cars, and ancillary equipment, although both levels provide passenger accommodation in the sleeping cars and in the lounge/cafe cars, where the upper level has large observation windows and TV monitors on which feature films can be shown.

North of the border, Canadian railways had been having similar problems. Canadian Pacific operations had become predominantly freight under the title CP Rail, although it still operated the 'Canadian' transcontinental service. The Canadian National was also still in the transcontinental business, with its 'Super-Continental', and also operated a fast inter-city service between Montreal and Toronto.

Interior of an Amtrak deluxe bedroom in a 'Superliner' car. In daytime a long sofa and swivel chairs are provided. Folding doors enable two rooms to form a single large suite.
Below: Amtrak experimented briefly with gas turbine power. This Turboliner is operating a New York-Niagara Falls service for which the name 'Empire State Express' was revived. The train is crossing the Mohawk River.

Above: A 'Metroliner' high-speed electric train on Amtrak's New York-Washington service.
Left: Another short-lived gas turbine experiment was conducted by the Canadian National Railways with Turboliners between Montreal and Toronto.

In 1977 the Canadian Government approved the setting up of a single company to manage passenger services in the country. Officially it was Via Rail Canada Inc, a subsidiary of the Canadian National, but for marketing purposes it took the brand name VIA Rail. The new organisation began to operate in 1978. Initially both transcontinentals ran as separate trains from Montreal and Toronto to Sudbury, where they combined as one train to Winnipeg, dividing there to continue to Vancouver via Calgary over the CPR line and via Edmonton over the CNR. From 28 October 1979 the through service by the CNR line was withdrawn between Sudbury and Winnipeg and both transcontinentals combined at Sudbury to travel to Winnipeg and the west coast by the CPR line, retaining the 'Canadian' title.

18. THE MODERN WORLD

AT THE END OF THE Second World War it seemed unlikely that new main lines would be built outside the undeveloped countries. The supposition was proved wrong when the Japanese National Railways embarked on a new high-speed electrified line from Tokyo to Osaka. Breaking with previous practice, the line was standard gauge, 4 ft 8½ in (1·435 m) and it by-passed the existing 3 ft 6 in (1·067 m) gauge line betweeen the two cities, which traversed the highly industrialised Tokaido region. The New Tokaido line was to carry fast passenger trains only, and in its length of 320·25 miles (515·4 km) it had 19 intermediate stations compared with nearly 100 on the older route.

The line was opened in October 1964 and operated with multiple-unit trains in 12-car, and later 16-car, formations. All axles in a train were motored, giving a total power in a 16-car formation of 15,877 hp (11,840 kW). Top speed was 130 mph (210 km/h), and the time of 3 hr 10 min by the fastest trains, making two intermediate stops, represented an average speed of 101 mph (162·75 km/h). Electrification was at 25kV, 60Hz, and the trains were rectifier-powered with tap-changer control. The rounded 'nose' ends of the trainsets combined with the velocity soon earned them the name of 'bullet trains' and the service of four trains an hour running at such speeds was an innovation in inter-city travel. Another aspect of the system which was unique at the time was the absence of lineside signals, instructions to the driver being conveyed by coded track circuits and displayed in the cab.

The new Tokaido line was the first of a series of *Shinkansen* (New Trunk Lines) planned by the Japanese National Railways (JNR). It was extended to Okayama in March 1972, and in 1975 was completed by a further extension to Hakata on the island of Kyushu, crossing under the strait in a tunnel 11·6 miles (18·7 km) long.

Two new Shinkansen running northwards from Tokyo came into operation in 1983. The Tohuku line was opened as far as Morioka on 23 June in that year, a distance of 308·5 miles (496·5 km); its

ultimate objective was Sapporo on the island of Hokkaido which would be reached by tunnelling under the sea for 33·4 miles (53·8 km). On 25 November 1983 the Joetsu line was opened, branching from the Tohuku line at Omiya and crossing the mountainous spine of the country to the port of Niigata on the Sea of Japan, a distance of 167·4 miles (269·5 km). The Japanese Alps were pierced in a tunnel 13·8 miles (22·2 km) long. In the rolling stock for these new lines, which had stiffer gradients, the motor horsepower was raised to 308·4 hp (230 kW) from the previous 248 hp (185 kW), and thyristor control replaced tap-changers. Maximum speeds were not increased. Environmental groups had objected to the noise of the first Shinkansen trains and the JNR had been put to much expense in erecting sound barriers. The new trains also had a snow plough incorporated in the nose end structure because of the heavy winter snowfall in the areas traversed. Shrouding of the underfloor equipment was increased, and blowers at the air intakes diverted snow from the traction motors and control

gear. Heated water sprinklers to melt snow were mounted at the trackside on the Joetsu and Tohuku lines and were brought into action automatically by a photo-electric sensing system.

By the time the new Shinkansen were opened in 1983 their speed levels had been surpassed by another purpose-built high-speed line. This was the Paris-Sud Est line of the French National Railways, the first of a programme of high-speed routes. The railways in France had spearheaded the advance towards higher speeds since the 1950s. When the Paris-Lyons electrification was completed in 1952 the 'Mistral' Paris-Nice express was scheduled to cover the 317·5 miles (511 km) from Paris to Lyons in 4 hr 15 min including a 2 minute stop at Dijon, giving an overall average speed of 74·7 mph (120·2 km/h). The highlight of the journey was the non-stop dash from Paris to Dijon at an average speed of 77·1 mph (124 km/h).

In 1955 high-speed trials with electric locomotives and a test train of three coaches produced a maximum speed of 205·7 mph (331 km/h) on two succes-

As the JNR's network of special high-speed lines (*Shinkansen*) has spread, new series of trains have been built. Class 210 illustrated is one of these later developments.

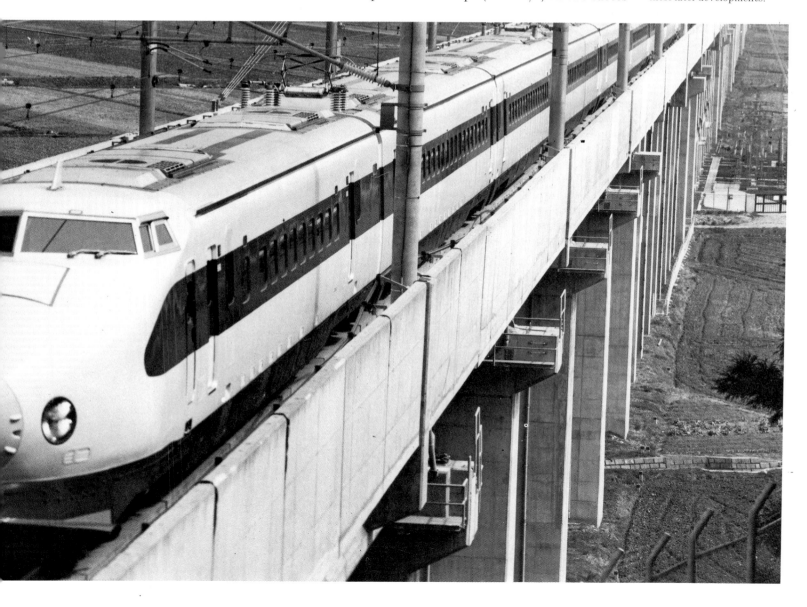

Right: The bar section of a TGV.
Far right: Interior of a first class section.

Below: The streamlined 'nose' of a TGV set at the Gare de Lyon in Paris.
Below right: The TGV route from Paris to Lyons has steep gradients, but the high speeds attained downhill help trains up the following rise without high power demand. Two TGVs pass in a clearly seen dip where the gradients change.

sive days. In the mid-1960s, with the Shinkansen in Japan holding the record for speed in regular passenger service, the Minister of Transport authorised the SNCF to plan for a maximum speed of 124·3 mph (200 km/h) for timetabled trains on existing routes. The first result was seen in the scheduling of the Paris-Toulouse express, the 'Capitole', to cover a modest 31·1 miles (50·1 km) at that speed in 1967.

In the meantime the Paris-Lyons electrification and its extensions were being worked to capacity, with further increases of traffic in prospect. A study of the line showed that elimination of freight traffic would roughly treble its passenger-carrying capacity between Paris and Lyons. It was also apparent that with axle-loads of up to 19·68 tons (20 tonnes) in wagons and sometimes as much as 22·64 tons (23 tonnes) in locomotives, existing tracks could not sustain speeds of 155 mph (250 km/h) and upwards without excessive expenditure on maintenance. A new line was the only means of meeting future demands and competitive pressures. Plans for the undertaking were prepared by the SNCF and approved by committees of enquiry. On 23 March 1976 a Government Decree declared the Paris-Sud Est high-speed line (*Ligne à Grande Vitesse*, or LGV) to be an enterprise of public utility.

The new line was electrified at 25kV, 50Hz. Leaving the former route at Combs-la-Ville, 18 miles (29 km) south of Paris, it rejoined it again at Sathonay, 5 miles (18 km) north of Lyons in the city suburbs. From Combs-la-Ville to Sathonay was a distance of 244 miles (390 km). The new line shortened the Paris-Lyons journey by 56 miles (90 km). A branch from Pasilly to the old route near Montbard shortened the distance from Paris to Dijon by 18 miles (29 km). Another branch diverged near Mâcon with connections to Geneva and the Savoy. It was an essential feature of the plan that the high-speed trains should extend their journeys over existing routes, observing the speed limits of the lines concerned. Those taking the branch at Pasilly continued to Dijon, Besançon, and Lausanne; the Mâcon branch served Geneva, Annecy, and Chambery; while south of Lyons there were through services to Marseilles and Montpellier. The only stations on the high-speed line were at Le Creusot, serving a community including Montceau, Les Mines, and Montchanin; and at Mâcon.

The line was planned for an initial service speed of 161·5 mph (260 km/h). It was calculated that a high-speed train of the type proposed, travelling at 161·5 mph (260 km/h) with its full power of 8,314 hp (6,200 kW), would be slowed only to 137 mph (220

km/h) after 2·2 miles (3·5 km) on a rising gradient of 1 in 28·6. This was therefore chosen as the maximum gradient on the route and it enabled the line to follow the contours of the ground in many places. No tunnelling was necessary but eight viaducts were built with spans ranging from 98 to 180 ft (30 to 55 m).

The trains on the new line are known as TGVs (*Trains à Grande Vitesse*). The first TGV, however, TGV 001, was an experimental five-car set powered by a 6,437 hp (4,800 kW) gas turbine with electrical transmission. Two important facts were learned from experience with this unit. One was that with suitable streamlining and a small increase in power

Below: The Paris-Toulouse 'Capitole' express of the French National Railways became the fastest train in France in May 1967 when authorised to travel at 125 mph (201 km/h). The locomotive in this picture is a 9200 class B-B for the 1,500V DC system.
Bottom: An experimental high-speed test car used by the French National Railways during development of the TGV.

a 10-car train could run from Paris to Lyons in 2 hours. Second, it was found that at high speeds there was sufficient adhesion to make it unnecessary for all axles to be motored. On one occasion in 1982 TGV 001 reached a maximum speed of 198·75 mph (318 km/h).

A TGV train on the Paris-Sud Est line is made up of 10-car units, each with two power cars and eight articulated trailers between them. In addition to the four motors of each power car, both axles of the adjacent trailer bogie are motored, the 12 motors in each unit totalling 8,448 hp (6,300 kW) at maximum output. Both power cars carry pantographs, but only the rear one is raised on the high-speed line, current being supplied to the leading car through cables on the car roofs. These power lines are not interconnected between units when two or more are running in multiple, and so each unit collects its own power supply. Separate pantographs are carried for DC operation. Because of the higher currents when running on 1,500V DC the roof power lines are not used but each power car collects current through its own DC pantograph. Many items of the control equipment are common to AC and DC working, and when the train passes from one system to the other are reconnected in the appropriate configuration by operating a multi-contact switch.

There are no lineside signals but instructions on the speed at which the train may travel are shown to the driver on a display in the cab. The driver must also observe lineside markers indicating the limits of block sections, since certain displays show the speed the train must not exceed on entering the section ahead and are an advance warning to begin reducing speed. Junctions and crossovers are laid out so that the angle of the diverging route is very small and can be taken at 136·7 mph (220 km/h). In conventional trackwork there would be a long gap where one rail crosses another but on the high-speed line the gap is closed by a flexible extension of the crossing 'nose' which is operated by a separate point machine working in synchronism with the machine controlling the switch rails.

The Paris Sud-Est line was opened throughout on 25 September 1983. A two-hour schedule was introduced between Paris and Lyons, and the maximum speed on the line was raised from 161·6 to 167·8 mph (260 to 270 km/h).

Italy and Germany both have programmes of building new lines by-passing older routes unsuitable for higher speeds. Italy, in fact, began the process before the Second World War with the Rome to Naples and Bologna-Florence *direttissime*. A third *direttissima*, from Rome to Florence, was under construction in 1984. The German Federal Railway was authorised in 1973 to begin a programme of building 590 route-miles (950 route-km) of new and better-aligned lines by-passing sections unsuitable for upgrading for higher speeds. These *Neubaustrecken*, like the *direttissime*, are for fast freight as

Italian State Railways ALe 724 class electric multiple-unit train for commuter and short-haul services.

Interior of an Italian National Railways cafeteria car.

well as passenger services although originally the Bundesbahn conceived them as high-speed passenger lines for speeds up to 185 mph (298 km/h).

When high speeds are run on existing lines there may be many places where speed limits are necessary on curvature in the interests of passenger comfort. Only a new line, such as the Paris-Sud Est, is likely to have curves with a minimum radius of 13,123 ft (4,000 m). In the 1960s British Railways began design work on a train which would improve inter-city times by taking curves at high speed without discomfort to the passengers. In simple terms, the cant already provided on the permanent way at curves would be increased artificially by tilting the coach bodies. There were other innovations in this Advanced Passenger Train (APT), notably a contour of the wheel treads which would minimise contact between flange and rail for guidance. Trials of a gas turbine prototype were sufficiently encouraging for construction of an electrically-powered APT to be authorised in 1974, and three prototypes with 25kV AC equipment were ready in 1979. Subsequent test running revealed numerous problems, particularly in the tilting mechanism and the special form of hydrokinetic braking. The difficulties were considered to have been sufficiently mastered for journeys with passengers to begin in December 1981 on the Euston-Glasgow route but the journeys were plagued with troubles, aggravated by severe weather, and the trains were withdrawn for redesign in several respects.

Above: The prototype BR High Speed Train and the first of three pre-production Advanced Passenger Trains meet at Swindon during trials, in the course of which the APT touched 151 mph (241·7 km/h).

Right: A Class 254 HST approaches Durham on a crew training run on the East Coast Main Line.
Opposite page, above: An Inter-City XPT train of the New South Wales Rail Authority. The design is closely based on BR's HST.
Opposite page, right: A prototype APT at Beattock on a proving run. The two power cars, identified by pantographs, are at the centre of the train. Future versions are likely to have a power car at one end.

Electrification of the main line from London Euston to Glasgow had been completed in 1974 and from 6 May in that year the service between Euston and Glasgow was increased by three trains daily in each direction. The 'Royal Scot' now made the journey of 401 miles (645·3 km) in 5 hours exactly while the times of the other trains averaged 5 hr 10 min. A publicity brochure issued at the time promised: 'There is still more to come. By 1977/78 the use of the first Advanced Passenger Trains will reduce the journey times between London and Glasgow to four hours. . .'. This did not happen, but the 'Electric Scots', as the conventional loco-motive-hauled trains on the route were called, followed the general policy then becoming established of improving a service all round rather than introducing one or two crack expresses. With so little to choose between the fastest and slower services, retention of the title 'Royal Scot' was a gesture to tradition rather than a spotlight for an outstanding train.

By 1970 competition from the air and on the roads made acceleration of services on non-electrified lines necessary and the commercial departments of British Railways could not afford to wait for the development of new technology as represented by the APT. Construction of a high-speed diesel train was therefore authorised embodying the latest developments in conventional railway practice. A prototype high-speed train (HST) was ready in under two years. Trial running was satisfactory and production units were ordered.

The new trains went into service under the brand name 'Inter-City 125', the figures standing for the new standard of travel at 125 mph (200 km/h) they introduced. They consist of two power cars and seven or eight air-conditioned coaches similar to those of locomotive-hauled trains. In each power car a 2,250 hp (1,678 kW) diesel engine running at 1,500 rpm drives an alternator, the output being rectified for the DC traction motors. The HST (as it continues to be called despite the marketing title) has proved popular and successful and trains of this type have accelerated services on major British Railways cross-country routes as well as to and from London. A version of the HST adapted for Australian conditions has been built there for the New South Wales State Railway Authority. Its brand name is Inter-City XPT and the train consists in its standard form of two power cars and five trailers, the latter of corrugated stainless steel construction. Diesel engines are the same as in the British HST but run at the lower rating of 2,000 hp, while the traction motors are geared for a maximum speed of 100 mph (160·9 km/h).

The term 'Inter-City', whether used in full or abbreviated, has become a widely used one for a fast train service at regular intervals. In West Germany a network of IC services is operated to a timetable that provides convenient interconnections at principal stations, usually with cross-platform interchange, so that a passenger whose journey cannot be made throughout in one IC express can usually finish it in another with the

Opposite, above: A German Federal Railway IC (Inter-City) express near Wolnach. *Opposite, centre:* Class 120 locomotives of the German Federal Railway are powered by three-phase motors fed from the single-phase catenary through electronic inverters. *Opposite, below:* The 'Britannia' international express (Hook of Holland to Innsbruck) at Janbach on the German Federal Railway.

Visual display units give continuously updated information to the traffic controller of the Stuttgart S-Bahn.

German research locomotive with a suspension system having different characteristics in the lower and higher speed ranges.

A diesel-powered Trans-Europ Express unit of the German Federal Railway.

minimum of inconvenience and delay. When the German Federal Railway began its IC services in 1971 the trains were first class only and ran at two-hour intervals. In 1978 certain IC trains included second class coaches as an experiment and in 1979 the whole network became two-class, with trains at intervals of one hour. Until 1980 French Railways trains in the 125 mph (200 km/h) group operating between Paris, Toulouse, and Bordeaux had been first class only but from 28 September in that year the 'Montaigne' express between Paris and Bordeaux included second class accommodation. The TGVs

were two-class from their introduction on 27 September 1981. At that time only the southern portion of the new line was in use. In Europe in the 1980s the 'first class only' train was a diminishing species.

Several railways used tilting coach bodies to enable speed round curves to be raised without discomfort to passengers. Originally the systems were 'passive', that is the bodies had a pendulum type suspension so that they could swing outwards under centrifugal force. The Japanese National Railways put 47 coaches of this type into service in 1973 in multiple-unit trains running between Nagoya and Nagano and reduced the time for the journey of 156·6 miles (252 km) from 3 hr 57 min to 3 hr 20 min. With the development of electro-hydraulic systems under electronic control, 'active' tilting systems responsive to sensors were introduced. One such system was on trial from 1975 to 1978 in a four-coach set of the Swiss Federal Railways on the 60 mile (96·5 km) run between Berne and Lausanne. The trains in which the coaches ran were accelerated to save 5 or 6 minutes on the journey but it was not considered worthwhile to convert more coaches to the system.

Another active system was adopted for the LRC ('Light, Rapid, Comfortable') diesel-hauled trains introduced on the Montreal-Toronto service by VIA Rail in 1981. With a 3,725 hp (2,778 kW) locomotive at the head, the trains are capable of 125 mph (200 km/h) although restricted at first to 95 mph (153 km/h) pending improvements to the permanent way.

Tilting through the air suspension system has been applied in rolling stock of the lightweight Talgo trains of the Spanish National Railways (RENFE). The Talgo coach body is supported under the roof by pillars from the underframe, and rests on the air bags of a pneumatic suspension. Normally

High-speed urban transport
without street congestion. The
cars on the Wuppertal elevated
railway are suspended from an
overhead monorail.

the levelling valves in the pneumatic system keep
the coach floor parallel with the plane of the track
but on curves of less than 4,920 ft (1,500 m) radius
the valves no longer operate and the air bags react
like ordinary springs to the centrifugal force, the
outer one extending and the inner contracting so
that the body tilts.

The Talgo tilt system is 'passive' in that no external energy is used. In Sweden, however, the
Swedish State Railways (SJ) have tested an 'active'
(hydraulic) tilting system for high-speed electric
trains on the main lines from Stockholm northwards
to Sundsvaal and south-westwards to Goteborg and
Malmo. There is growing interest in the possibilities
of vehicle tilting as an alternative to costly realign-
ment of main lines for high speeds but the problems
to overcome are both technical and psychological.
Passengers have complained of discomfort and
nausea induced by the apparent rise and fall of the
horizon as seen from the carriage windows.

Freight transport by rail takes place increasingly
in block trains conveying a particular type of load
and running direct between the loading and unloading points. Examples are coal from collieries to power
stations, oil from refineries to storage depots, stone

from quarries to distribution points, and many other
bulk loads moving between private sidings. Other
products are transported as far as possible in full
wagonloads. For miscellaneous items of the kind
which once formed a large part of goods traffic there
are numerous parcels services, often by express and
high-speed passenger trains. In general, railways
have more freedom than in the past to select the
types of traffic they can handle most economically
and with the greatest advantage to the customer.

The new pattern of freight traffic has greatly
reduced the number of marshalling yards. Sorting
by hump shunting is still required at key points,
however, and the methods of automation developed
in the 1950s have been further refined. Up to that
period railbrake operators had judged the appropriate braking pressures to apply by the length and
weight of the cuts. Towards the end of the decade
radar systems were brought into use to measure
the speed and 'rollability' of cuts coming off the
hump and control the railbrake pressures accordingly. By the 1980s measurements from this and
other sources were being processed by computer to
give more precise control. The installation at the
automated Mulhouse-Nord yard on the SNCF

in 1984 employed three microprocessors, one for setting the points and controlling the railbrakes, another for storing certain operational data, and the third collecting statistical information from which the programs can be modified to improve the working of the yard if necessary. Routeing instructions are supplied to the control computer from a keyboard. All other operations are automatic, such as measurements of the speed at which cuts are travelling at the moment they buffer up with wagons already in the siding, and of the length of free track in each siding after each cut is received. This information continuously modifies the control of the railbrake. The computer also reviews its own performance over the preceding 120 operations and makes corrections as shunting proceeds. Any of the microprocessors can take over the work of one of the others in case of a failure.

Early applications of computers in railway work were for statistical and accounting purposes, material for processing being sent to central bureaux and the printouts collected later. With the development of time-sharing systems, enabling operators at computer terminals dispersed over a large area to communicate with a central computer, seat reservation systems were developed. The next step was for computers to monitor the movement of traffic on a railway in step with the changing situation, enabling them to supply information on demand regarding the whereabouts of individual loaded and empty wagons, other vehicles, and locomotives. This is known as 'real time' working and is the basis of various systems adapted from the original TOPS system of the Southern Pacific Railroad in the USA. The version of TOPS developed by British Railways for its own requirements has played an important

Computer-controlled displays on colour TV screens have replaced the conventional signalling control panel regulating S-Bahn traffic in the Mid-Neckar Region of West Germany.

part in selling the idea of freight transport by rail to industry, enabling firms to know where their wagon-loads are at any moment and dispelling the old prejudice that a wagon sent by rail was liable to be 'lost' in a yard *en route* instead of being despatched expeditiously to its destination. TOPS also helps railway management to provide the standard of service they have set themselves. Lists of wagons in a yard can be printed out on demand, either in full or selecting those which have been there for more than a stated time. Operating weaknesses can be detected and action taken at once. When wagons are requested by a yard with freight for despatch, the computer locates those of suitable types which are ready for loading and may make it possible for them to be sent loaded instead of empty to their new assignment.

In passenger working the computer may hold the timetable and compare the actual running of trains with the timetable plan, again providing management with useful data for improving the working where weaknesses exist. In signalling the computer soon established itself as the basis of the train describer – the system which shows signalmen the positions and identities of trains in the areas under their control. This is basically a logic operation of identifying movements detected by the track circuits with the descriptions of trains entered from a keyboard as they come into the controlled area. Originally a 'wired logic' system was used, but if changes were made in the track layout or operating procedures the wiring had to be scrapped and the circuits rewired. With a computer the changes can be made more easily and quickly by modifying the program. This task alone would leave the computer with much spare time and so other work is found for it. Typical offshoots of the basic train describer

LRC (Light, Rapid, Comfortable) train-set with automatic tilting cars introduced by Via Rail, Canada, for accelerated inter-city services.

function are printout of train reports for management use, provision of train running information on demand for inquiry offices, the control of platform indicators and recorded announcements, and the operation of visual display units (VDUs) showing sections of track and the reporting numbers of trains moving on them on television type screens, for the use of senior traffic regulators and terminal station staff. The computerised train describer has in fact become a traffic information system.

The small size of computing installations made possible by the microprocessor and 'microchips' in general is particularly useful when computers are installed in railway vehicles for processing information transmitted from the track. In the British Railways APT system coded instructions regarding speed were stored in transponders mounted on the sleepers. When the APT passed over them they were energised by energy radiated from the train and the message was transmitted. It was decoded by two microprocessors working independently and only displayed to the driver if both agreed. A second computer was carried as a standby and brought into use automatically if the other one failed. This duplication was necessary to maintain the safety standards insisted on in railway signalling and would have been impracticable before microprocessors had 'shrunk' computers to their present size.

The interlocking of railway points and signals is a logic operation which for many years has been performed mechanically, or electrically by means of relays. Today the reliability of circuits formed on silicon chips has reached the level where they can be used in electronic interlocking systems. British Rail in collaboration with two manufacturers has developed microprocessor-based interlocking equipment that was due to be installed as a pilot scheme at Leamington Spa in the mid-1980s. In 1983 service trials began of an automatic route-setting system based on two microcomputers for controlling three junctions on an 8 mile (13 km) stretch of BR Southern Region's Brighton main line. One computer took information from the train describer system; the other was linked with the computer in which the Region's master timetable is stored. The two microcomputers continuously compared the actual running of trains with the schedules and calculated the optimum pattern of train movement and route-setting.

Before electronics were allowed to take part in the actual operation of signalling they had proved themselves in remote control systems allowing conventional relay interlockings over a wide area to be controlled from one signalbox, and the indications of signal aspects, point settings and train movements to be sent back from site for display on the signalling panel in the box. Concentration of control in this manner became economic when electronics enabled many channels of information to be carried by one pair of wires.

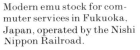

Modern emu stock for commuter services in Fukuoka, Japan, operated by the Nishi Nippon Railroad.

Bi-level Vista-Dome coaches for inter-urban services of the Kinki Nippon Railway, a Japanese private system.

The steps to the upper level inside a bi-level Vista-Dome coach.

Interest continues in vehicles able to run on rail or road. A train of 14 RoadRailer cars leaves Alexandria, Virginia, on a high-speed test run.

A twin-unit gas turbine locomotive, with separate fuel car, hauls heavy freight on the Union Pacific Railroad.

Radio communication with trains is becoming widely used. Transmitter/receiver stations are spaced at intervals along the rail route and connected by landline to a control centre. When a message from a train is picked up at two lineside sites, the strongest signal is selected automatically. Systems of this kind carry both ordinary speech and standard coded messages transmitted by simply pressing a push-button. Such messages are decoded and displayed visually in the cab or at the control centre. Communication is maintained in tunnels by 'piping' signals from the

nearest lineside station along radiating cable. The same cable picks up signals from a train in the tunnel and conveys them to the transmitter in the open. Radio service for travellers is often provided in inter-city expresses, connecting them with the ordinary telephone system so that they can call a number. Originally calls had to be made through an operator on the train but some railways have in-

stalled coin-operated telephones from which callers can dial a number themselves.

Another growing use for radio is for remote control of shunting locomotives from the trackside. The driver alights, carrying a small portable transmitter, and can watch the movements of the locomotive as it responds to the control signals. From his position beside the line he is better able to see potential danger to other railwaymen working in the shunting yard than he could from the cab. The electronic controls of the modern electric or diesel locomotive are readily adaptable to control by radio signals.

Electronic devices on railways today begin with the small chip of silicon containing the equivalent of hundreds of individual components, and end with the large slice of semiconductor material mounted on a heat sink to dissipate the heat generated by the passage of heavy currents. These power-handling devices take two forms: the diode, which rectifies an alternating current input to produce direct current; and the thyristor, which both rectifies the input and controls the output. Both are used in the traction circuits of electric locomotives and motor-coaches. In a diode rectifier the input and output voltages are nearly the same, the voltage drop across the diodes

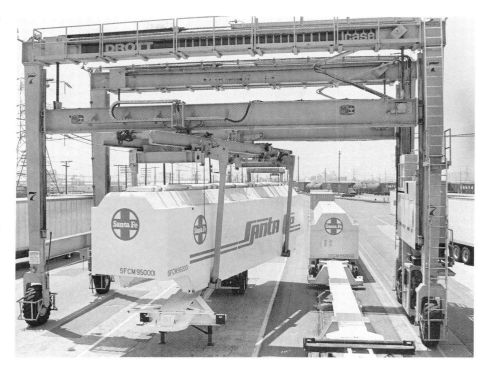

Transferring a container from road trailer to freight train at a Santa Fe terminal.

Class 80 diesel-electric locomotives of the New South
Wales Railways haul hopper
wagons on undulating track.

being small. Control of the output voltage must therefore take place on the input side, normally by switching between different tappings on a transformer. The thyristor takes a fixed AC input voltage and produces a DC output that is continuously variable from zero to maximum. At first the thyristor blocks the incoming half-cycle until it has passed maximum and fallen nearly to zero, when the thyristor is switched on and begins to pass current. The point of switch-on is gradually advanced until the thyristor conducts throughout the half-cycle and supplies full power to the load. This system is called 'phase-angle control'.

Thyristors can also be operated on a DC input in a 'chopper' circuit in which power is supplied to the load in pulses, which are lengthened, or occur at shorter intervals, until the thyristors conduct continuously and the traction motors operate at full power. The French TGV trains are controlled by a chopper system when running on DC lines, and choppers are becoming increasingly common in high-power locomotives. An advantage of the system is that there is no loss of energy as heat such as occurs in the resistances used in conventional control of DC motive power.

The third application of thyristors is in inverter circuits which convert a DC input into AC. With suitable grouping and control of the thyristors, a three-phase output variable in voltage and frequency can be obtained, and used to drive induction motors.

Electronics have achieved a number of goals which have been sought by traction engineers since the earliest days of railway electrification. They may be summarised as:

Stepless control of power, avoiding the abrupt increases of tractive effort which occur with electro-mechanical switching and are liable to set up wheelspin.
Elimination of energy losses in resistances and the switching necessary in conventional DC control to connect the traction motors in different groupings during acceleration.
The use of induction motors, which are mechanically simple and without commutators, while avoiding earlier problems of a limited range of running speeds.
The German Federal Railway has taken a leading part in the development of locomotives with induc-

tion motors and inverter drive. Five prototypes with the Bo-Bo wheel arrangement and a rating of 7,500 hp (5,593 kW) were ordered in 1977 and commissioned in 1979–80. The railway's supply is 15kV, 16⅔Hz and the locomotive equipment rectifies the single-phase AC input before it reaches the inverters, which operate on DC. Since commissioning the locomotives have worked heavy freight trains in the 1,476–1,575 tons (1,500–1,600 tonnes) range and 125 mph (200 km/h) passenger services with loads of 590·5 tons (600 tonnes). By mid-1983 one of the five had run 434,960 miles (700,000 km) with 15 occasions when a failure made it necessary to substitute another locomotive. The incidence of such failures declined steadily and in 1982 only one occurred. Similar three-phase equipment has been supplied by German industry for locomotives in Switzerland, Norway and Austria.

The combination of electronic techniques can produce a fully automatic railway. In May 1983 the first 5·6 miles (9 km) of a new Metro line were opened in Lille, northern France, where trains run without driver or guard, controlled by a two-way flow of information between the trains, stations, and the computer in the control room at one end of the line. Sliding glass doors at the edge of the station platforms remain closed until a train arrives. It stops with an error of no more than 11·8 in (30 cm) so that its vehicle doors are opposite the doors at the platform edge. A signal from the train is picked up by an antenna in the track, and after a one second check that all conditions are correct another signal from the train causes both sets of doors to open. A countdown begins, at the end of which the instruction to depart is given to the train by the station. Stops are normally 14 seconds but at certain busy points are 30 seconds.

After unloading at the terminus, the train runs forward into a shunting neck, and in so doing interrupts a signal beamed across the track by an oscillator. If all conditions are correct, the points are reversed and the train returns to the other platform for its next journey. Trains are despatched from the terminus by the computer, which inserts extras in rush hours and prolongs or curtails station stops *en route* according to whether trains are running ahead of or behind schedule. The interval between trains when the line was opened was two minutes, but it was intended to reduce this to one minute. On the opening day the people of Lille enjoyed free rides throughout the afternoon to familiarise themselves with the experience of riding in a train with no one at the controls.

Systems such as the full automation of the Lille Metro are of most interest to rapid transit lines, both surface and underground, but the other electronic developments are likely to be used in operating some of the lines in the major projects of new construction under way or planned in the 1980s. In diesel-electric traction electronics have superseded servo-driven regulators for matching engine and generator output. Governor movements are detected by a sensor which transmits an 'increase' or 'decrease' signal to thyristors controlling the generator excitation. It is now general practice for the generator to be an alternator, its AC output being rectified for the DC traction motors. With DC generators there was a limit to the power that could be supplied to the motors without commutation problems, and these could also occur at fast rotational speeds, so that power units were generally medium-speed and relatively heavy diesel engines. The commutator is simply a mechanical rectifier, and the substitution of static semiconductor diodes allows the use of

Road trailers on rail on the Gotthard line of the Swiss Federal Railways.

faster-running engines developing more power per unit of weight.

The biggest new construction project nearing completion in 1984 was the Baikal-Amur line in the Soviet Union, which has been called 'the railway building enterprise of the century'. Total length of the line, from Ustkut to Komsomolsk-on-Amur, with a north-south connection to the Trans-Siberian at a point appropriately called 'Bam', is over 2,175 miles (3,500 km). A similar route to the north of the present Trans-Siberian line was considered when a railway to the Pacific coast was first being planned but was rejected as too difficult. Today it has the strategic advantage of being further from the Chinese frontier, but it also opens up territory rich in mineral resources which can be exploited with modern methods in spite of the harsh environment. Over the central section of the route the temperature varies from 35°C in summer to –50°C in winter. For over half the distance the ground is locked in permafrost all the year. Seven mountain ranges, one large river and numerous water-courses are crossed, while in some areas the line has to be laid over swampy ground and scree.

An Italian State Railways Class E633 Bo-Bo-Bo electric locomotive (3,000V DC) heads bi-level coaches of a French design built under licence in Italy.

Above: The Juvisy signalling centre, French National Railways.

Right: This VAL system train on the Lille Metro line, Northern France, carries no crew and is controlled electronically.

The remoteness of many working sites made the transport of materials difficult. Temporary roads had to be built, and certain supplies, such as food and fuel, were brought in by helicopter. The line has been opened in sections since 1980. Opening throughout was dependent on when work on tunnels could be finished, including one some 9·3 miles (15 km) long where the frozen ground had caused delays, but it was hoped to take place in 1985.

In China the Ministry of Railways launched a modernisation plan to cover the period 1978–85. Some construction projects which had been limping forward slowly were given new impetus, among them the Chinghai-Tibet Railway, a strategic line 1,375 miles (2,213 km) long, much of it at an altitude of 13,123 ft (4,000 m). Other major lines have been completed in recent years, including the Xinzheng-Liuzhou Railway, 550 miles (885 km), and a line 284·5 miles (474 km) long in Southern Sinkiang.

China remains a stronghold of steam traction although it has some modern 25kV electrification and a fleet of powerful diesels. In 1983 the Da Tong locomotive works, some 248 miles (400 km) north-west of Peking, was reported to be building between 200 and 300 2-10-2 steam locomotives of the 'Quian Jin' ('Forwards') class. The resources of China in coal and manpower make it probable that steam traction will continue on the Chinese National Railways into the next century.

One of the biggest and most important railway construction ventures completed anywhere in the world since the Second World War was the work on the 2,461 miles (3,960 km) of the Australian transcontinental route from Sydney to Perth. In New South Wales 422 miles (679 km) of standard gauge line from Parkes to Broken Hill, originally laid as a light development line, were brought up to mainline standards. In South Australia 247 miles (398 km) of new standard gauge line were laid to connect Broken Hill with Port Pirie and the Trans-Australian line. On the other side of the continent Western Australia built 450 miles (724 km) of standard

gauge line linking Kalgoorlie with Perth, Fremantle and Kwinana. This huge undertaking was completed in November 1969; the first through freight service between Fremantle and Sydney was launched on 12 January 1970. A new passenger service between Perth and Sydney began on 1 March of the same year. It was named the 'Indian-Pacific' and for the first time passengers could travel across Australia without changing trains at breaks-of-gauge, between the coasts of the two oceans.

The variety of gauges in Australia was at the root of a more recent construction project. Passengers for Alice Springs in the heart of the Northern Territory used to change at Marree from a standard gauge train of the Central Australian Railway into a 3 ft 6 in (1·067 m) gauge train of the same system for the rest of the journey. The narrow-gauge line was of limited capacity and liable to flooding and an alternative route was surveyed, starting at Tarcoola on the Trans-Australian line and running nearly due north for 516·3 miles (831 km) to Alice Springs. The new line, of standard gauge, was opened on 9 October 1980. A chain of 28 microwave radio installations along the route provides communication between trains and stations. They are spaced about 18·6 miles (30 km) apart and are powered by batteries kept charged by solar cells,

with no other source of energy. The old line north of Marree has been abandoned. With the opening of the new route a through sleeping car train was put on between Adelaide and Alice Springs. It kept the name, the 'Ghan', by which the old narrow gauge train was known for many years. Tradition relates the name to the days when Afghans manned the camel trains which provided communications in the Australian outback. Alice Springs will not remain a terminus. An extension of the railway to Darwin was approved and work was expected to begin in 1985.

More railway construction will be seen in Europe. In 1983 President Mitterand of France announced another *Ligne à Grande Vitesse* to provide a 'TGV Atlantique' service. The new line will leave the existing line close to the Montparnasse terminus in Paris and continue for 81·4 miles (131 km) to Courtalain, where it will divide into two branches, one of 46 miles (74 km) to Le Mans and the other of 57 miles (92 km) to Tours. Continuing over existing lines from these two towns, TGV trains will serve destinations along the Atlantic coast from Brest to Hendaye.

Construction continues of other 'special-purpose' railways for the haulage of huge tonnages of minerals and other products from mines and producing areas

Luxury air conditioned double-deck, inter-urban, electric multiple units designed and built for the State Rail Authority of New South Wales. The stainless steel cars operate with matched power cars and trailers in either four car or eight car sets. Top speed is 130 km/ph.

Facing page, top: A 2-10-2 locomotive of the Chinese State Railways. The Chinese still have a massive programme of steam construction underway.

Facing page, bottom: A stainless steel diesel multiple-unit train for suburban services in Adelaide, South Australia.

French National Railways B-B locomotive No 10004 equipped with traction motors controlled by a static commutation system, current directions being switched electronically in a stationary winding.

to ports and industrial complexes. On some of these lines already operating, the trains are unmanned and the locomotives fully automatic, controlled by coded track circuits. In such circumstances the automation system need not be as elaborate as on a passenger-carrying line such as the Lille Metro where the controls have to cover the length of station stops and operation of doors. Locomotives for both passenger and freight service today are often fitted with controls by which a driver can preset a particular speed or tractive effort, which will be maintained irrespective of gradients until another setting is chosen. The quick response of electronics has made these systems more attractive. With electro-mechanical switchgear there was a tendency to overshoot and correct at every change of gradient which led to rapid wear of contacts.

While some countries are already committed to induction motors for traction, in France a new approach to achieving a traction motor without a commutator has taken shape. In 1983 a 7,510 hp

M179 stock for RER (Réseau Express Inter-Régional) services in Paris. RER trains are equipped for AC/DC operation to allow through running between the RER's 1,500V DC electrified tracks and 25kV AC main lines of the French National Railways.

(5,600 kW) locomotive with 'static commutation' was demonstrated on the French National Railways. A commutator is simply a mechanical switch on the armature shaft which reverses the current in the windings as they revolve so that the turning force acts continuously in the same direction. The motors in the new French locomotive can be regarded as DC motors turned 'inside out'. The armature windings are stationary while the magnet system revolves. Groups of thyristors are switched on and off in a sequence which changes the direction of currents in the windings at the proper moment in each revolution to maintain the constant turning force. It is likely that motors of this type will be installed in the TGV Atlantique trains.

Also appearing on the horizon is the electric train in which the motive power comes from the reaction between the currents in windings on the train and others extending along the track. This arrangement is known as a 'linear motor' and it does away with the traditional dependence on adhesion between wheel and rail. Linear motors can be used in conjunction with magnets which maintain a gap between the vehicle and its guiding track. A system developed by British Rail Research has been adopted for vehicles carrying passengers between Birmingham Airport and the National Exhibition Centre, adjacent to the BR Birmingham International station. The gap between the supporting magnets and the guide rail in this installation is held within the limits of plus or minus 0·5 in (1·3 cm). Some Maglev (magnetic levitation) systems of this kind are being designed for very high speeds. In Germany an experimental Maglev vehicle has reached a top speed of 137 mph (220 km/h) but further development aims at 250 mph (400 km/h) by a vehicle built in two sections and seating 96 passengers.

For the greater part of a century railways pursued their own lines of development and were served by specialist industries. Today, they draw on the whole field of technology and their horizons are broadening.

An experimental Maglev vehicle in West Germany. The magnets are inside the massive underframe below the car body, their poles above and below the track acting to lift the vehicle out of contact with it while in motion.